TOTTERING-BY-GENTLY®

TOTTERING-BY-GENTLY®

OUT & ABOUT WITH
THE TOTTERINGS

ANNIE TEMPEST

YOUNG AT HEART...

...slightly older in other places...

F

FRANCES LINCOLN LIMITED
PUBLISHERS

Frances Lincoln Limited
4 Torriano Mews
Torriano Avenue
London NW5 2RZ
www.franceslincoln.com

Out & about with the Totterings
Copyright © The O'Shea Gallery 2010
Text copyright © Annie Tempest 2010
Illustrations copyright © Annie Tempest 2010

Illustrations archived and compiled by
Raymond O'Shea

British Library Cataloguing in Publication Data
A catalogue record for this book is available from
the British Library.

ISBN 978-0-7112-3084-2

Printed in China

Bound for North Pimmshire

9 8 7 6 5 4 3 2 1

Photo © Garlinda Birkbeck

BOOKS BY ANNIE TEMPEST

2007   *At Home with the Totterings*
(The O'Shea Gallery)

2003   *Tottering-by-Gently Vol III*
(The O'Shea Gallery)

2002   *Lady Tottering's Journal*
(Orion in association with The O'Shea Gallery)

2001   *Tottering Hall*
(Orion in association with The O'Shea Gallery)

1998   *Tottering-by-Gently* (paperback)
(The O'Shea Gallery)

1998   *Tottering-by-Gently Vol II*
(The O'Shea Gallery)

1996   *Tottering-by-Gently Vol I*
(Country Life Books)

1988   *Westenders*
(Muller)

1987   *Henry on Hols*
(Muller)

1986   *Hooray Henry!*
(Muller)

1985   *How Green Are Your Wellies?*
(Muller, Blond & White)

1985   *Turbocharge Your Granny*
(Muller, Blond & White)

BOOKS ILLUSTRATED/CONTRIBUTED TO BY ANNIE TEMPEST

2002   *Why the Reindeer has a Velvet Nose* by Robin Page
(Bird's Farm Books)

2000   *The Guest from Hell* by Alistair Sampson
(Orion in association with The O'Shea Gallery)

1999   *Will I See You in Heaven?* By Michael Seed
(Blake Publishing)

1998   *Berry's Best Cellar Secrets* by Jonathan Ray
(Berry Bros. & Rudd)

1992   *Where Did I Go Wrong?* by R. Rushbrooke
(St. Paul's Publications)

1992   *Crime-check!*
(ABI)

1991   *I Will See You in Heaven Where Animals Don't Bite* by Michael Seed
(St. Paul's Publications)

1991   *Best Behaviour* by Mary Killen
(Random Century)

1989   *The Recycled Joke Book* by Anneka Rice
(Mentorn Enterprises)

1988   *Best Cartoons of the Year*
(Robson Books)

1988   *Publish and Be Damned!* by International PEN
(Heinemann Kingswood)

Gentle reader,

Beware what you say to Annie Tempest, or you'll find yourself in Tottering Hall, that last outpost of Empire at the back of *Country Life* where the kindly sun never sets.

Let slip that your great-aunt was famous from the Andes to the Indies for her undies, or that the Cypriot climate is so-o-o good for your health (income tax at 4.25%), or that in Scotland "Viscount" is pronounced "Vacant", or that a Vacant has 16 pearls on his coronet (more than any other species of Peer, making one's Noble Friends madly jealous), and in two shakes of a duck-island's tail you'll be Dicky and Daffy's next guest.

Which are you? I'm the one with the –er – Vacant expression and the race between the receding hairline and the receding chin, which the Roman nose is winning. It's an honour to play a small part in a great national institution. Enjoy!

MONCKTON OF BRENCHLEY
Viscount Monckton of Brenchley

TOTTERING HALL

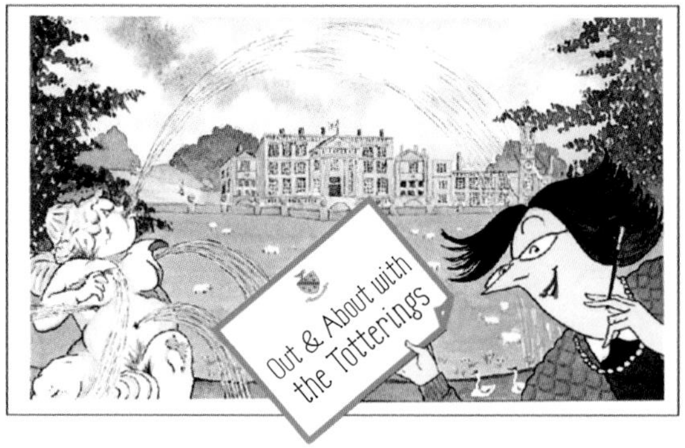
Out & About with the Totterings

THE TOTTERING PORTRAIT GALLERY

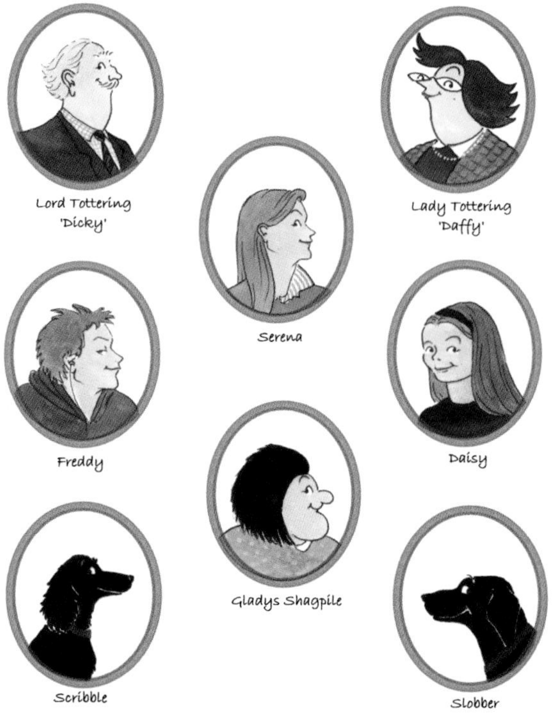
Lord Tottering 'Dicky'
Lady Tottering 'Daffy'
Serena
Freddy
Daisy
Gladys Shagpile
Scribble
Slobber

TOTTERING-BY-GENTLY ®
ANNIE TEMPEST

Annie Tempest is one of the top cartoonists working in the UK. This was recognized in 2009 with the Cartoon Trust awarding her the Pont Prize for her portrayal of the British Character. Annie's cartoon career began in 1985 with the success of her first book, *How Green Are Your Wellies?* This led to a regular cartoon, 'Westenders' in the *Daily Express*. Soon after, she joined the *Daily Mail* with 'The Yuppies' cartoon strip which ran for more than seven years and for which, in 1989, she was awarded 'Strip Cartoonist of the Year'. Since 1993 Annie Tempest has been charting the life of Daffy and Dicky Tottering in Tottering-by-Gently – the phenomenally successful weekly strip cartoon in *Country Life*.

Daffy Tottering is a woman of a certain age who has been taken into the hearts of people all over the world. She reflects the problems facing women in their everyday life and is completely at one with herself, while reflecting on the intergenerational tensions and the differing perspectives of men and women, as well as dieting, ageing, gardening, fashion, food, field sports, convention and much more.

Daffy and her husband Dicky live in the fading grandeur of Tottering Hall, their stately home in the fictional country of North Pimmshire, with their extended family: daughter Serena, and grandchildren, Freddy and Daisy. The daily, Mrs Shagpile, and love of Dicky's life, Slobber, his black Labrador, and the latest addition to the family, Scribble, Daisy's working Cocker Spaniel, also make regular appearances.

Annie Tempest was born in Zambia in 1959. She has a huge international following and has had eighteen one-woman shows, from Mexico to Mayfair. Her work is now syndicated from New York to Dubai and she has had eleven collections of her cartoons published. This latest book, *Out and About with the Totterings,* is the latest volume of the 'Biennial Collection' of all the *Country Life* cartoons to be published in chronological order. This book covers the period January 2004 to December 2005.

THE O'SHEA GALLERY

Raymond O'Shea of The O'Shea Gallery was originally one of London's leading antiquarian print and map dealers. Historically, antiquarian galleries sponsored and promoted contemporary artists who they felt complemented their recognized areas of specialization. It was in this tradition that O'Shea first contacted *Country Life* magazine to see if Annie Tempest would like to be represented and sponsored by his gallery. In 1995 Raymond was appointed agent for Annie Tempest's originals and publisher of her books. Raymond is responsible for creating an archive of all of Annie's cartoons.

In 2003, the antiquarian side of his business was put on hold and the St. James's Street premises were finally converted to The Tottering Drawing Room at The O'Shea Gallery. It is now the flagship of a worldwide operation that syndicates and licenses illustrated books, prints, stationery, champagne, jigsaws, greetings cards, ties and much more. It has even launched its own fashion range of tweeds and shooting accessories under the label Gently Ltd.

The Tottering Drawing Room at The O'Shea Gallery is a wonderful location which is now available for corporate events of 45–125 people and is regularly used for private dinner parties catering for up to 14 people. Adjacent to St. James's Palace, the gallery lies between two famous 18th century shops: Berry Bros. & Rudd, the wine merchants and Locks, the hatters. Accessed through French doors at the rear of the gallery lies Pickering Place – not only the smallest public square in Great Britain, with original gas lighting, but it was also where the last duel in England was fought. A plaque on the wall, erected by the Anglo-Texan Society, indicates that from 1842–45 a building here was occupied by the Legation from the Republic of Texas to the Court of St. James.

Raymond O'Shea and Annie Tempest are delighted to be able to extend Tottering fans a warm welcome in the heart of historic St. James's where all the original Tottering watercolours can be seen along side a full product and print range.

January 1st, 2004

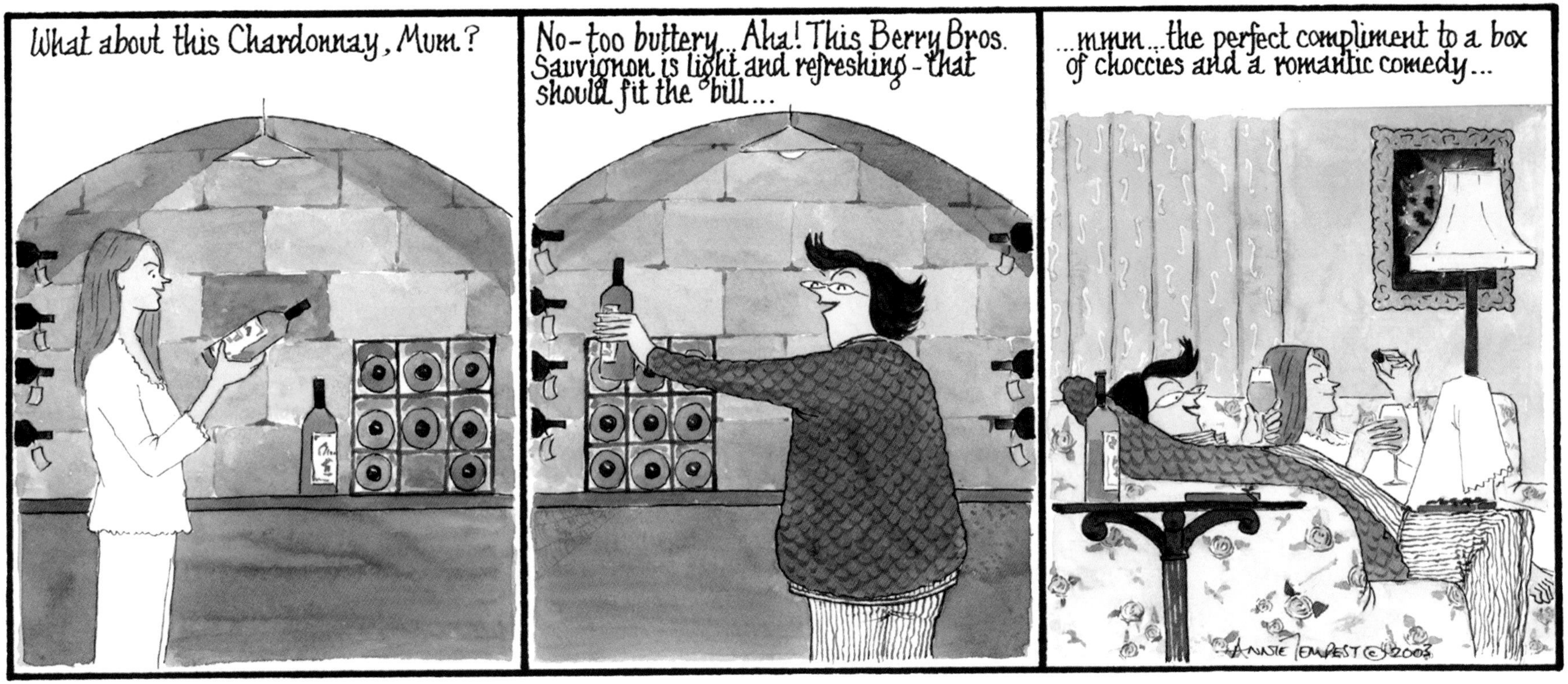
What about this Chardonnay, Mum?
No-too buttery... Aha! This Berry Bros. Sauvignon is light and refreshing - that should fit the bill...
...mmm... the perfect compliment to a box of choccies and a romantic comedy...
ANNIE TEMPEST © 2003

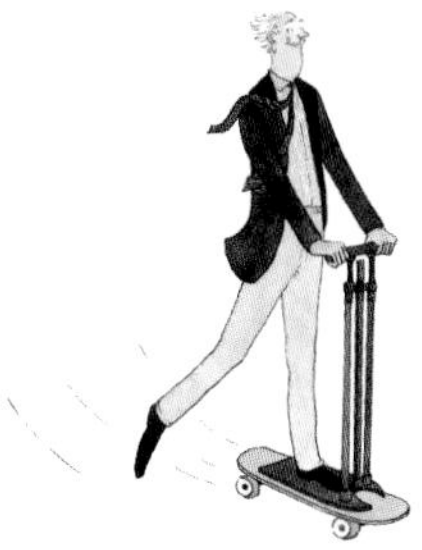

January 8th, 2004

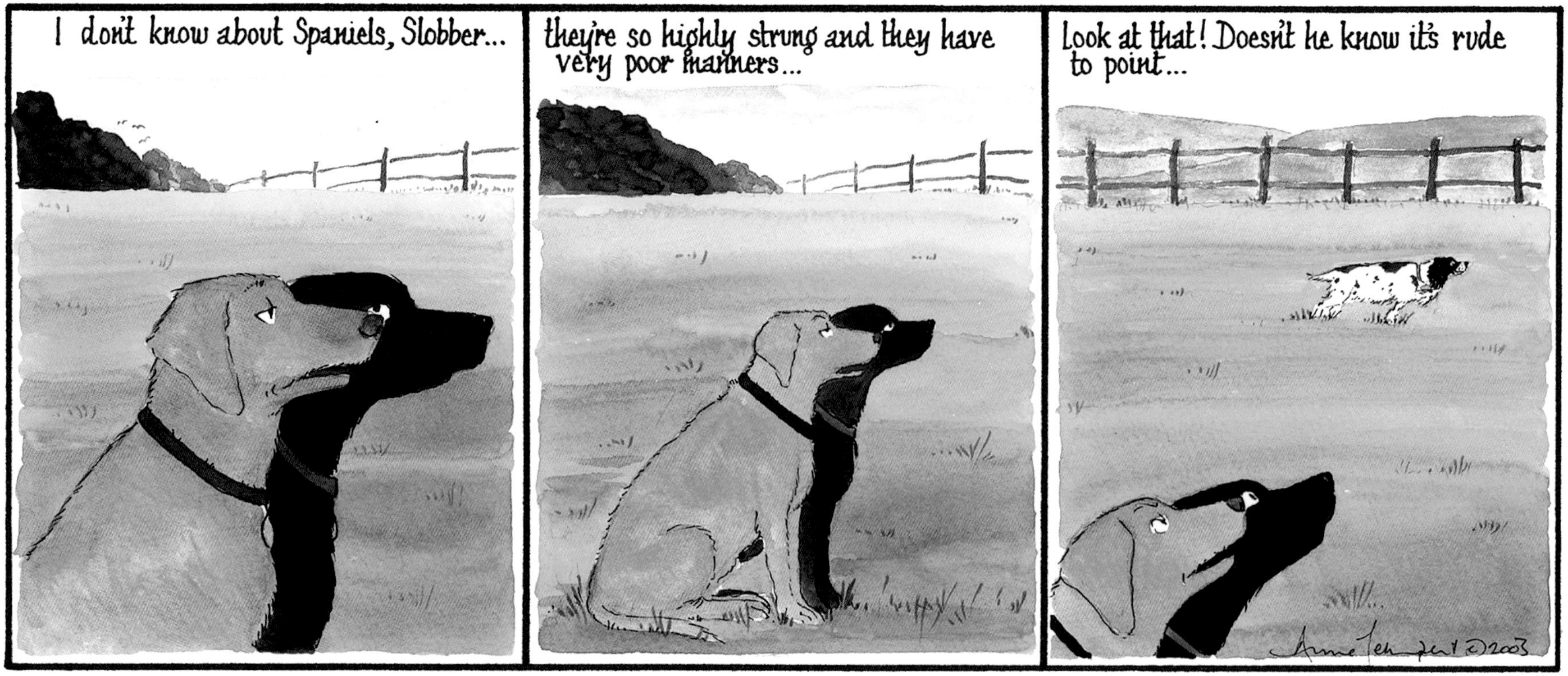
I don't know about Spaniels, Slobber...
they're so highly strung and they have very poor manners...
Look at that! Doesn't he know it's rude to point...

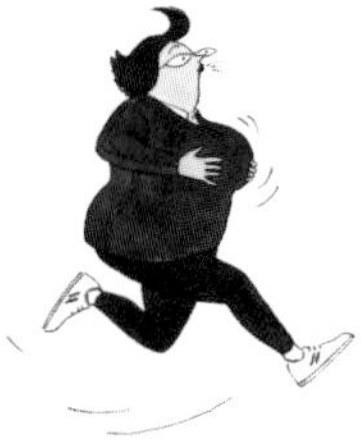

January 15th, 2004

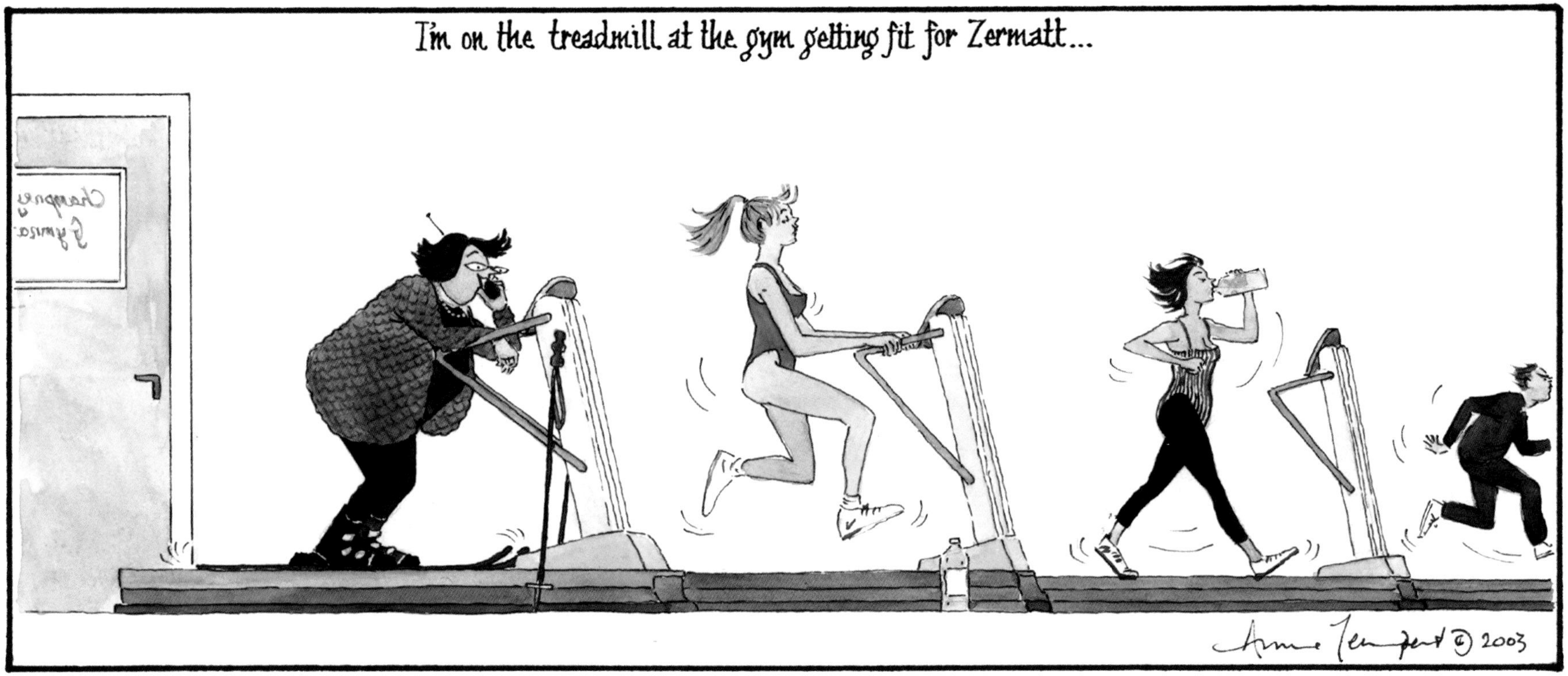
I'm on the treadmill at the gym getting fit for Zermatt...

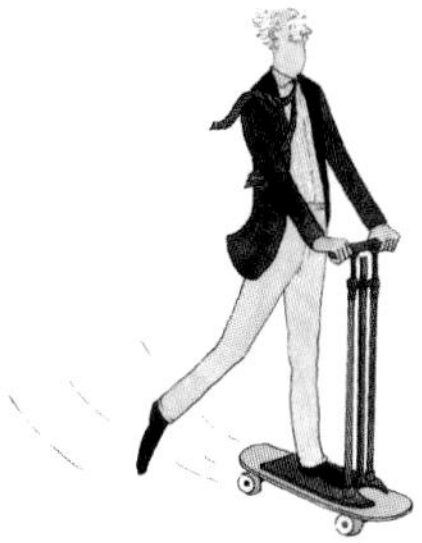

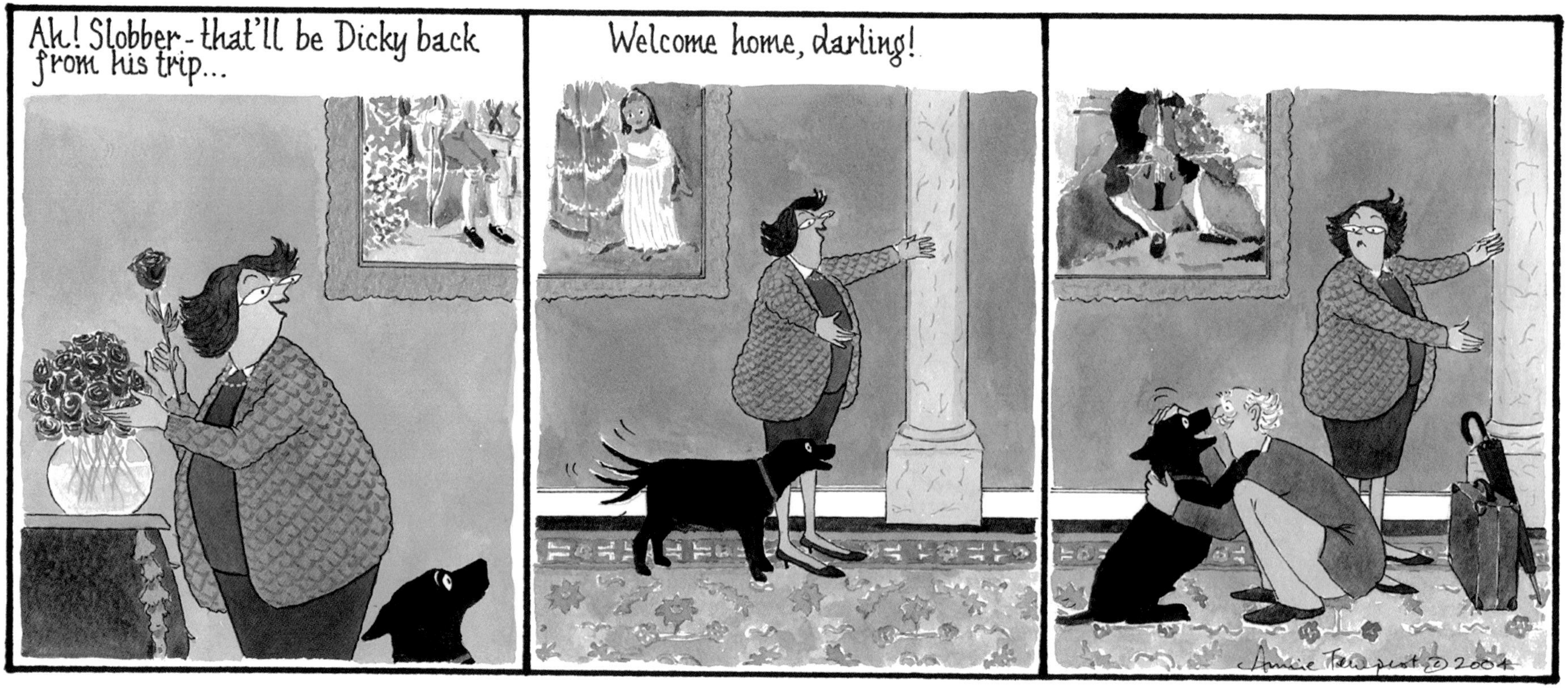
Ah! Slobber - that'll be Dicky back from his trip...
Welcome home, darling!
Annie Tempest © 2004

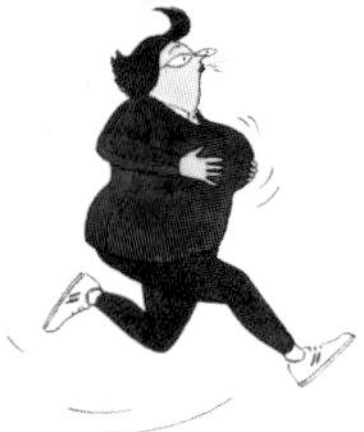

It's Freddy's metal detector – It's great fun...

Every time it goes *beep beep beep* – you get this wonderful surge of adrenalin while you dig for that hoard of Roman coins...

...which usually turns out to be another fascinating piece for my rusty nail collection.

beep!

beep!

beep!

Annie Tempest © 2003

February 5th, 2004

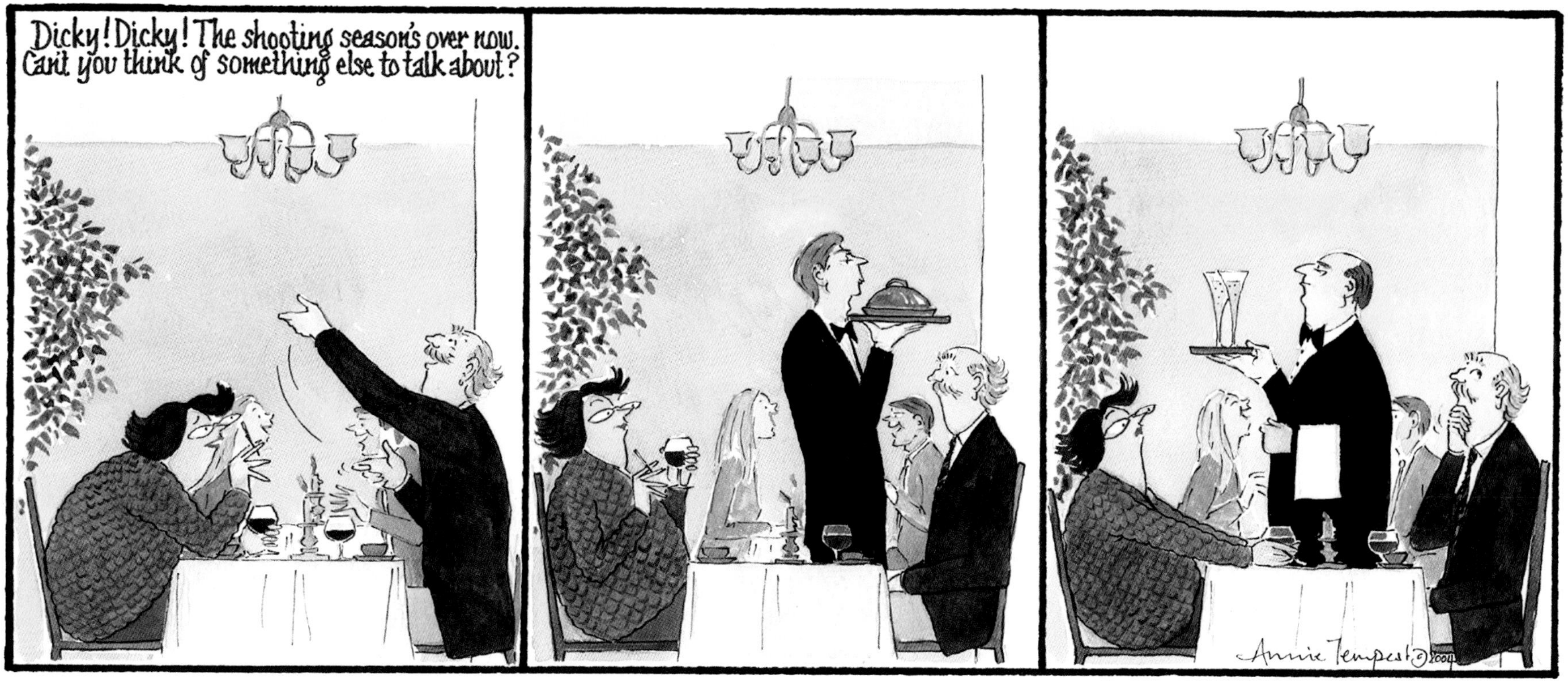
Dicky! Dicky! The shooting season's over now.
Can't you think of something else to talk about?
Annie Tempest © 2004

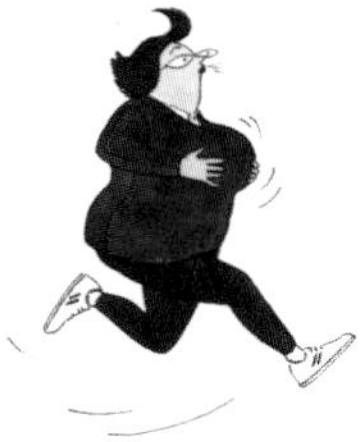

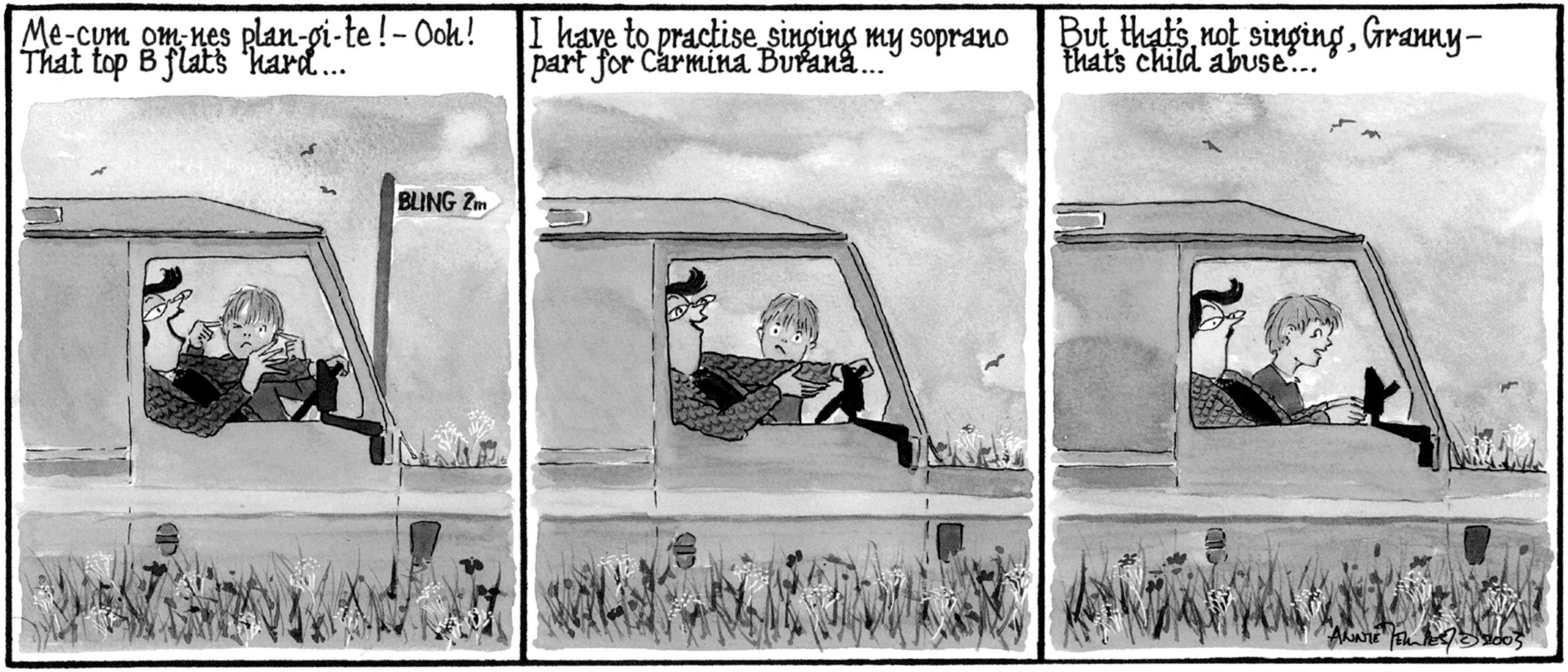
Me-cum om-nes plan-gi-te! - Ooh! That top B flat's hard...
BLING 2m
I have to practise singing my soprano part for Carmina Burana...
But that's not singing, Granny - that's child abuse...
ANNIE TEMPEST © 2003

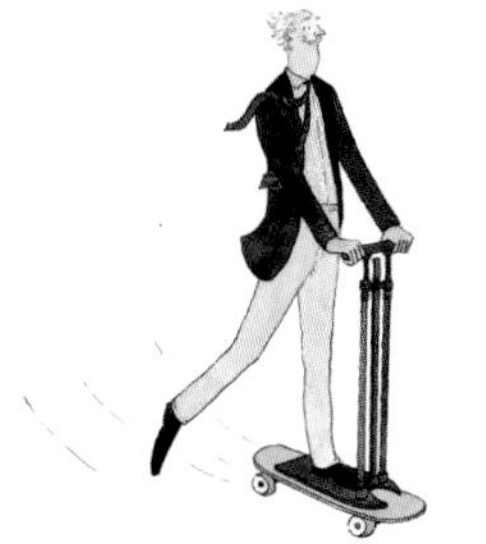

February 19th, 2004

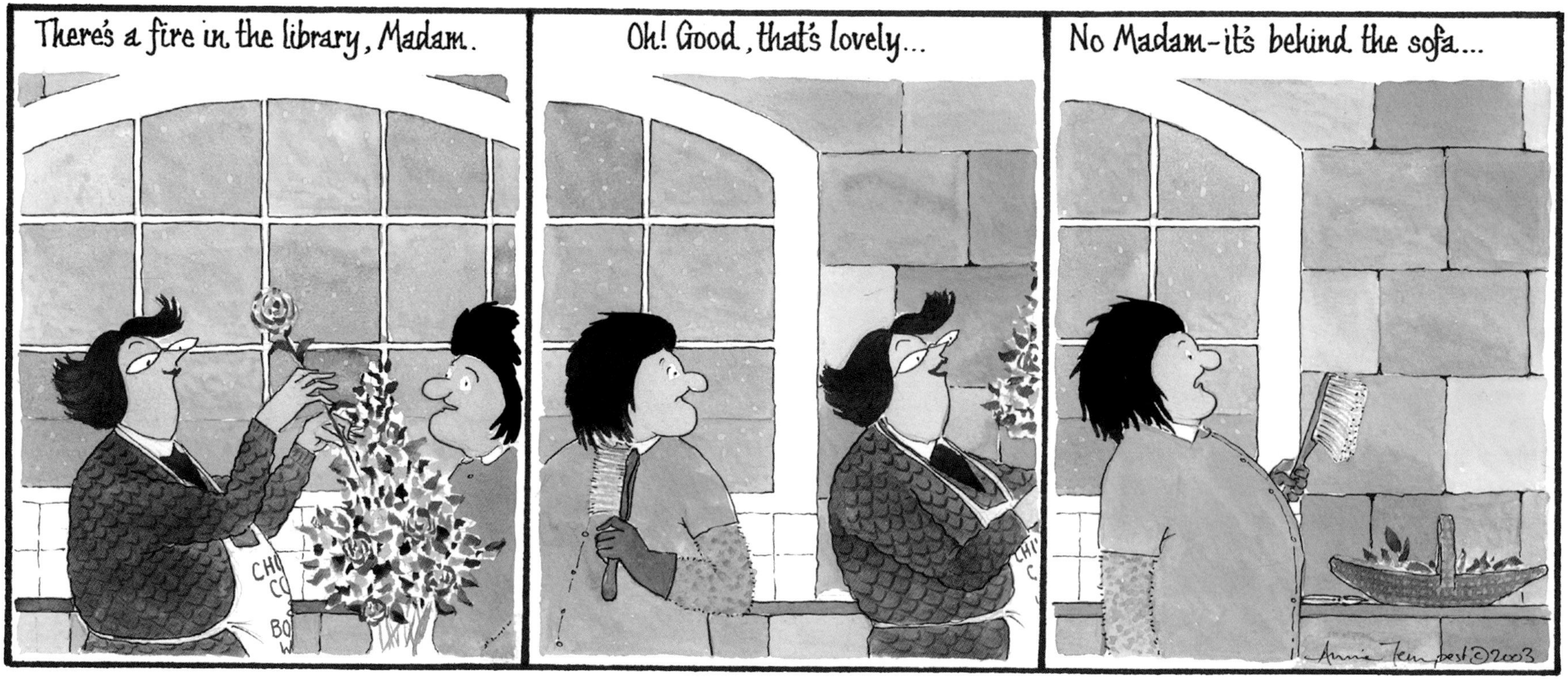
There's a fire in the library, Madam.
Oh! Good, that's lovely...
No Madam–it's behind the sofa...
Annie Tempest ©2003

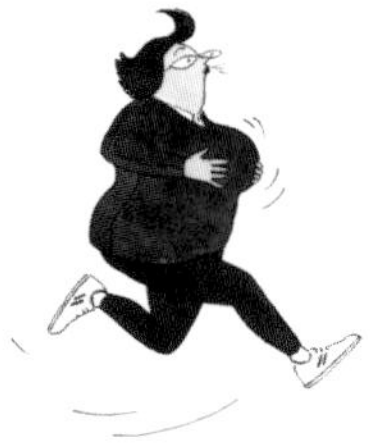

February 26th, 2004

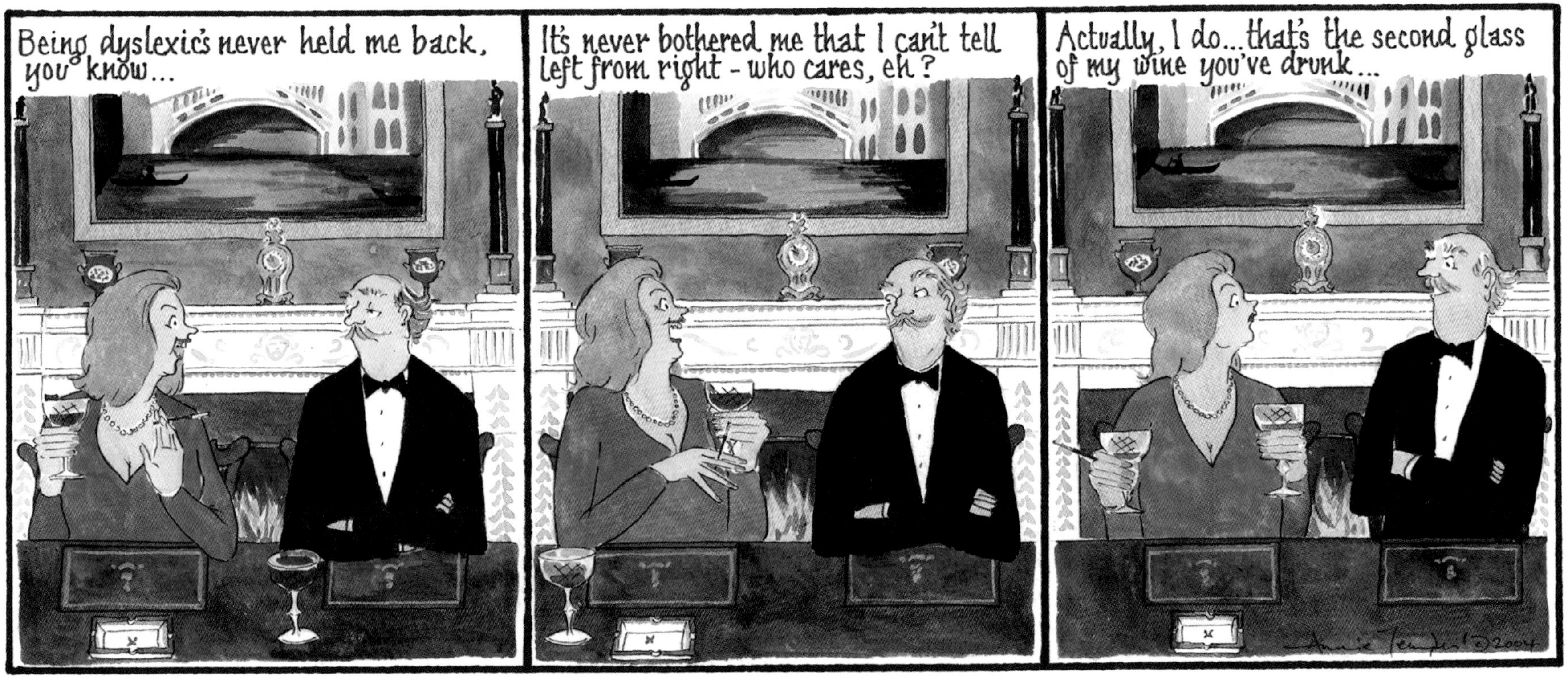
Being dyslexic's never held me back, you know...
It's never bothered me that I can't tell left from right - who cares, eh?
Actually, I do... that's the second glass of my wine you've drunk...

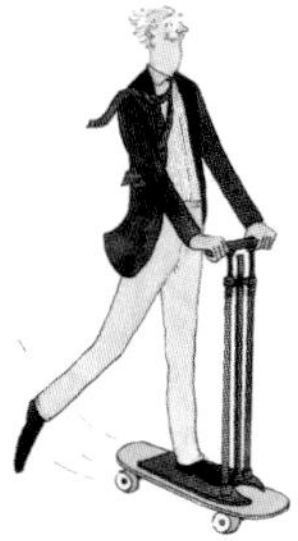

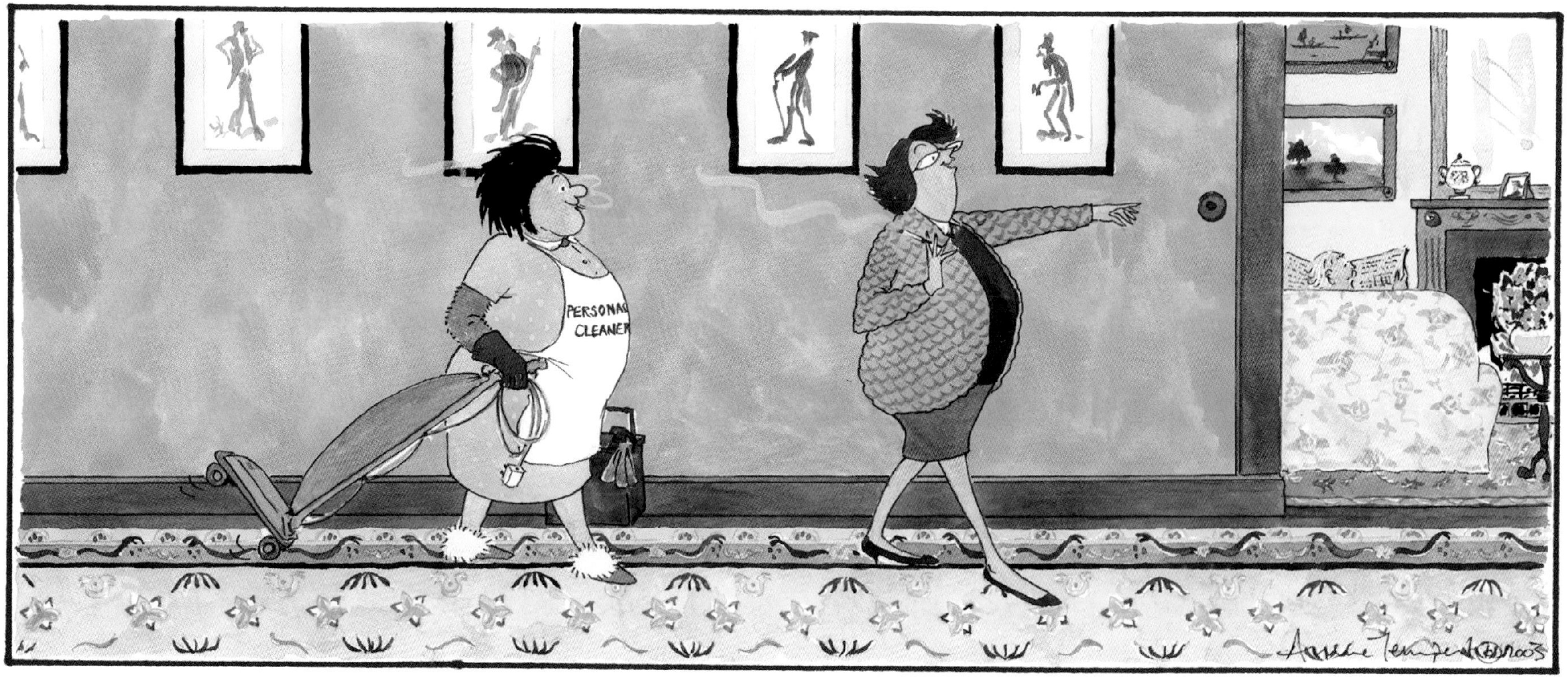
PERSONAL CLEANER

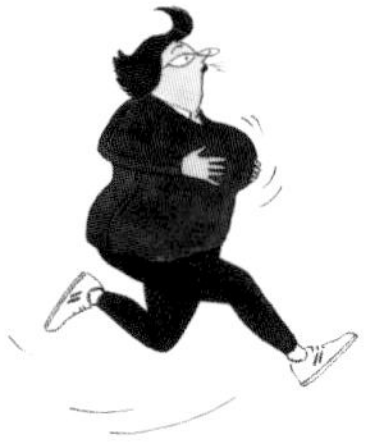

March 11th, 2004

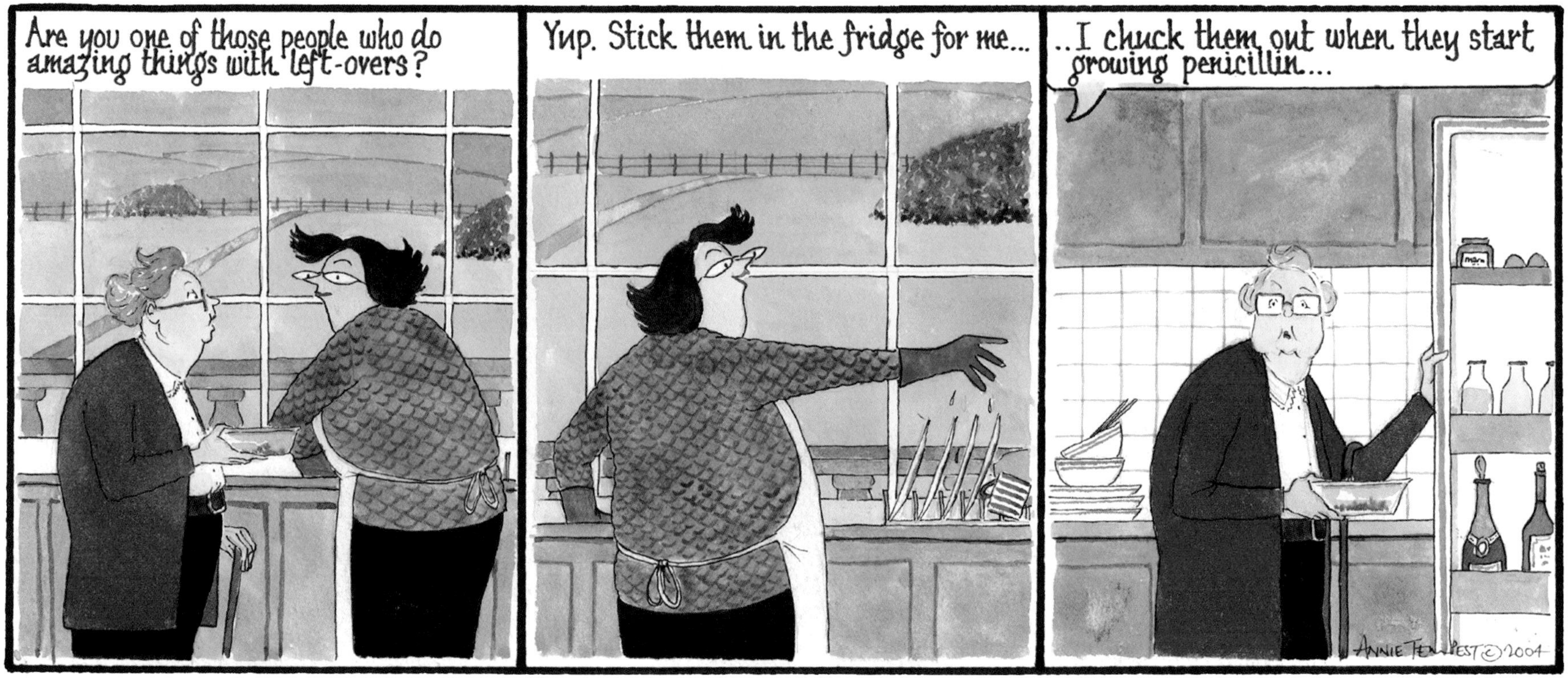

Are you one of those people who do amazing things with left-overs?
Yup. Stick them in the fridge for me...
..I chuck them out when they start growing penicillin...

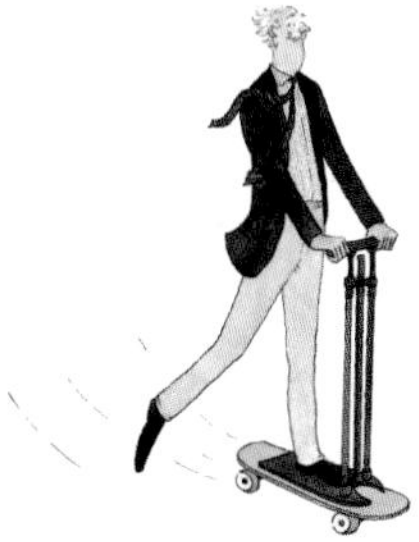

March 18th, 2004

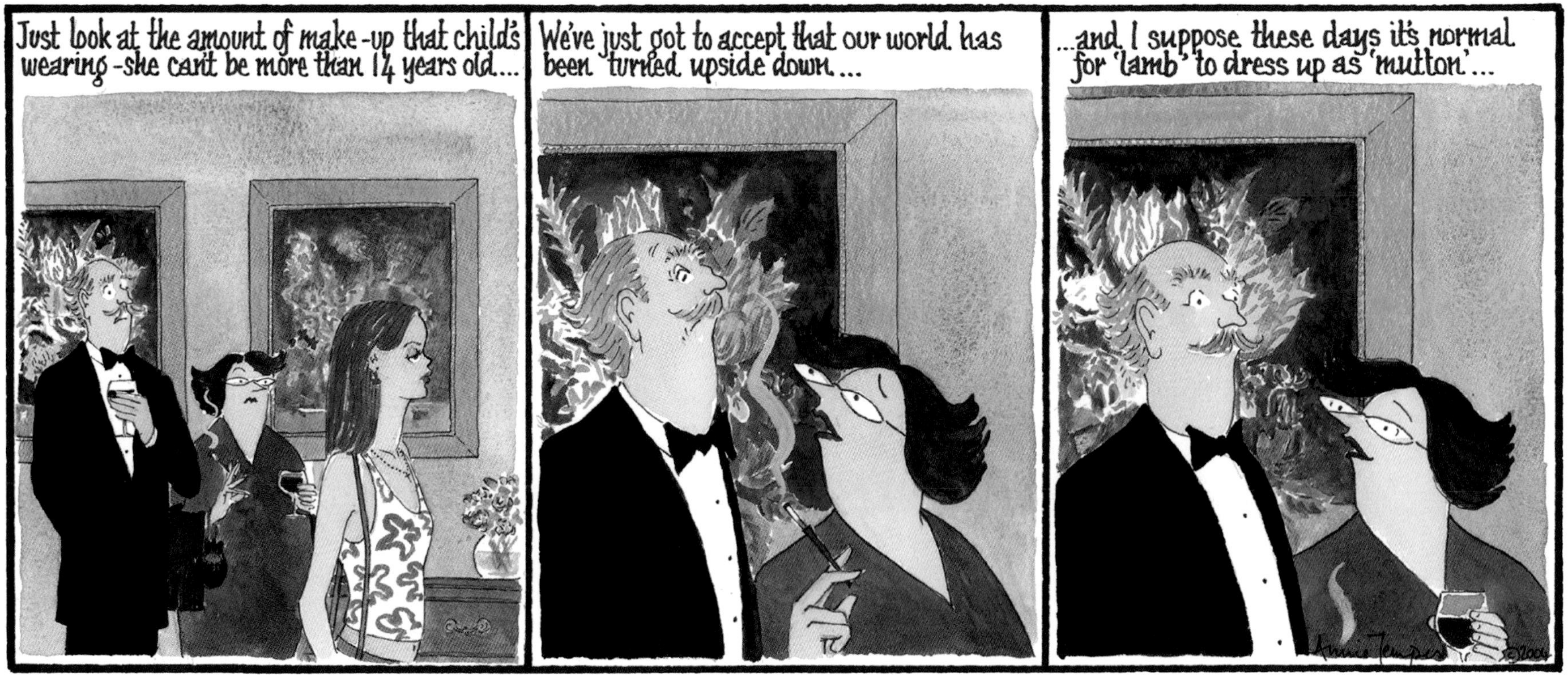
Just look at the amount of make-up that child's wearing - she can't be more than 14 years old...
We've just got to accept that our world has been 'turned upside down...
...and I suppose these days it's normal for 'lamb' to dress up as 'mutton'...

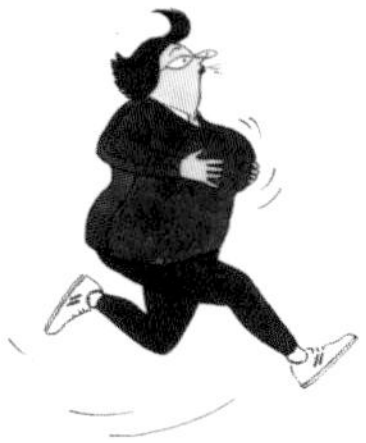

March 25th, 2004

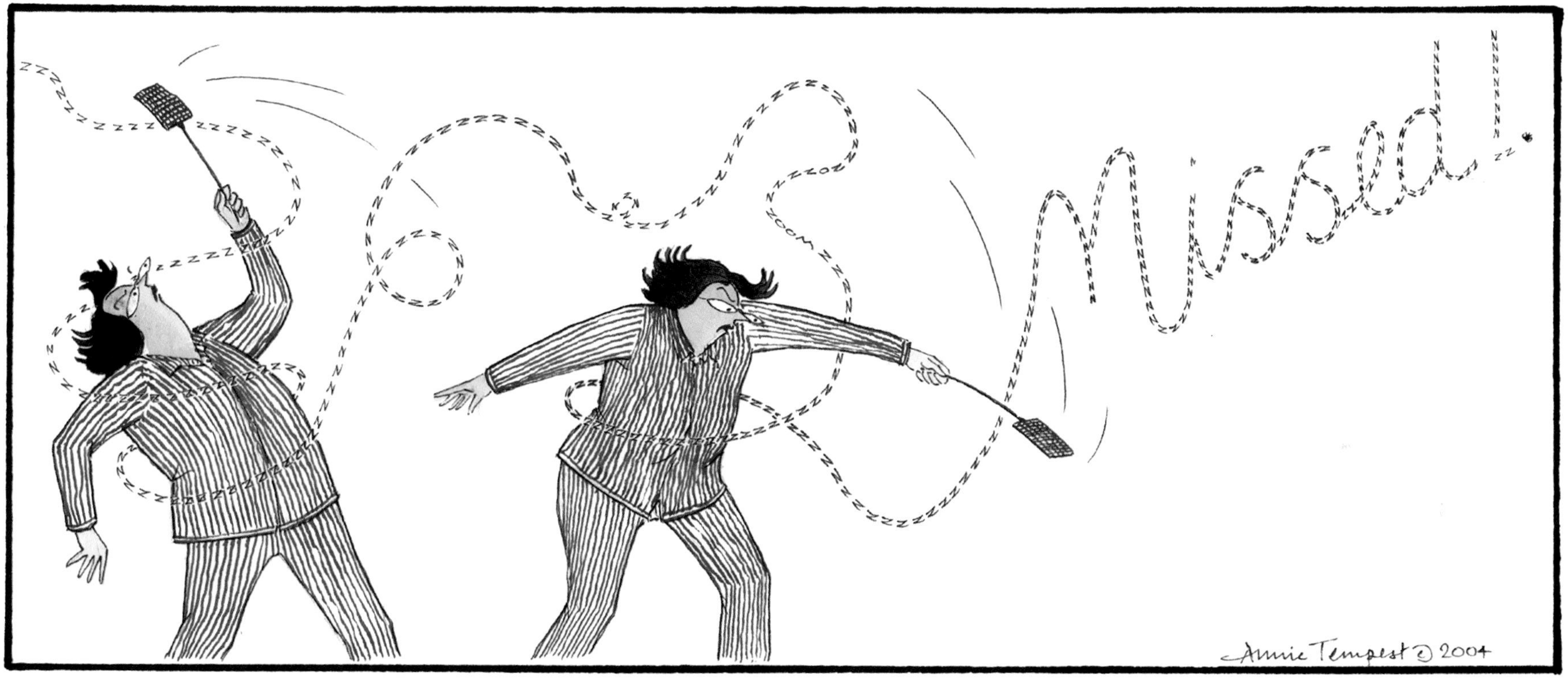
Missed!
Annie Tempest © 2004

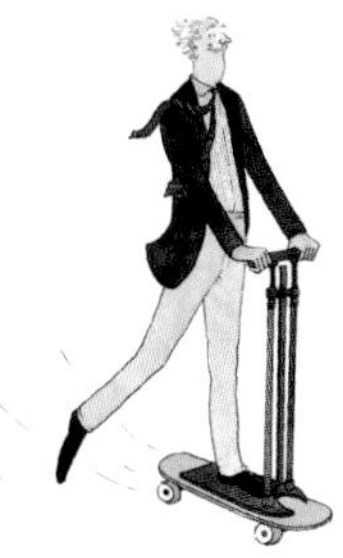

April 1st, 2004

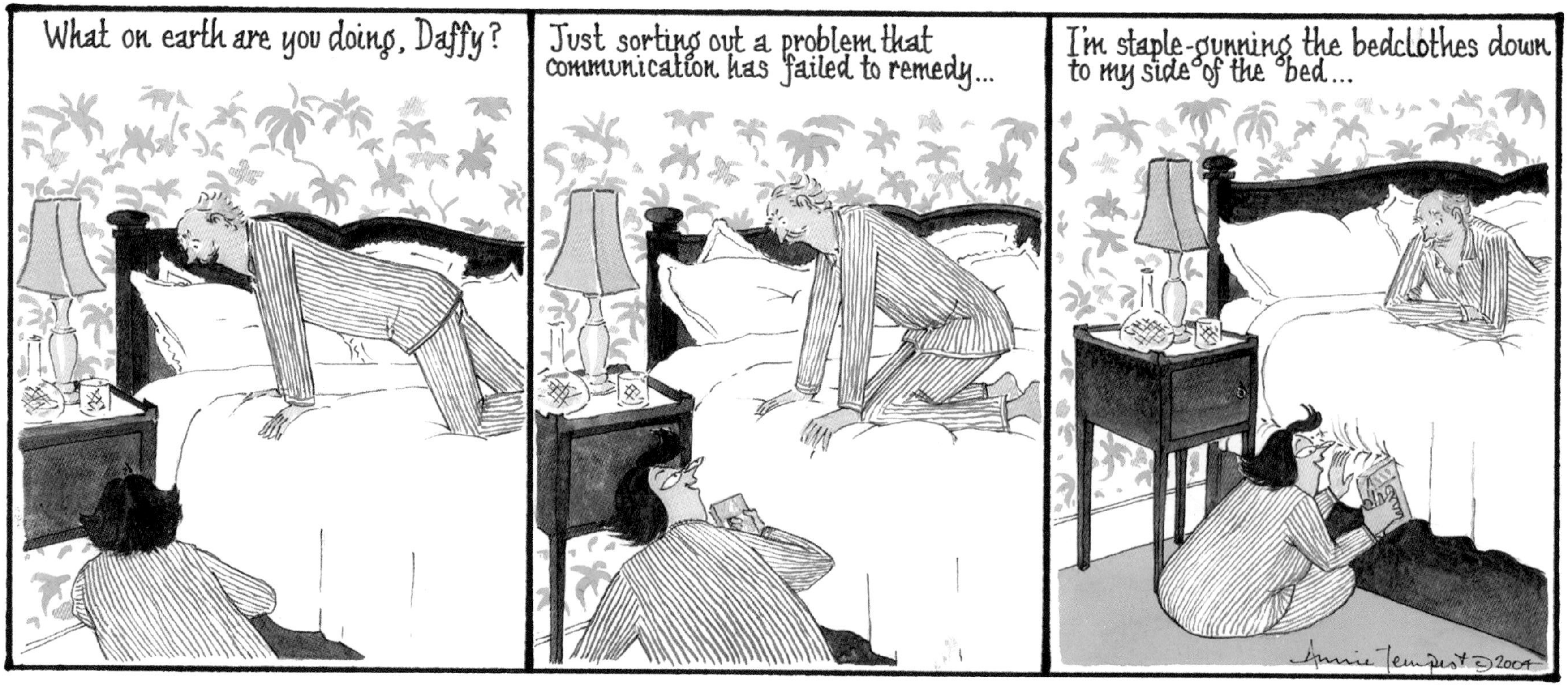
What on earth are you doing, Daffy?
Just sorting out a problem that communication has failed to remedy...
I'm staple-gunning the bedclothes down to my side of the bed...
Annie Tempest ©2004

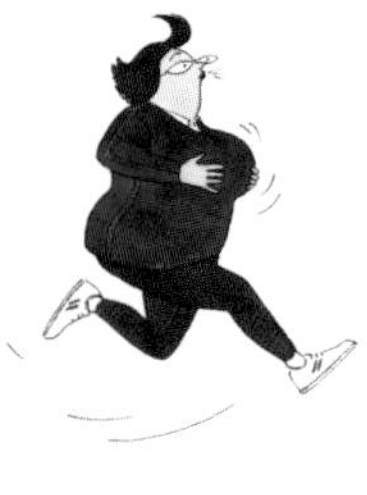

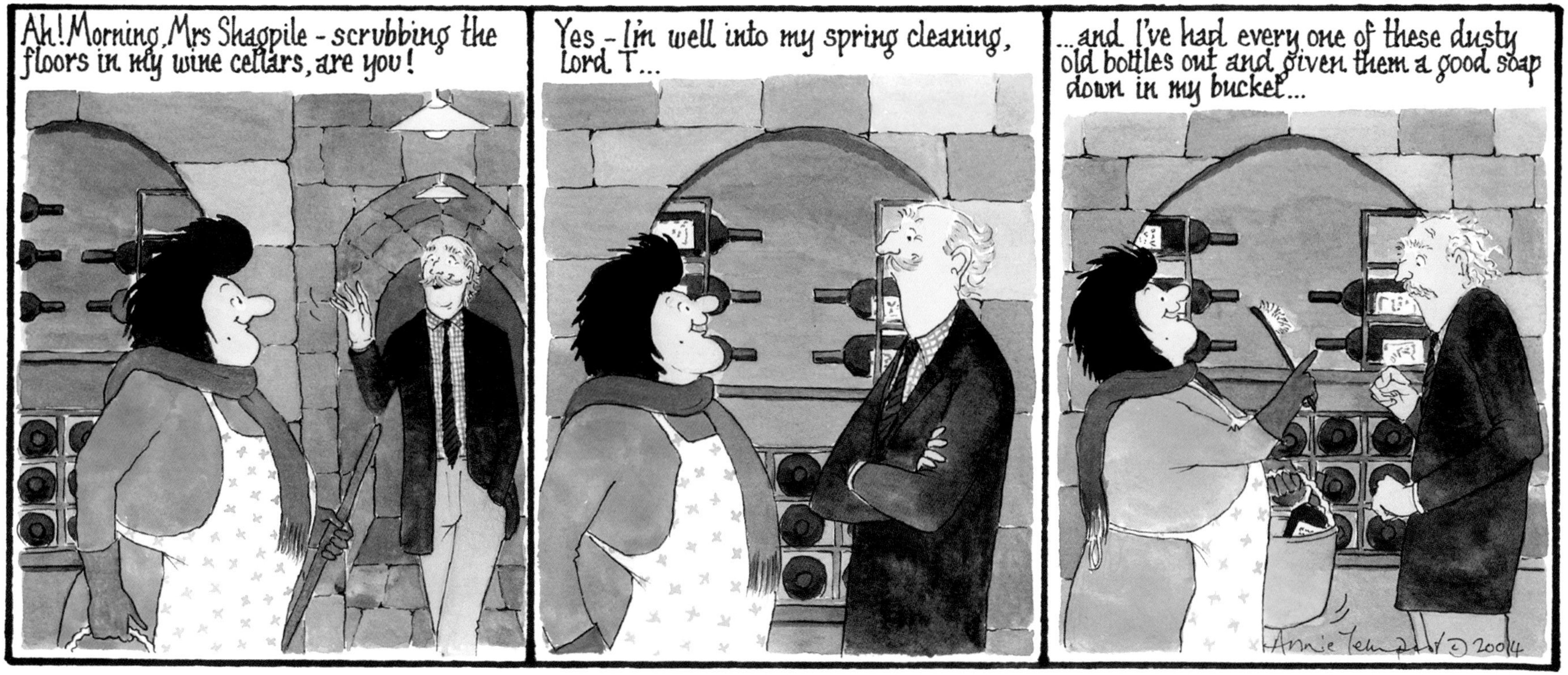
Ah! Morning, Mrs Shagpile - scrubbing the floors in my wine cellars, are you!
Yes - I'm well into my spring cleaning, Lord T...
...and I've had every one of these dusty old bottles out and given them a good soap down in my bucket...
Annie Tempest © 2004

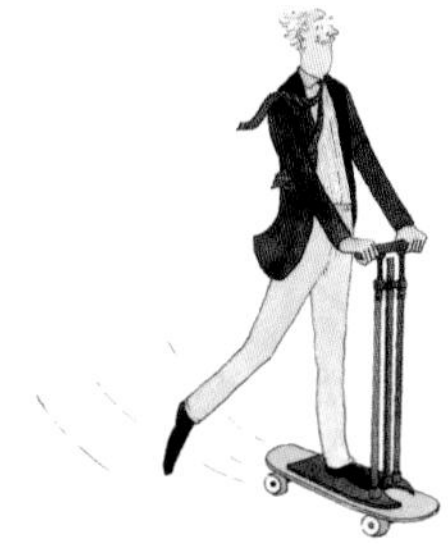

April 15th, 2004

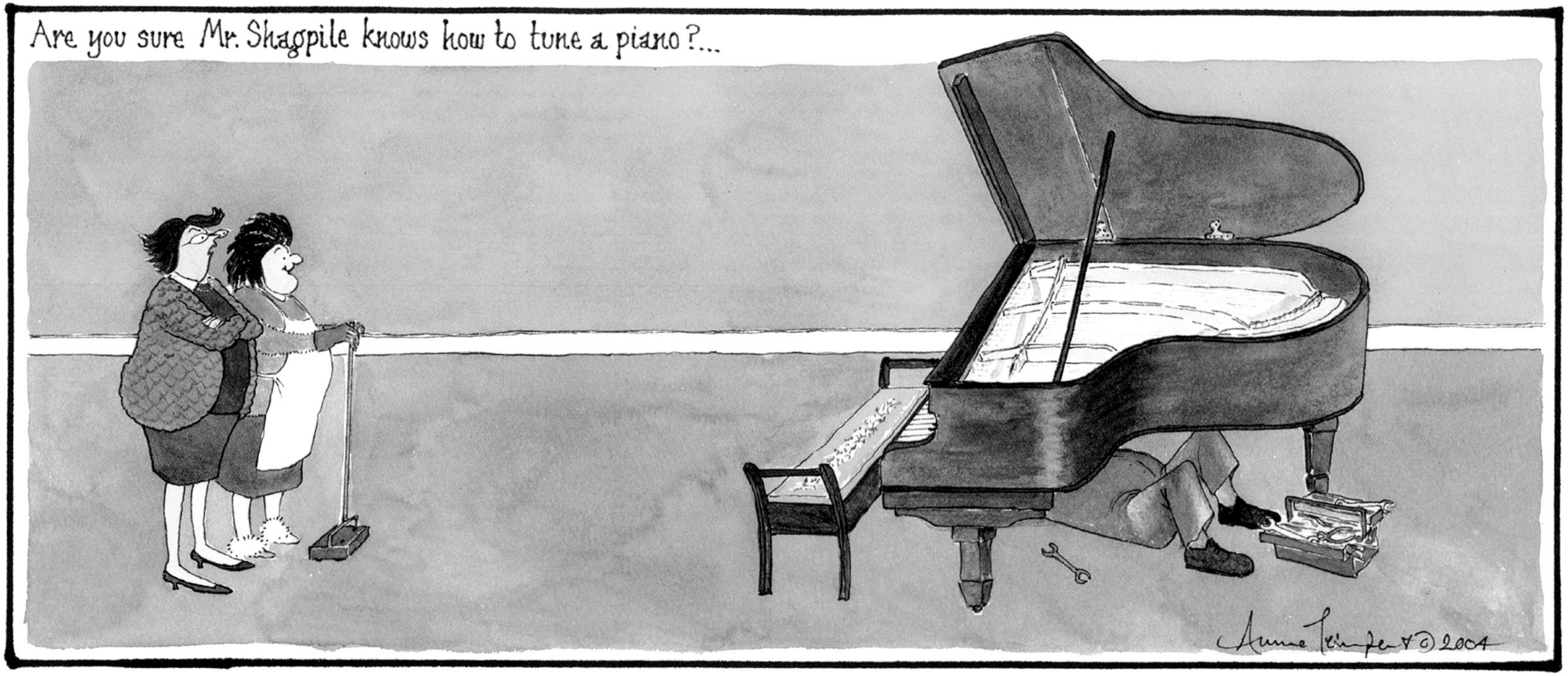
Are you sure Mr. Shagpile knows how to tune a piano?...

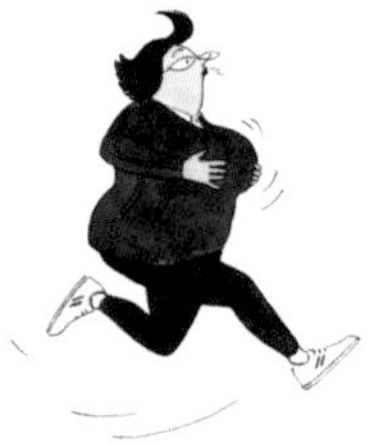

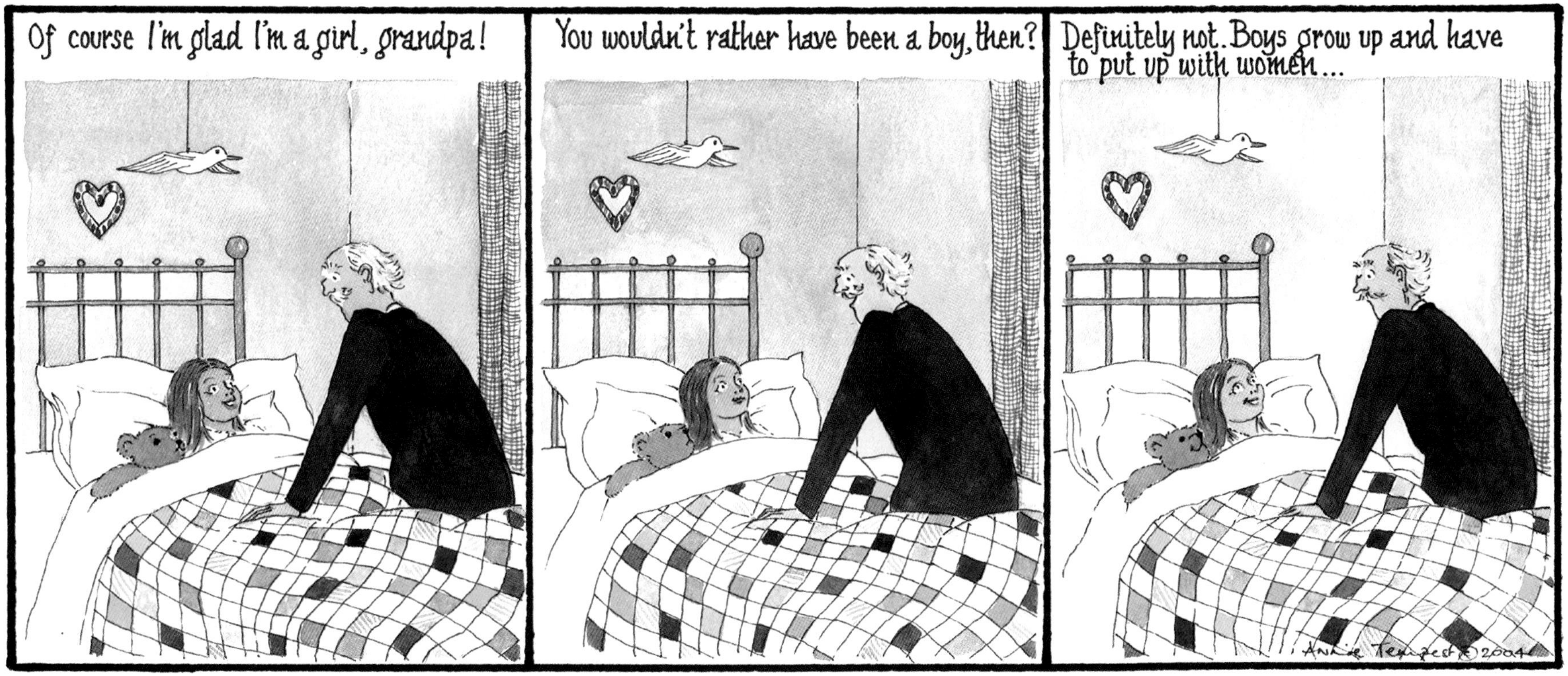
Of course I'm glad I'm a girl, grandpa!
You wouldn't rather have been a boy, then?
Definitely not. Boys grow up and have to put up with women...
Annie Tempest © 2004

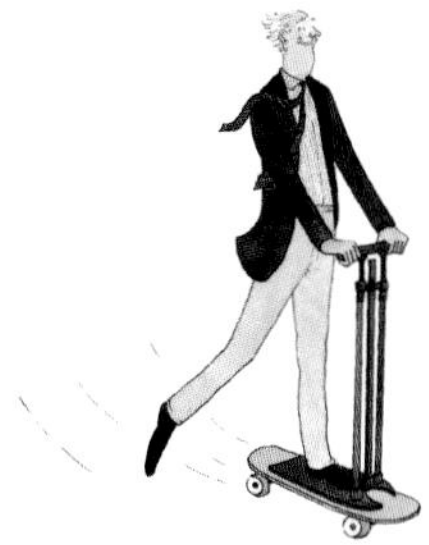

April 29th, 2004

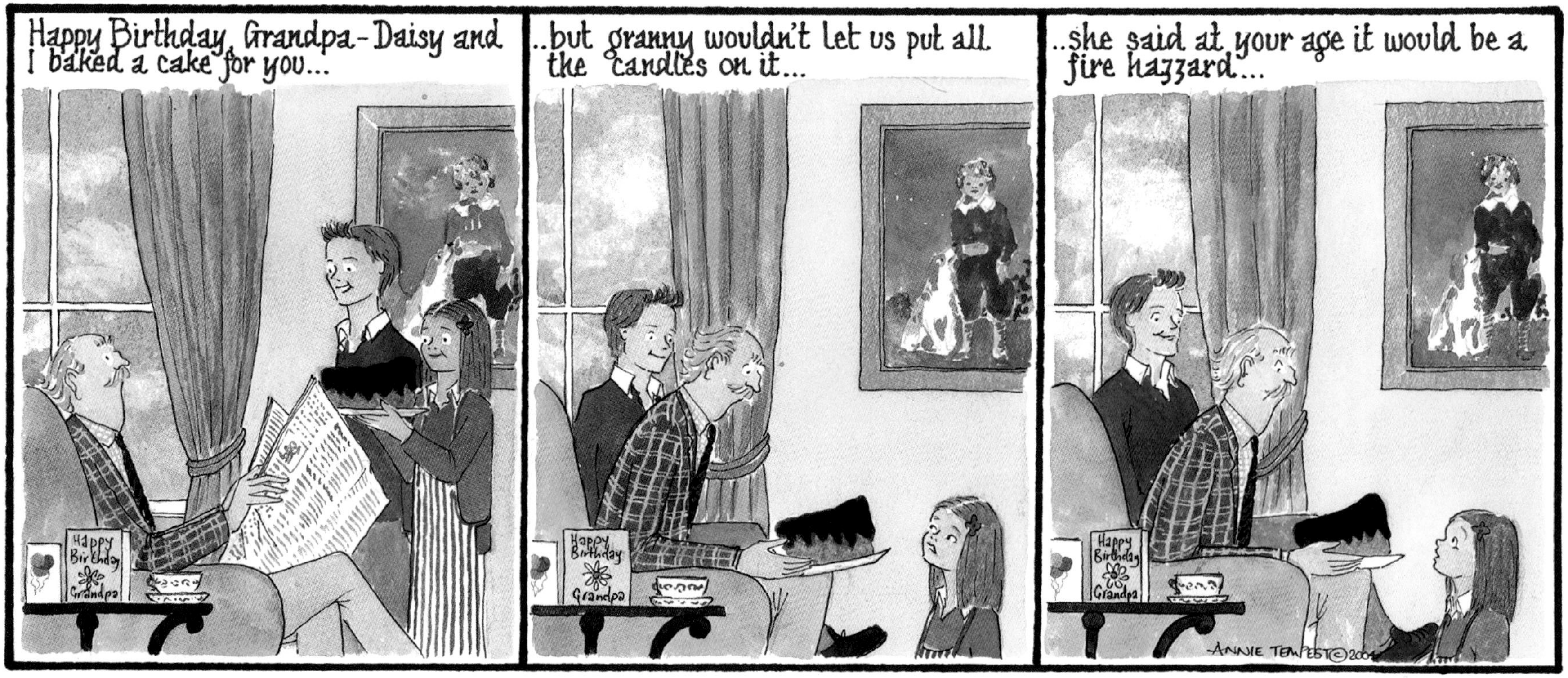
Happy Birthday, Grandpa - Daisy and I baked a cake for you...
Happy Birthday Grandpa
..but granny wouldn't let us put all the candles on it...
Happy Birthday Grandpa
..she said at your age it would be a fire hazzard...
Happy Birthday Grandpa
ANNIE TEMPEST © 2004

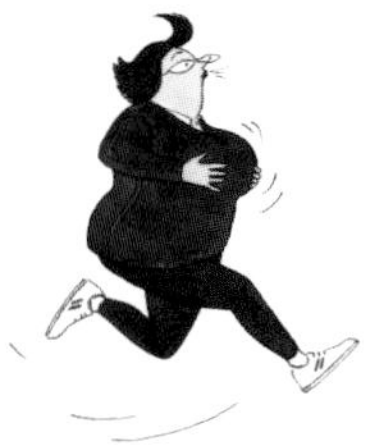

May 6th, 2004

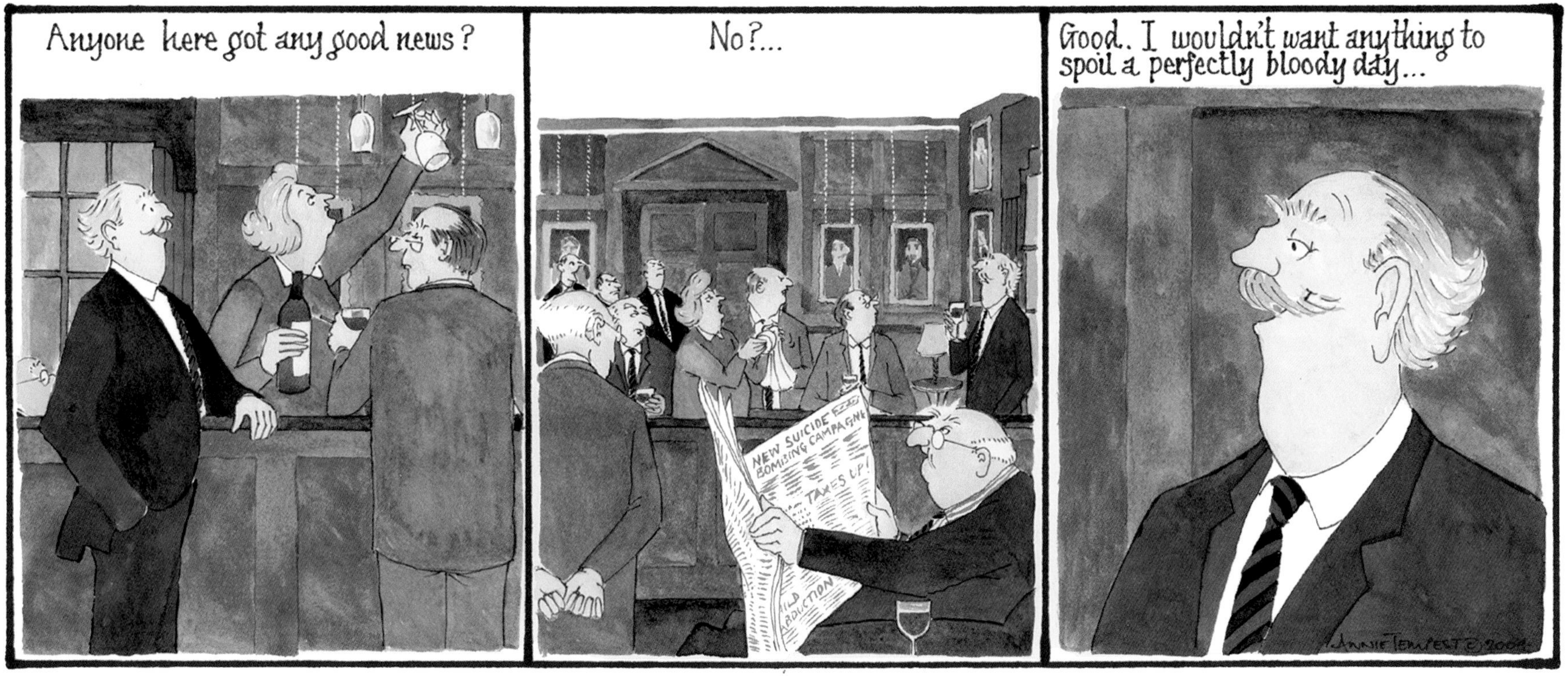
Anyone here got any good news?
No?...
NEW SUICIDE BOMBING CAMPAIGN
TAXES UP!
Good. I wouldn't want anything to spoil a perfectly bloody day...
ANNIE TEMPEST © 2004

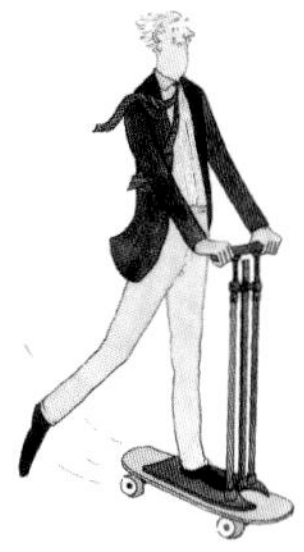

May 13th, 2004

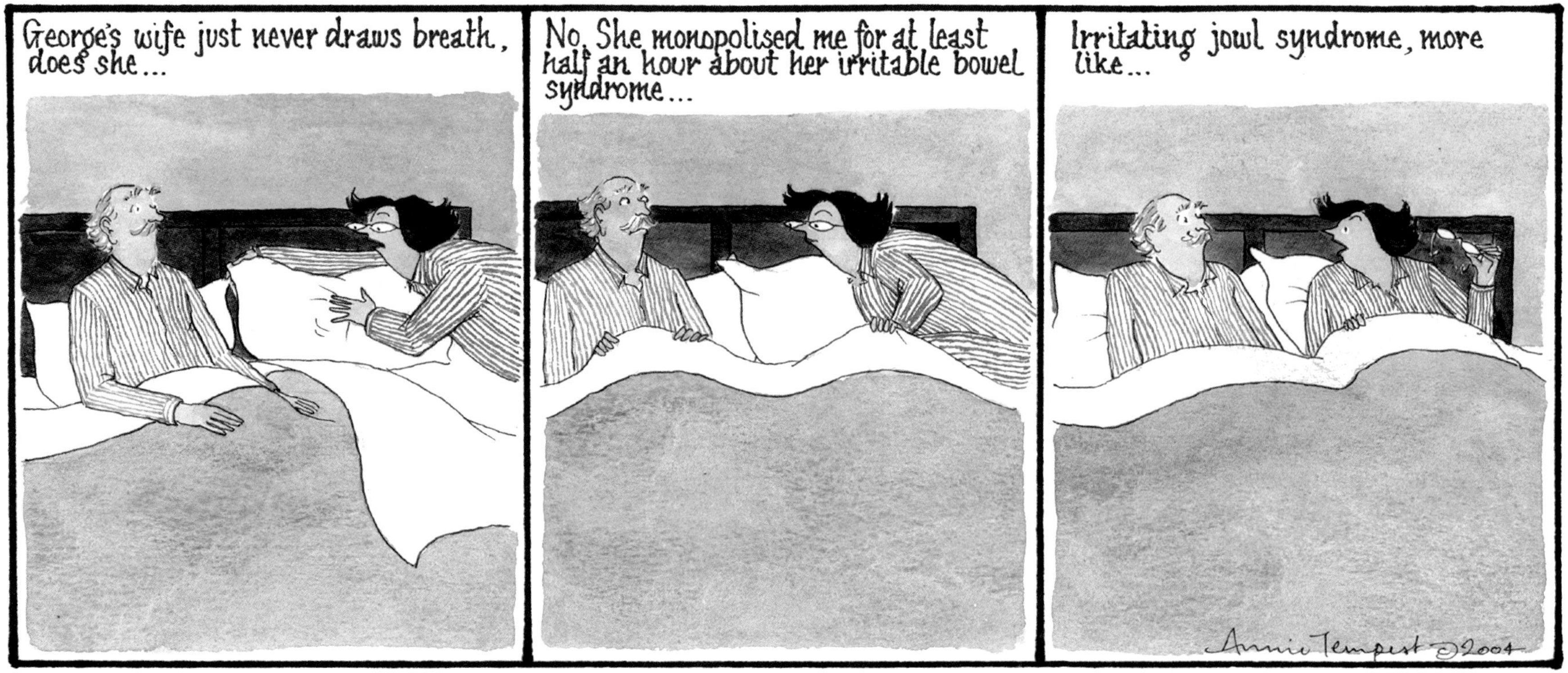
George's wife just never draws breath, does she...
No. She monopolised me for at least half an hour about her irritable bowel syndrome...
Irritating jowl syndrome, more like...
Annie Tempest ©2004

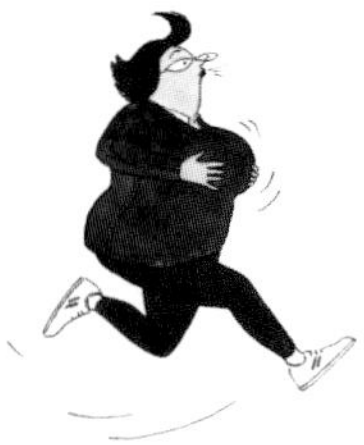

May 20th, 2004

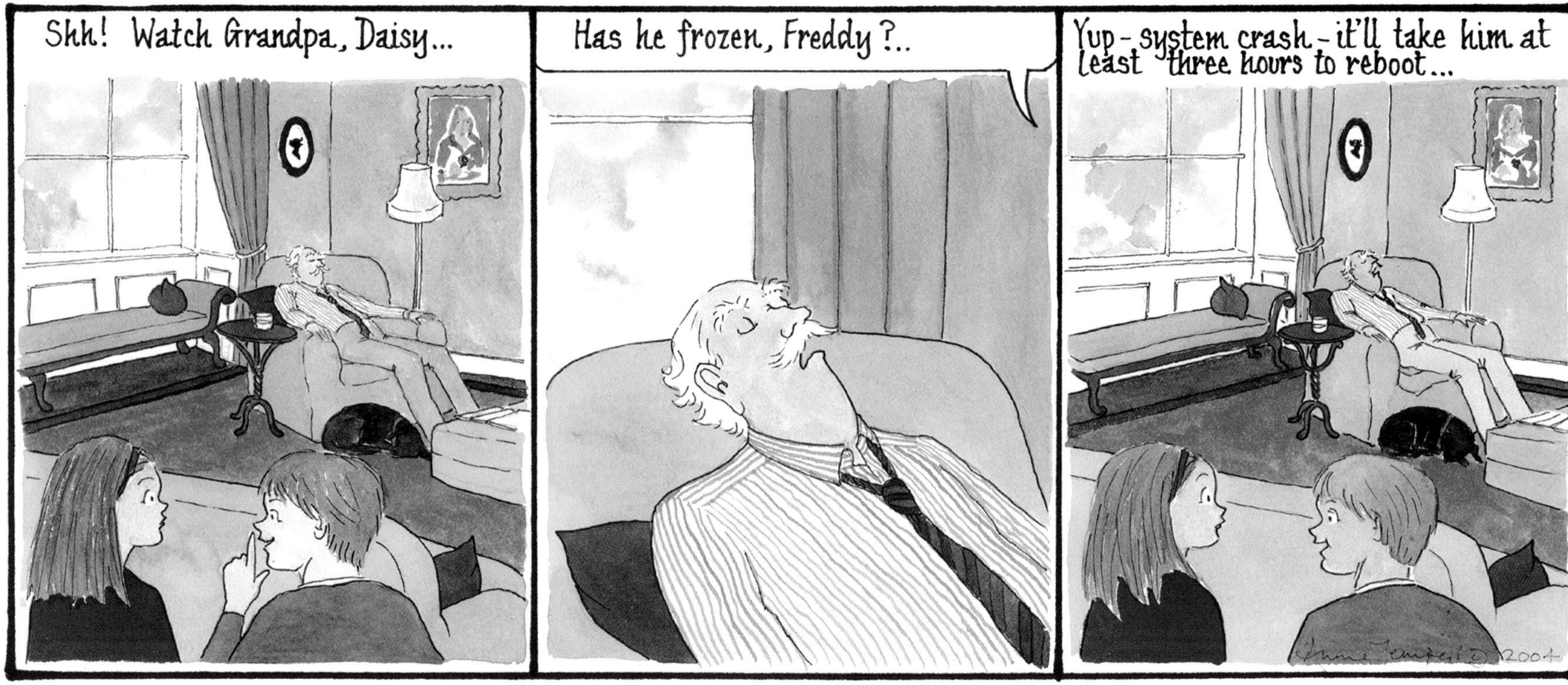
Shh! Watch Grandpa, Daisy...
Has he frozen, Freddy?..
Yup - system crash - it'll take him at least three hours to reboot...

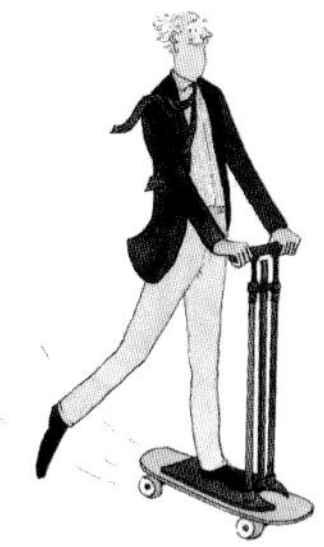

May 27th, 2004

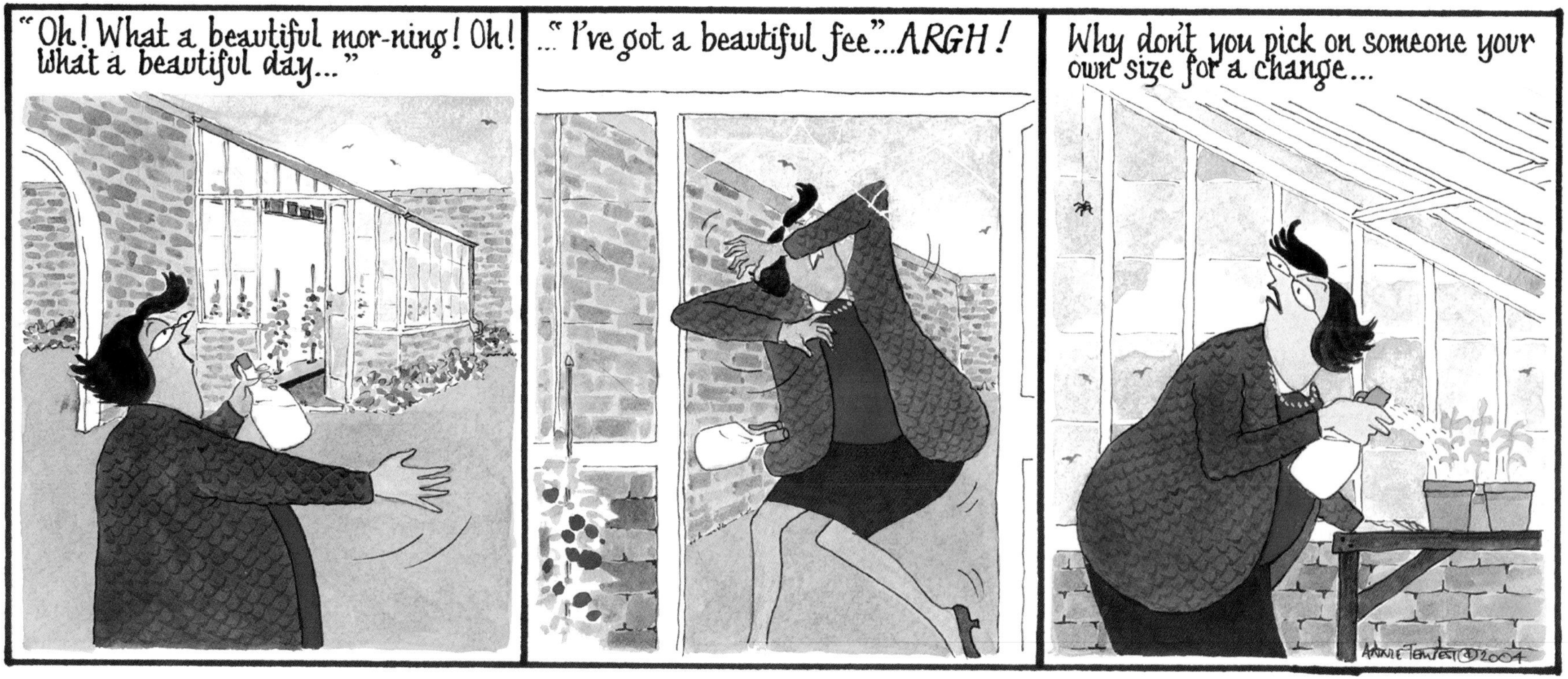
"Oh! What a beautiful mor-ning! Oh! What a beautiful day..."
..."I've got a beautiful fee"...ARGH!
Why don't you pick on someone your own size for a change...
ANNIE TEMPEST © 2004

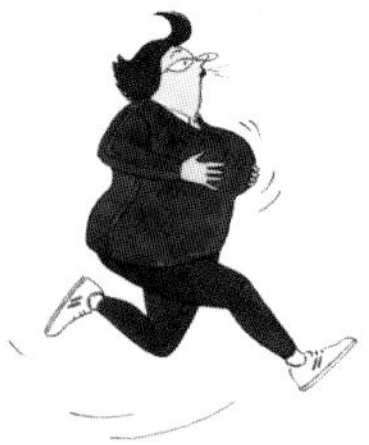

June 3rd, 2004

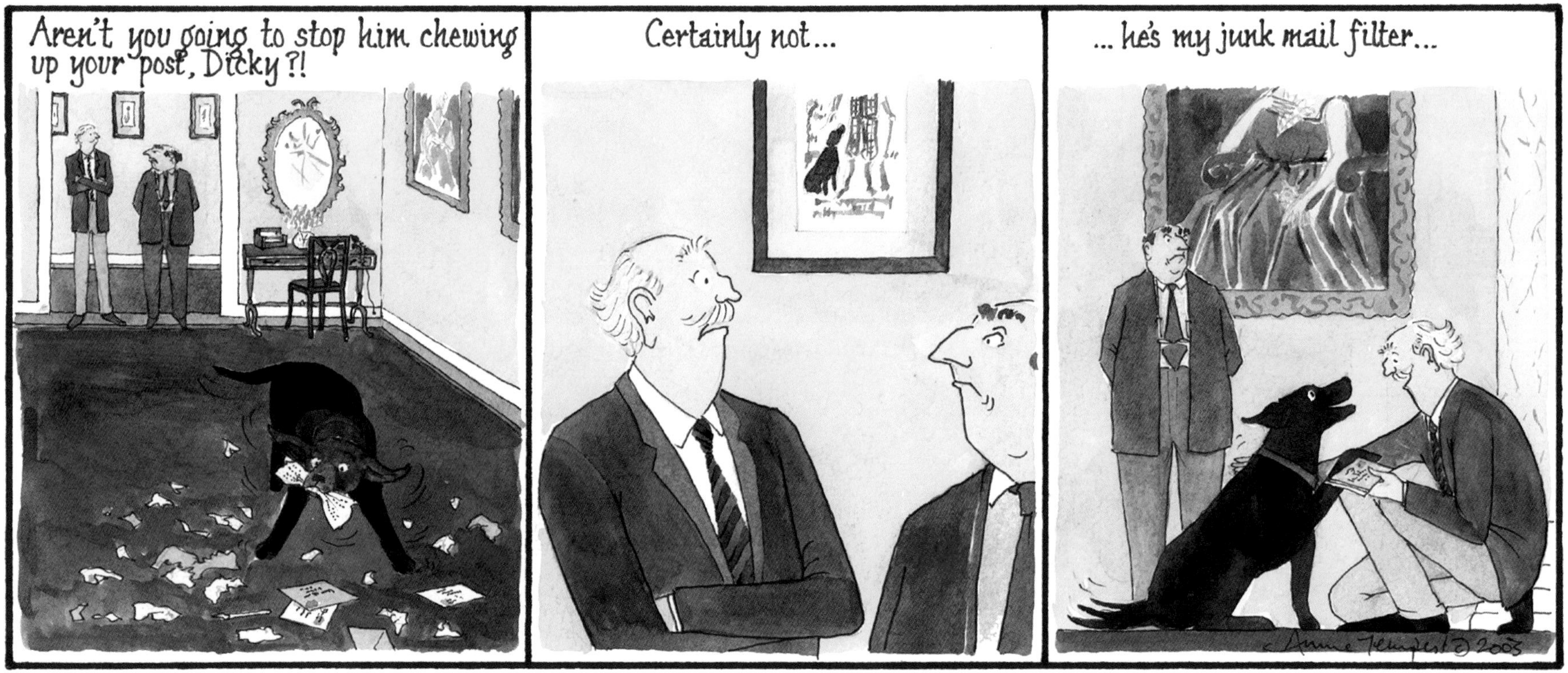
Aren't you going to stop him chewing up your post, Dicky?!
Certainly not...
... he's my junk mail filter...

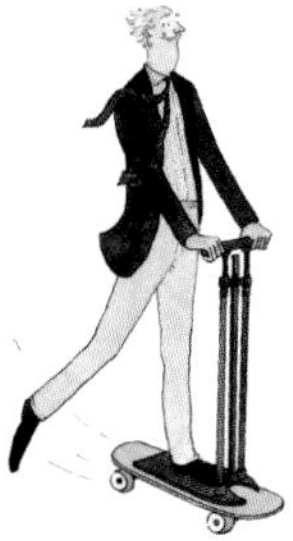

June 10th, 2004

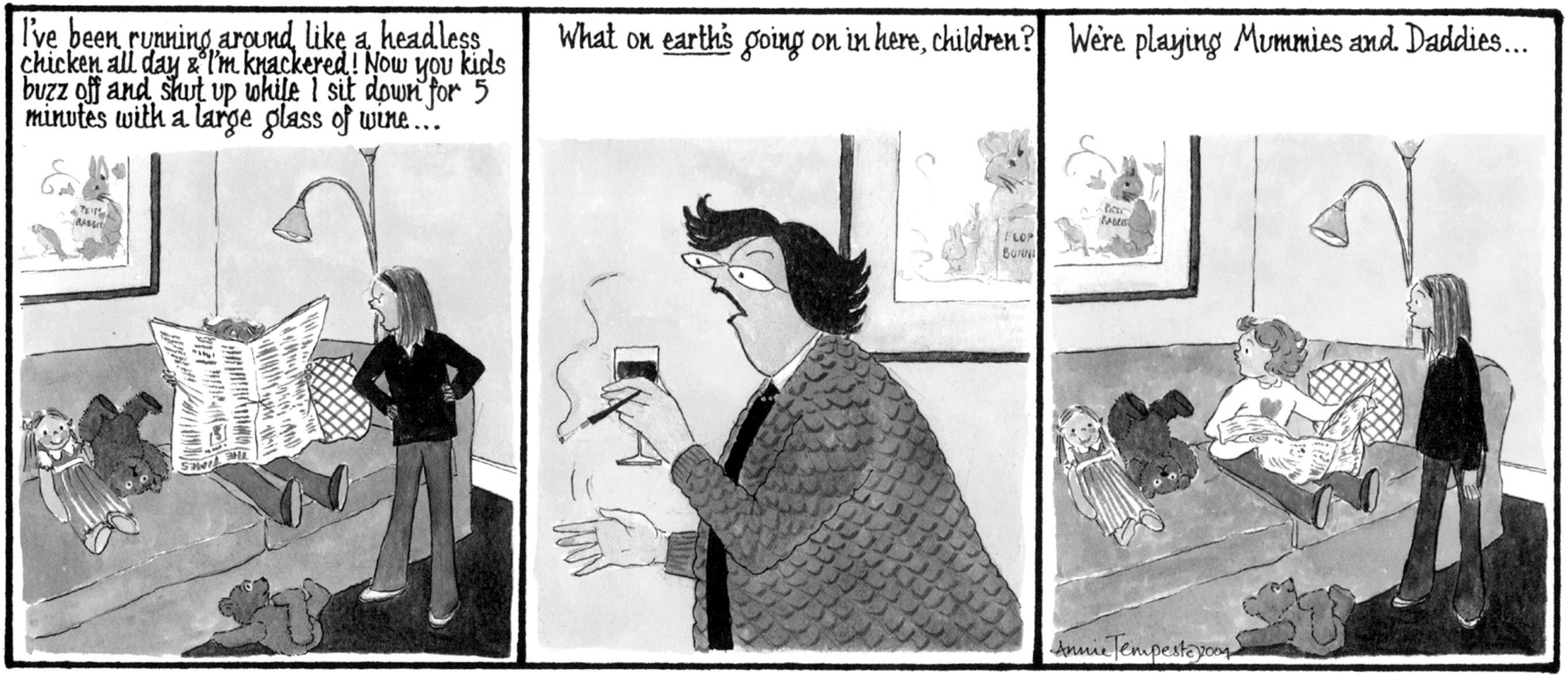

I've been running around like a headless chicken all day & I'm knackered! Now you kids buzz off and shut up while I sit down for 5 minutes with a large glass of wine...
What on earth's going on in here, children?
We're playing Mummies and Daddies...
Annie Tempest ©2004

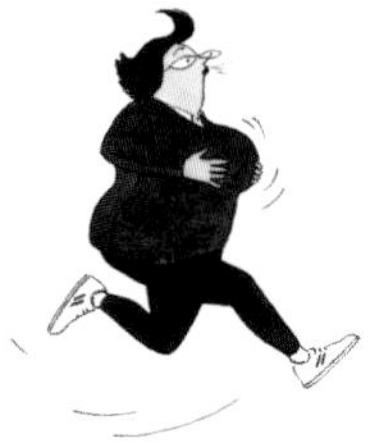

June 17th, 2004

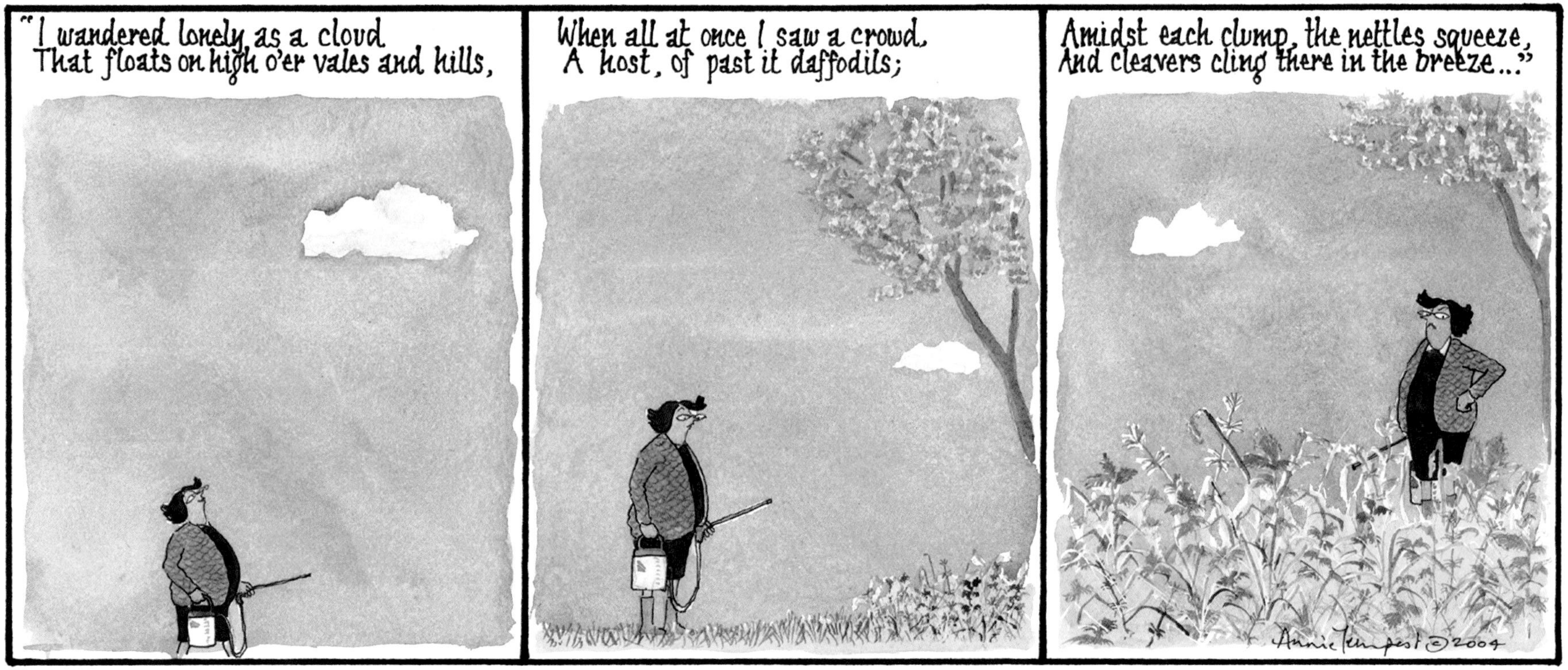
"I wandered lonely as a cloud
That floats on high o'er vales and hills,
When all at once I saw a crowd,
A host, of past it daffodils;
Amidst each clump, the nettles squeeze,
And cleavers cling there in the breeze..."
Annie Tempest ©2004

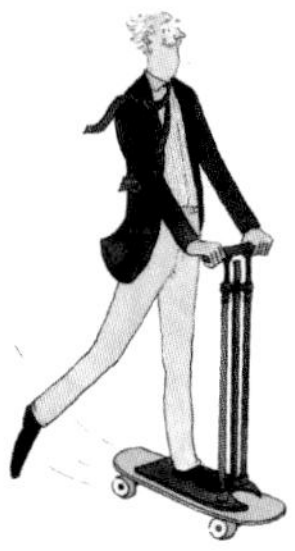

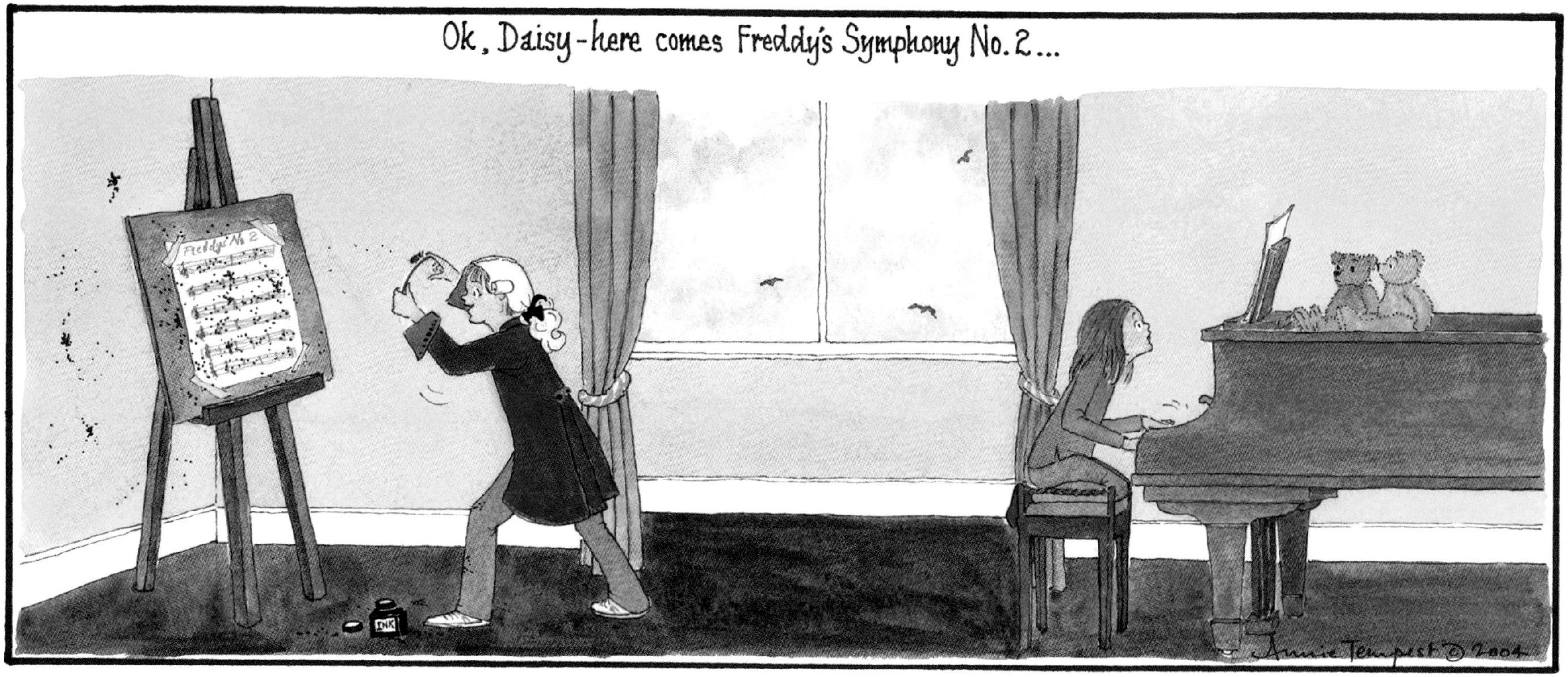
Ok, Daisy-here comes Freddy's Symphony No. 2...
Freddy's No 2
INK
Annie Tempest © 2004

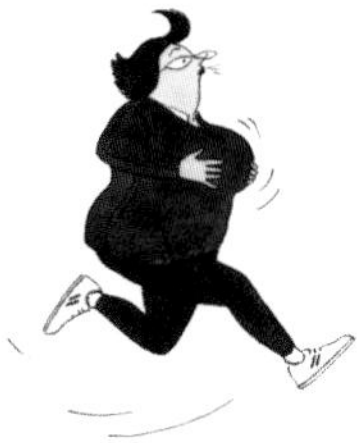

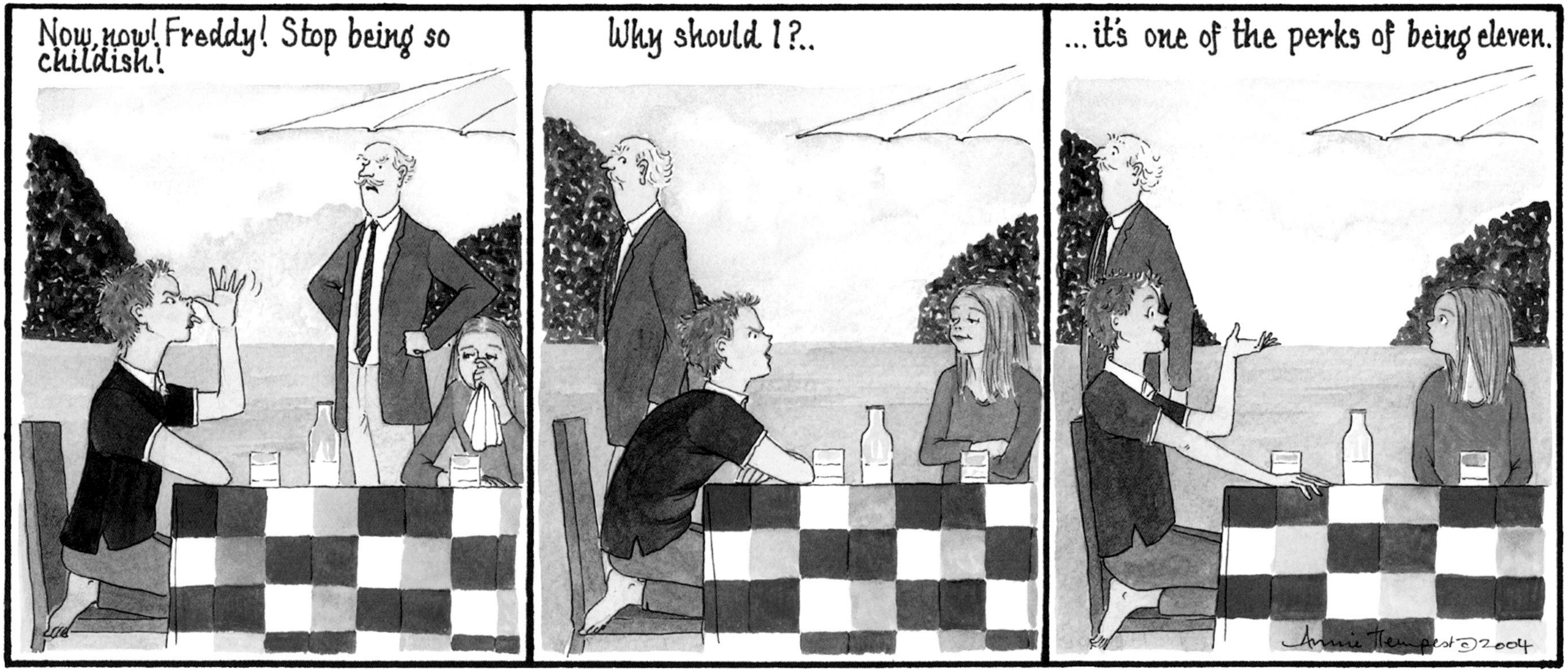
Now, now! Freddy! Stop being so childish!
Why should I?..
... it's one of the perks of being eleven.
Annie Tempest © 2004

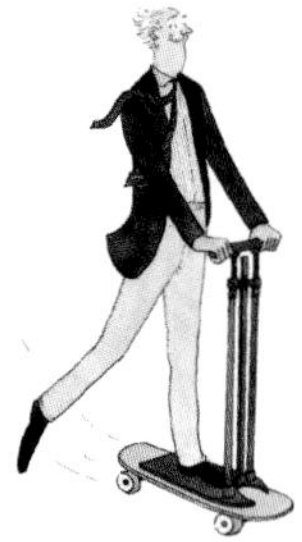

July 8th, 2004

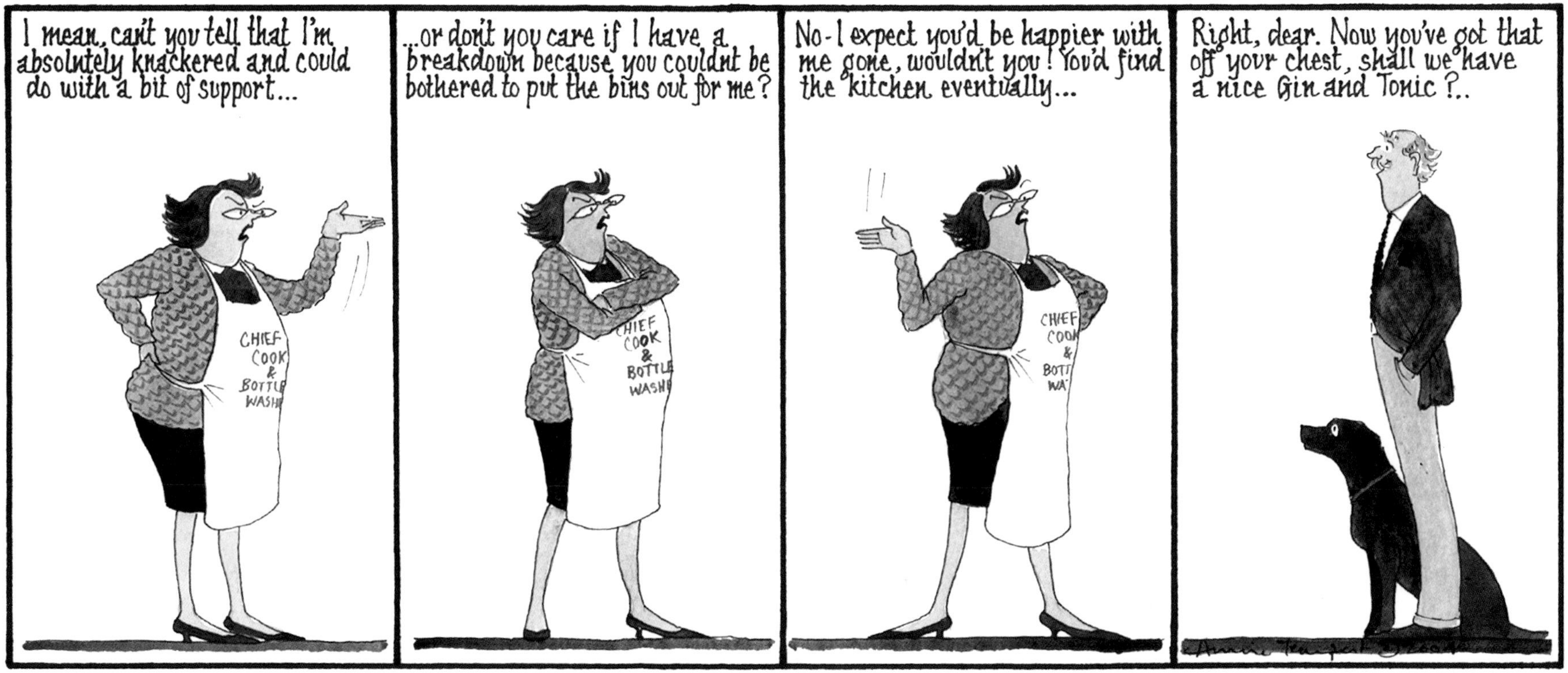
I mean, can't you tell that I'm absolutely knackered and could do with a bit of support...
CHIEF COOK & BOTTLE WASH
...or don't you care if I have a breakdown because you couldnt be bothered to put the bins out for me?
No-I expect you'd be happier with me gone, wouldn't you! You'd find the kitchen eventually...
Right, dear. Now you've got that off your chest, shall we have a nice Gin and Tonic?..

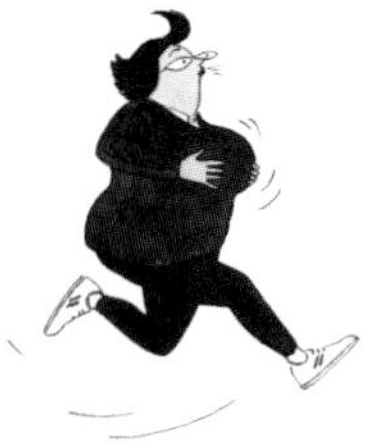

July 15th, 2004

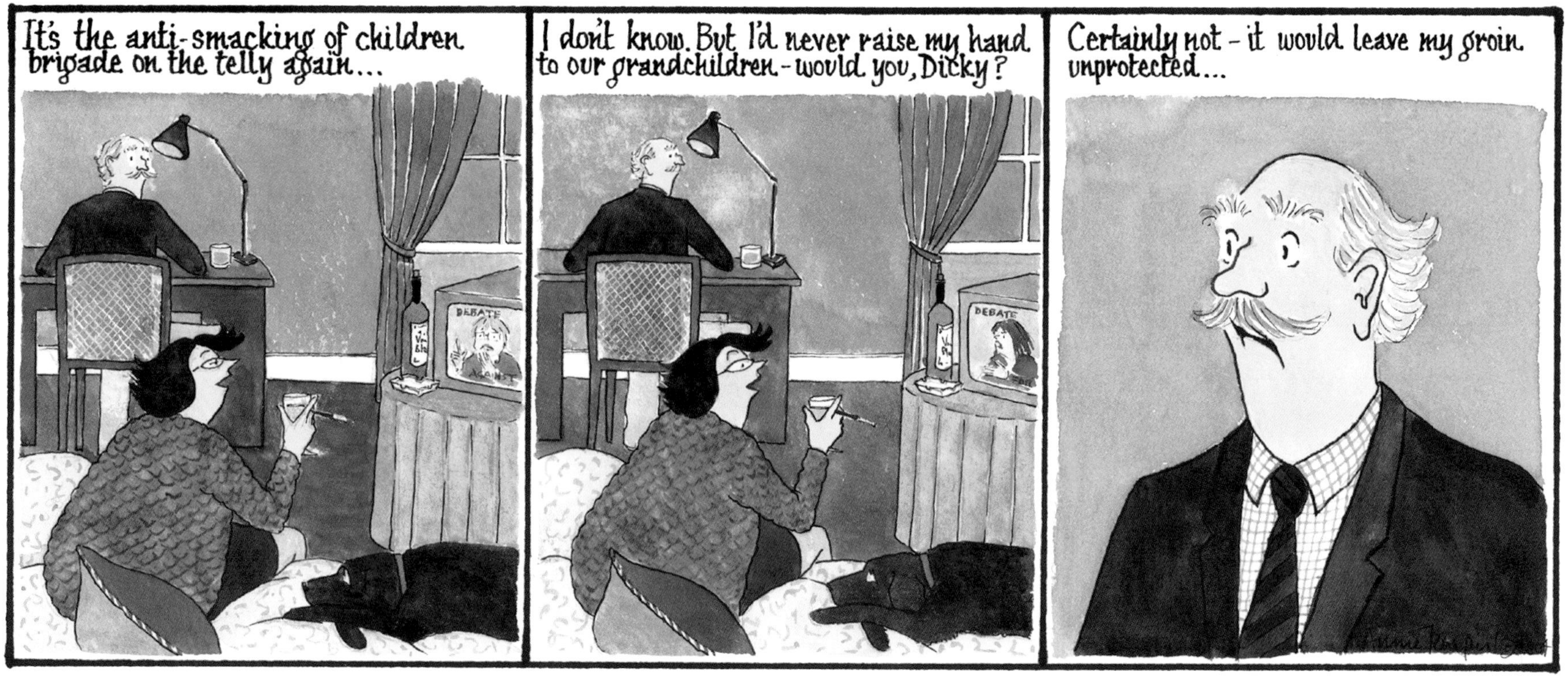
It's the anti-smacking of children brigade on the telly again...
DEBATE
I don't know. But I'd never raise my hand to our grandchildren - would you, Dicky?
DEBATE
Certainly not - it would leave my groin unprotected...

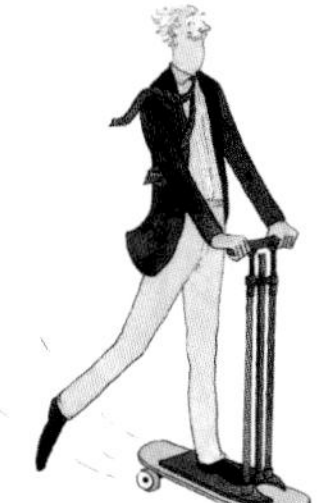

July 22nd, 2004

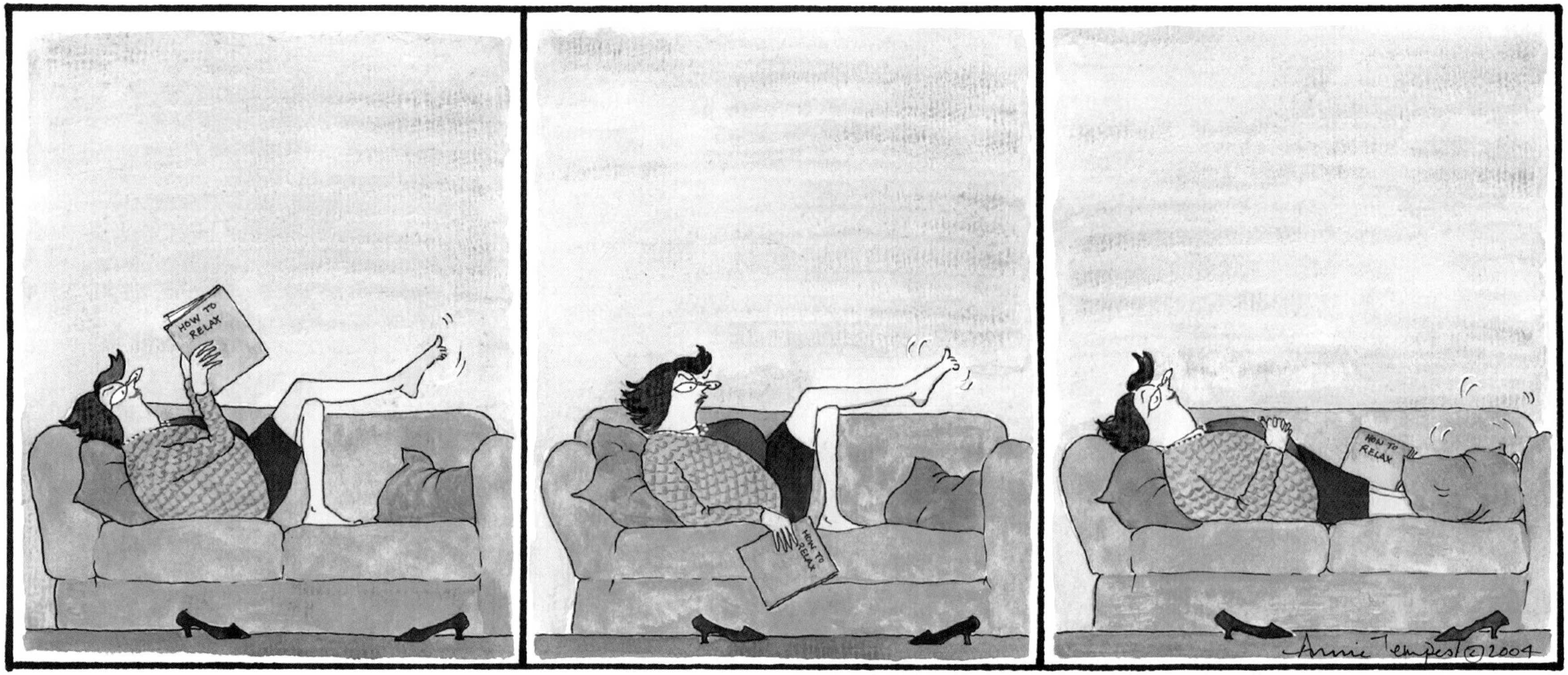
HOW TO RELAX
HOW TO RELAX
HOW TO RELAX
Annie Tempest © 2004

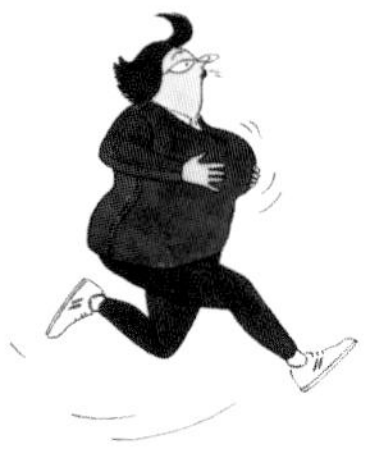

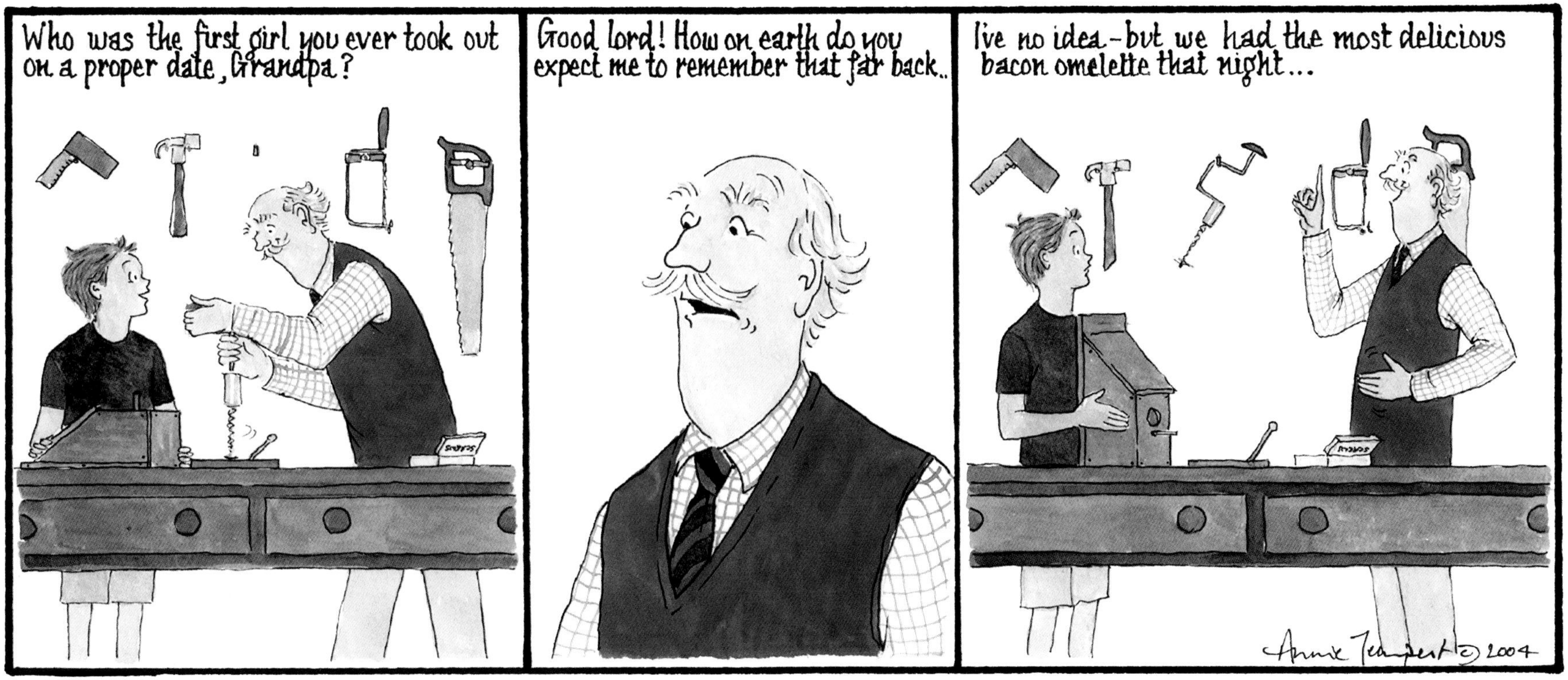
Who was the first girl you ever took out on a proper date, Grandpa?
Good lord! How on earth do you expect me to remember that far back..
I've no idea - but we had the most delicious bacon omelette that night...
Annie Tempest © 2004

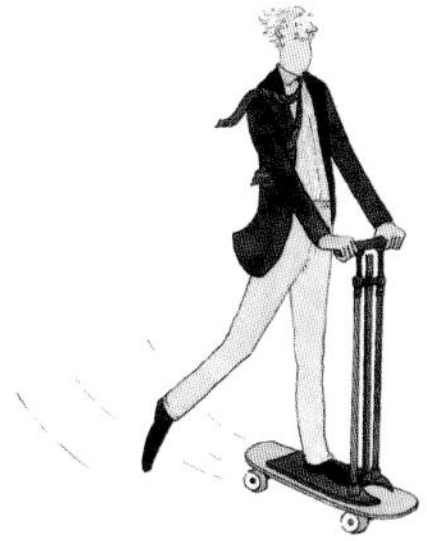

August 5th, 2004

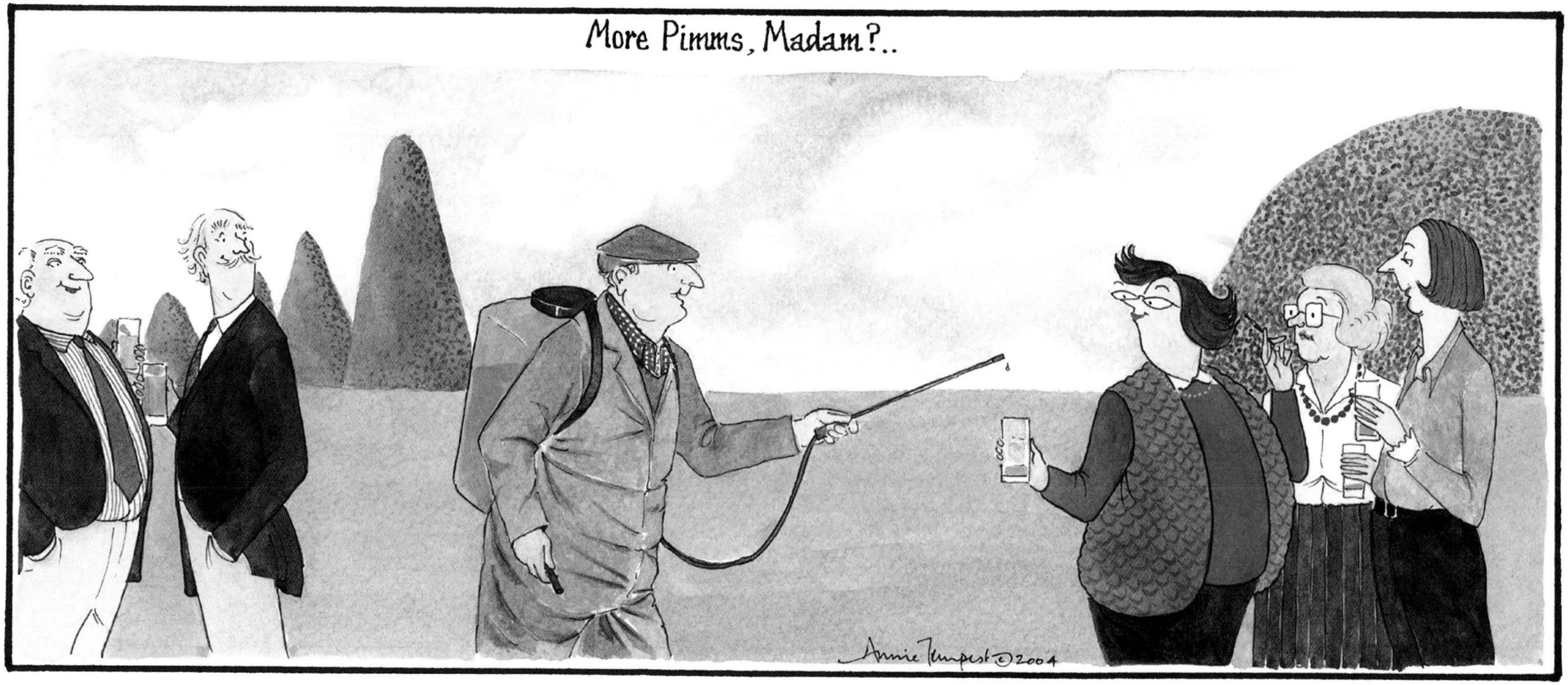
More Pimms, Madam?..
Annie Tempest ©2004

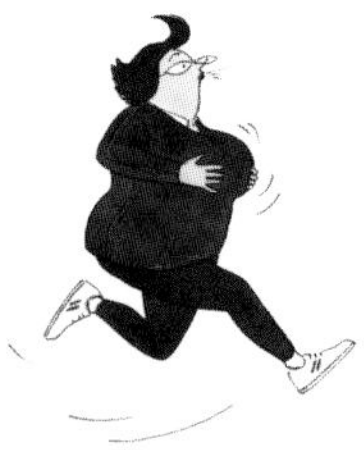

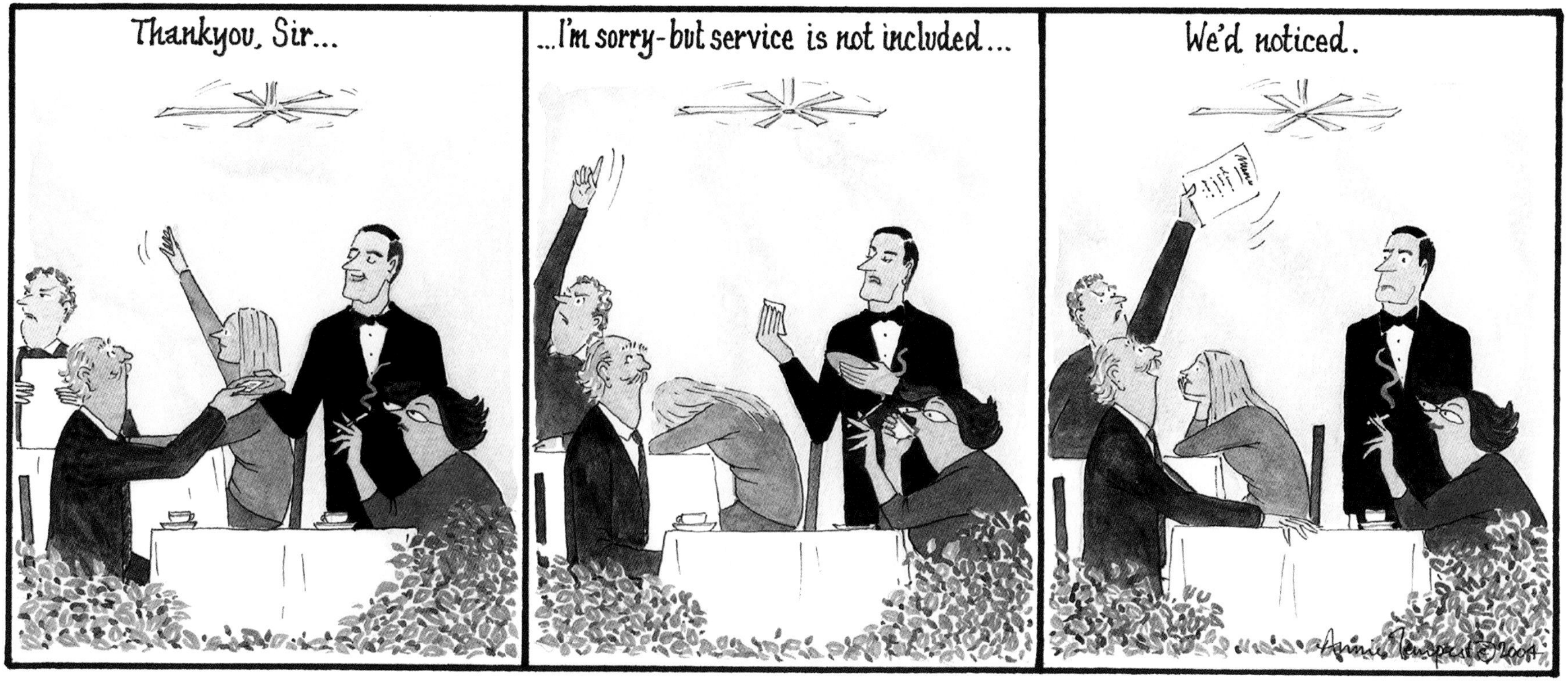
Thankyou, Sir...
...I'm sorry-but service is not included...
We'd noticed.
Annie Tempest © 2004

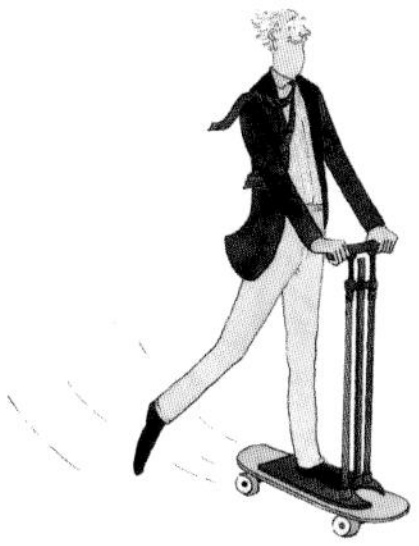

August 19th, 2004

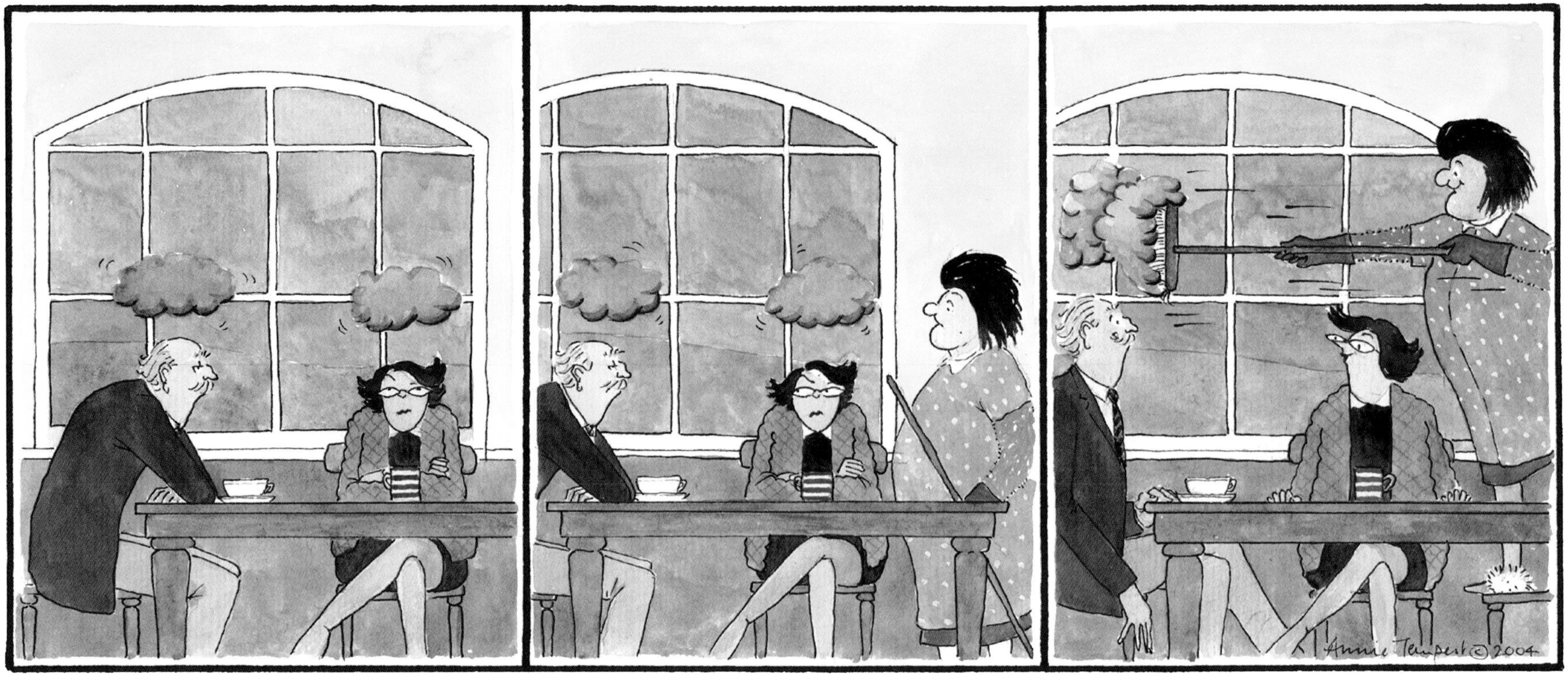
Annie Tempest © 2004

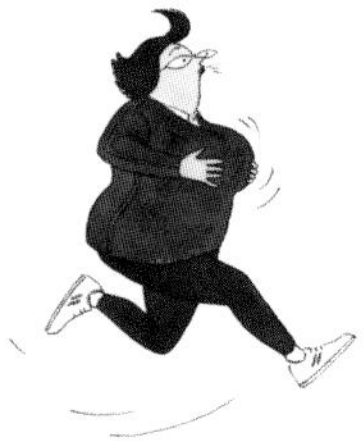

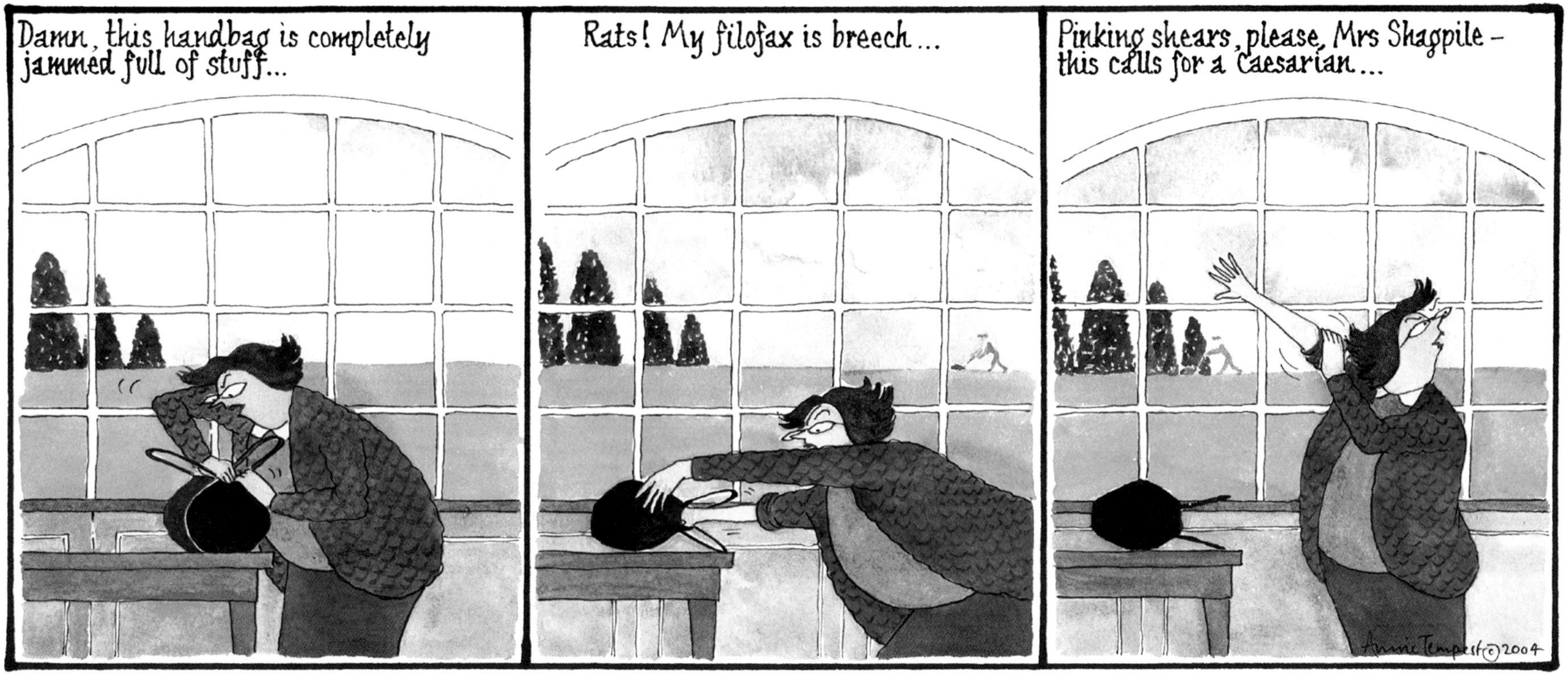
Damn, this handbag is completely jammed full of stuff...
Rats! My filofax is breech...
Pinking shears, please, Mrs Shagpile – this calls for a caesarian...
AnnieTempest©2004

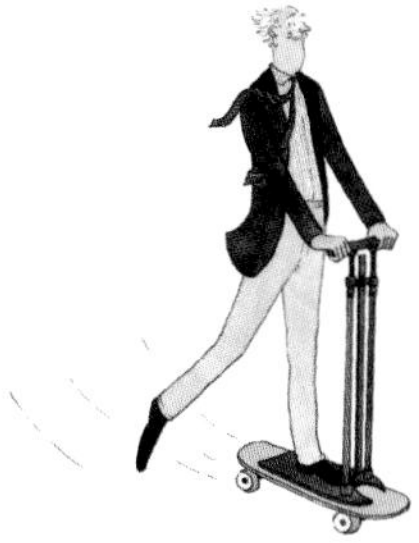

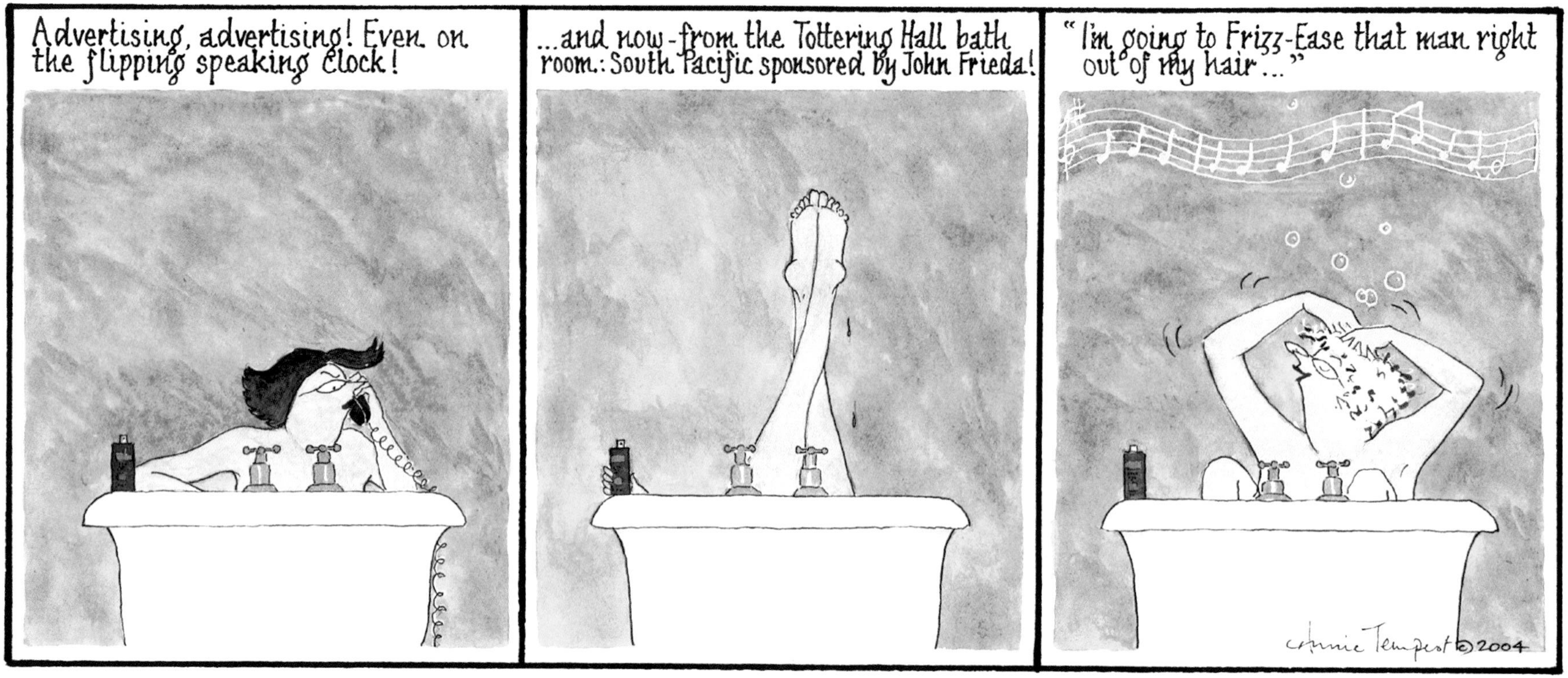
Advertising, advertising! Even on the flipping speaking clock!
...and now - from the Tottering Hall bath room.: South Pacific sponsored by John Frieda!
"I'm going to Frizz-Ease that man right out of my hair..."
Annie Tempest © 2004

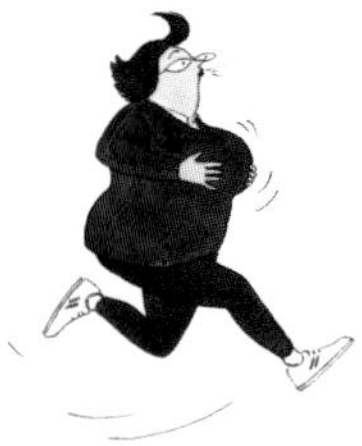

September 9th, 2004

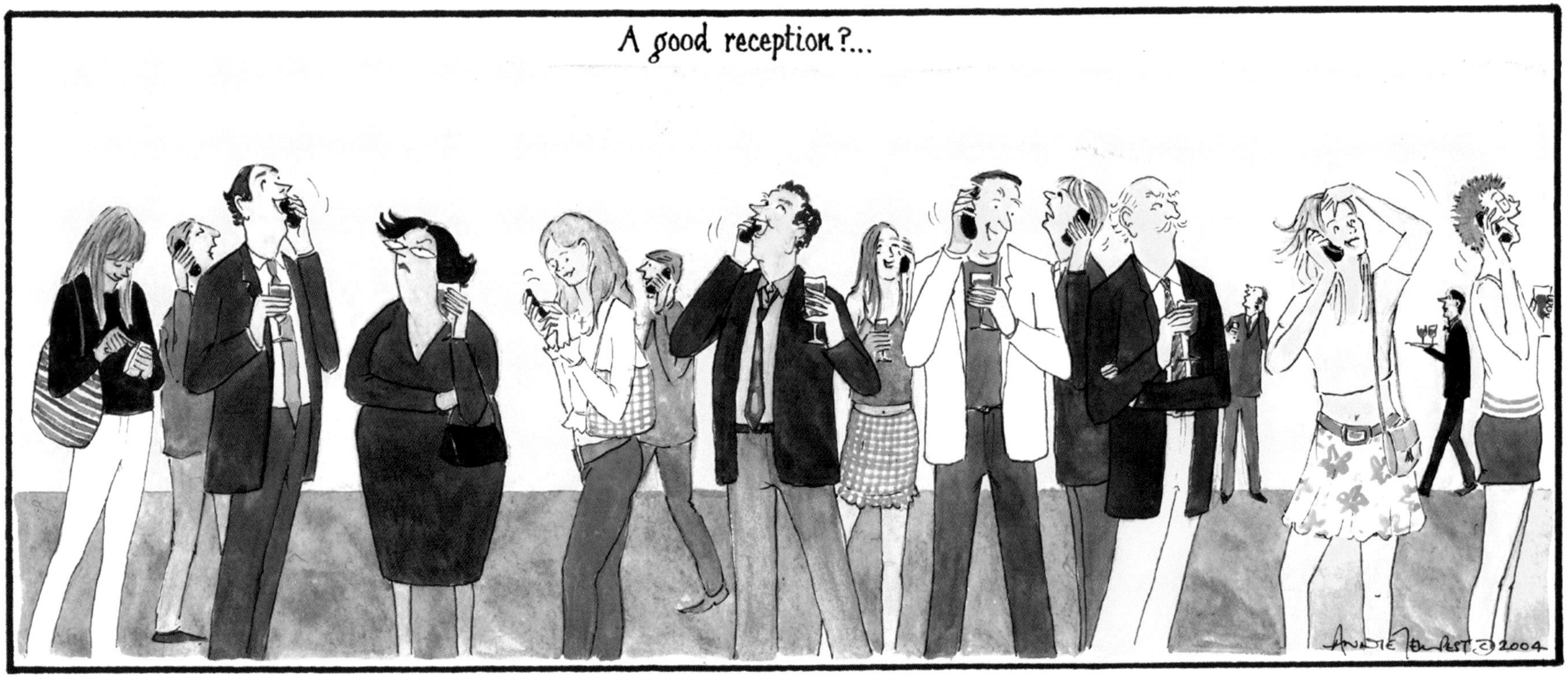

A good reception?...

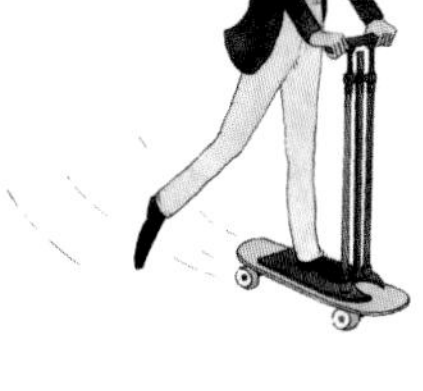

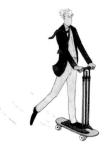

September 16th, 2004

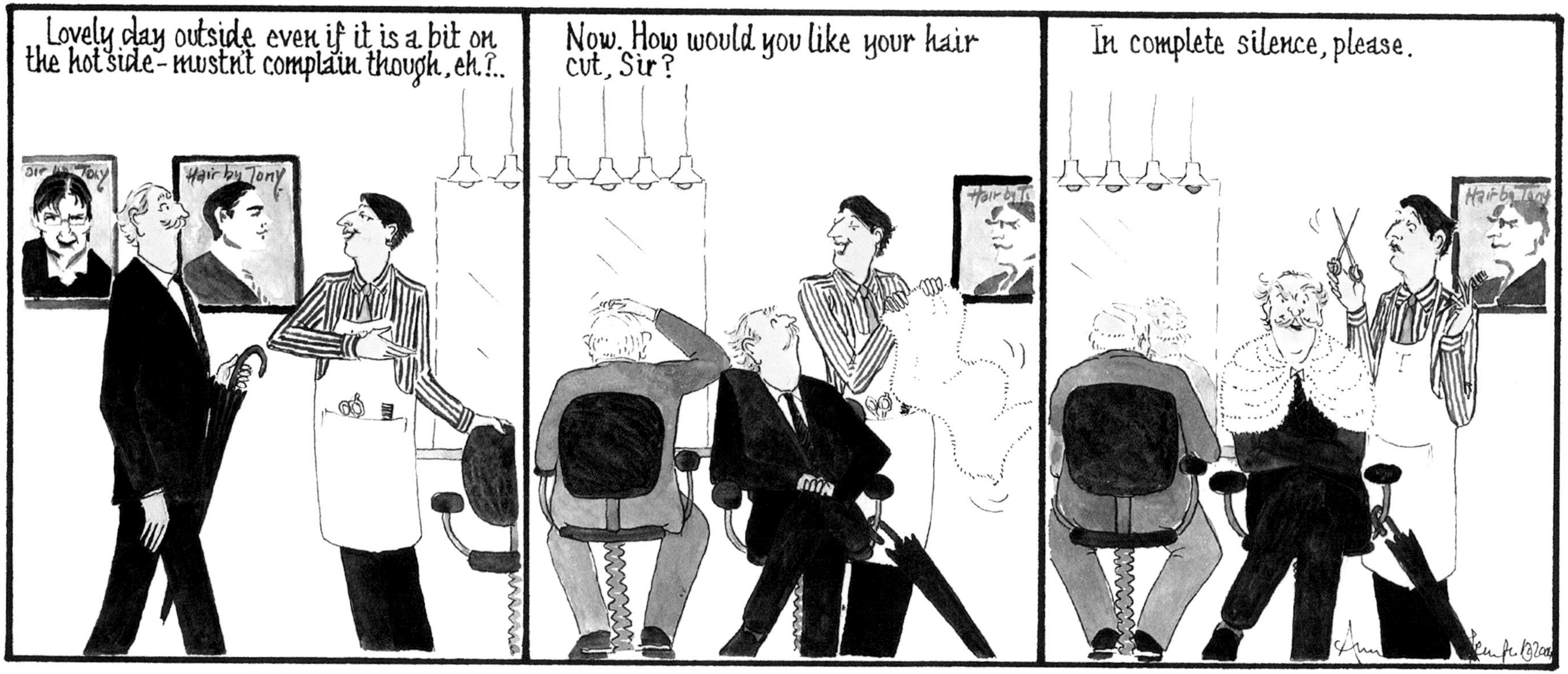

Lovely day outside even if it is a bit on the hot side - mustn't complain though, eh?..
Hair by Tony
Now. How would you like your hair cut, Sir?
In complete silence, please.

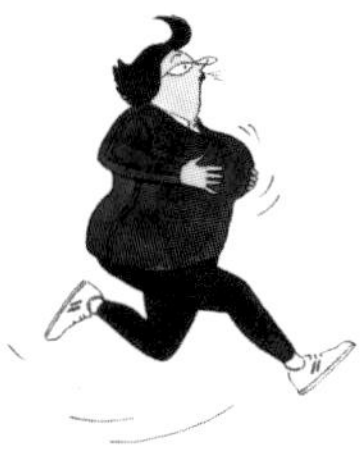

September 23rd, 2004

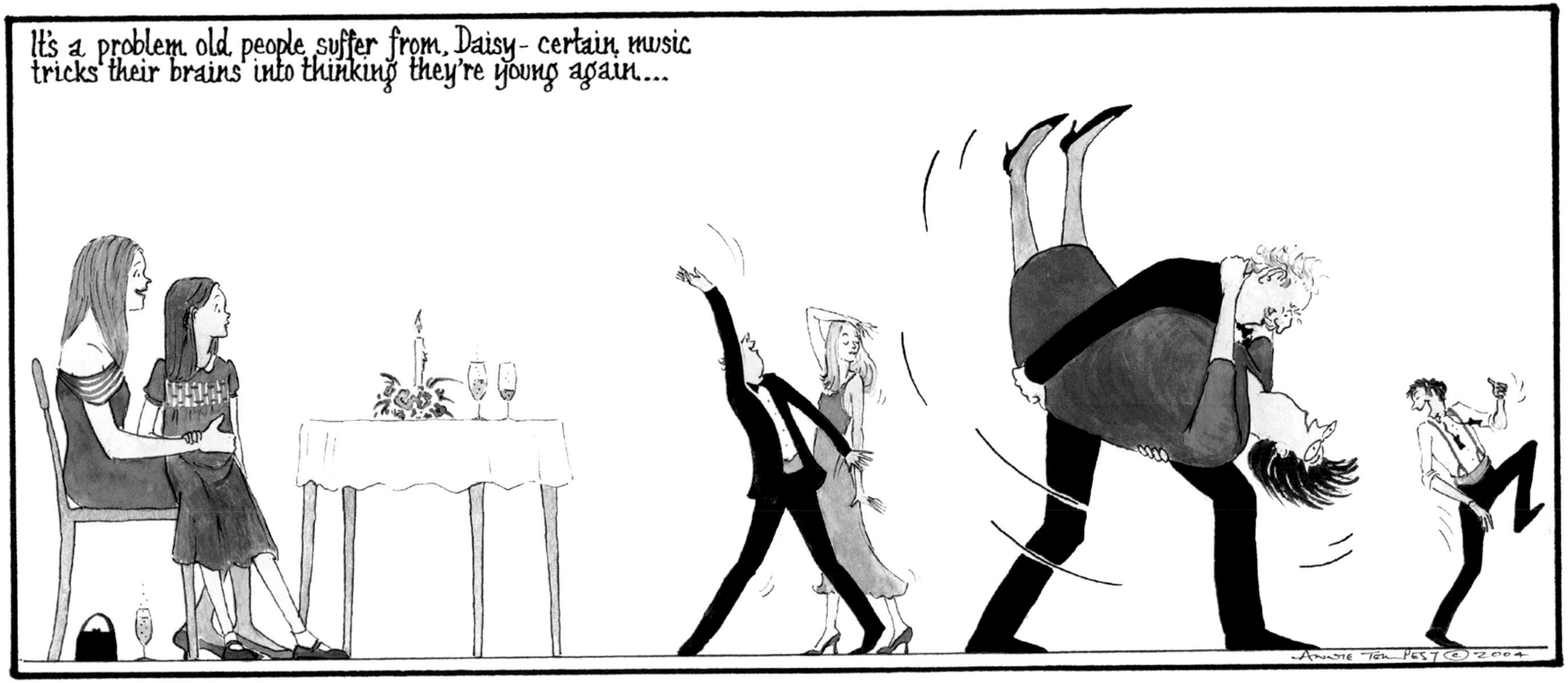
It's a problem old people suffer from, Daisy - certain music tricks their brains into thinking they're young again....
ANNIE TEMPEST © 2004

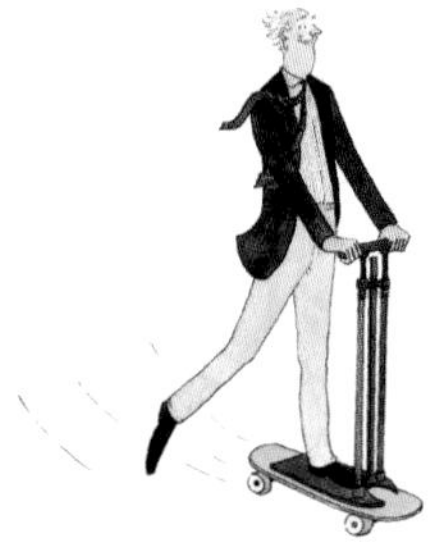

September 30th, 2004

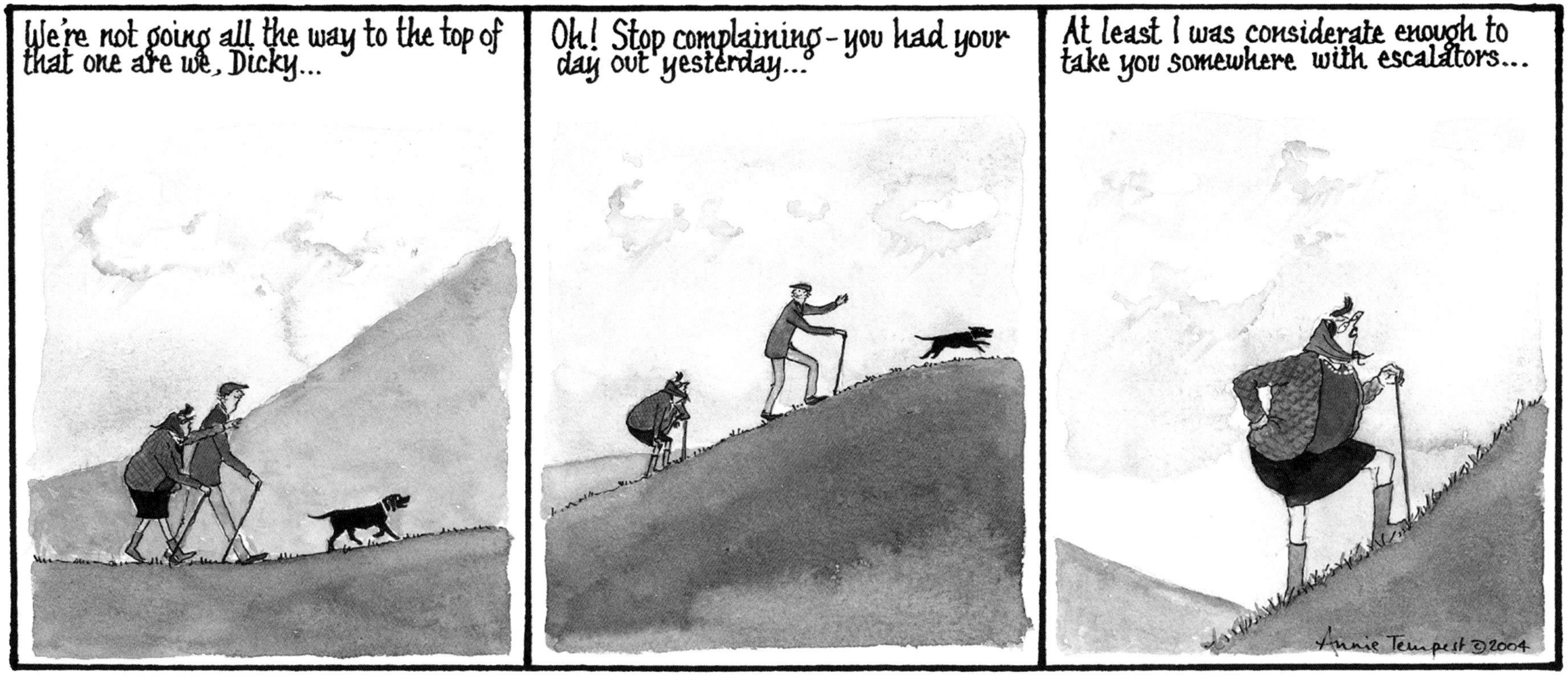
We're not going all the way to the top of that one are we, Dicky...
Oh! Stop complaining - you had your day out yesterday...
At least I was considerate enough to take you somewhere with escalators...
Annie Tempest ©2004

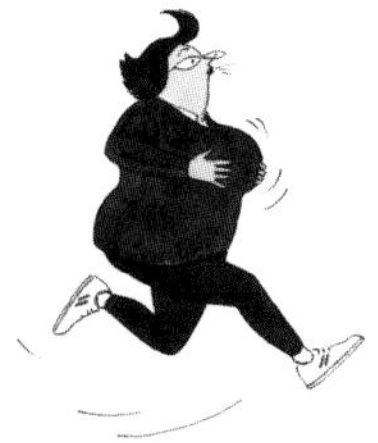

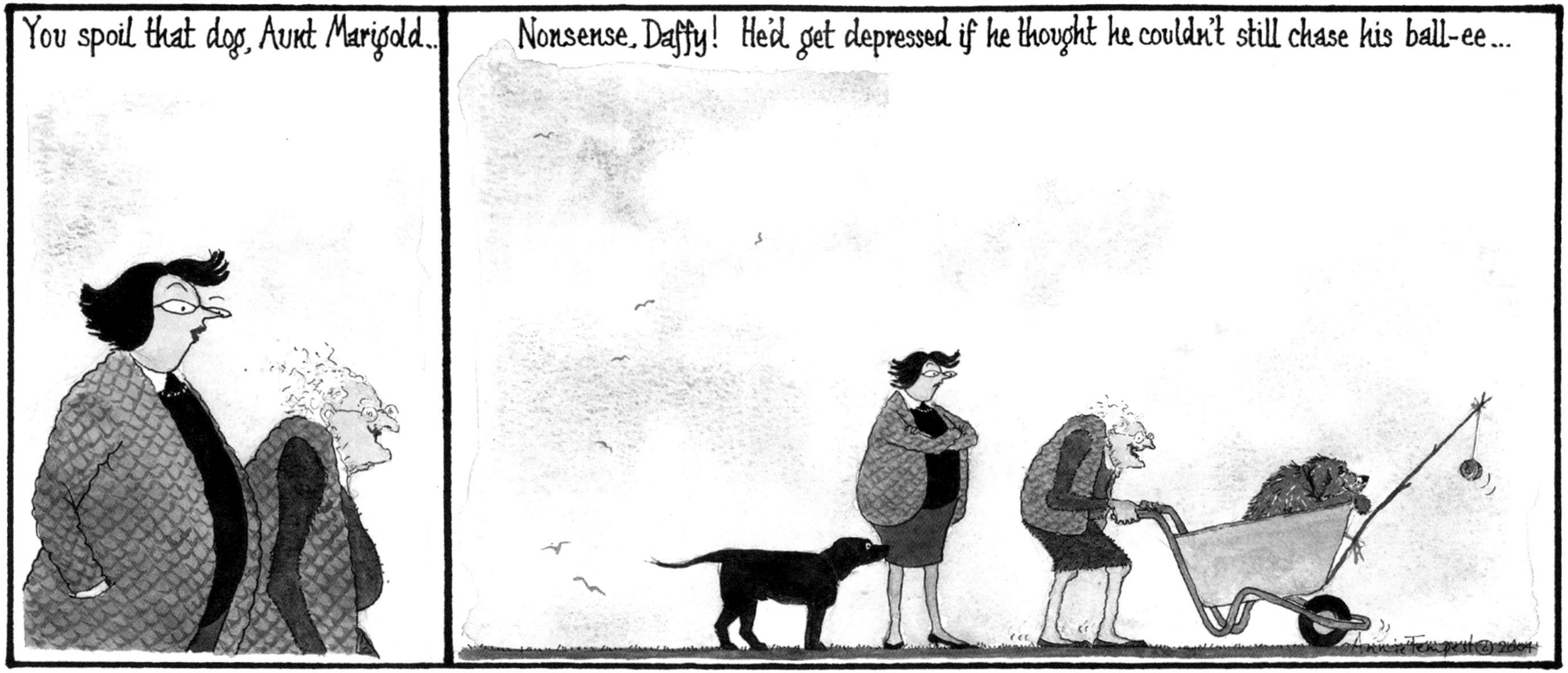
You spoil that dog, Aunt Marigold..
Nonsense, Daffy! He'd get depressed if he thought he couldn't still chase his ball-ee...

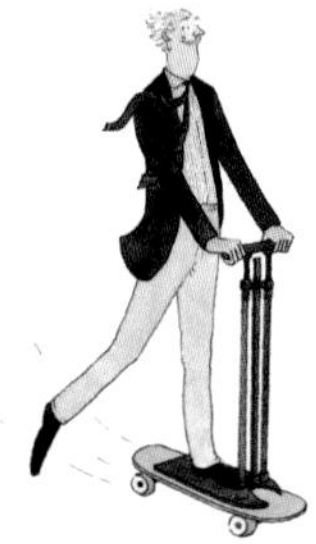

October 14th, 2004

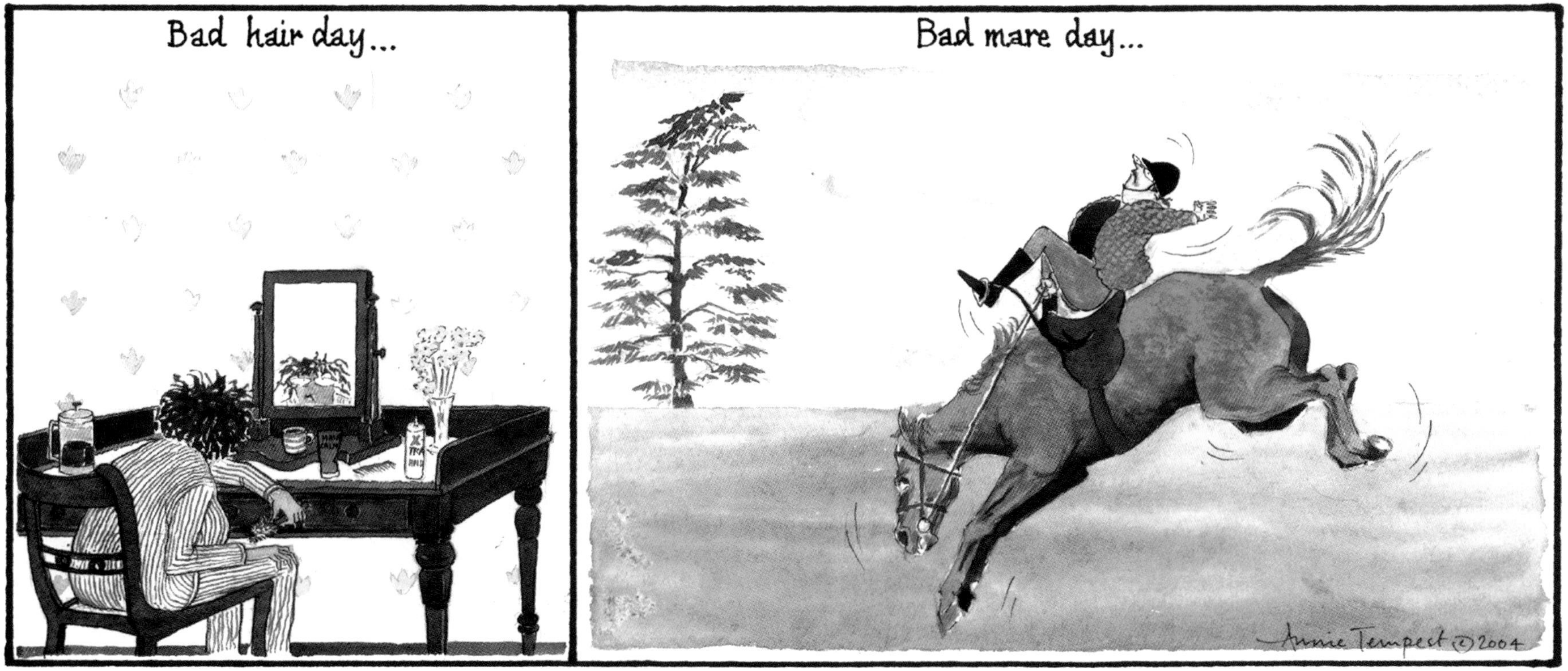
Bad hair day...
Bad mare day...
Annie Tempest © 2004

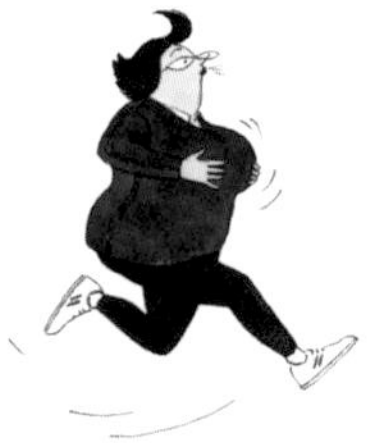

October 21st, 2004

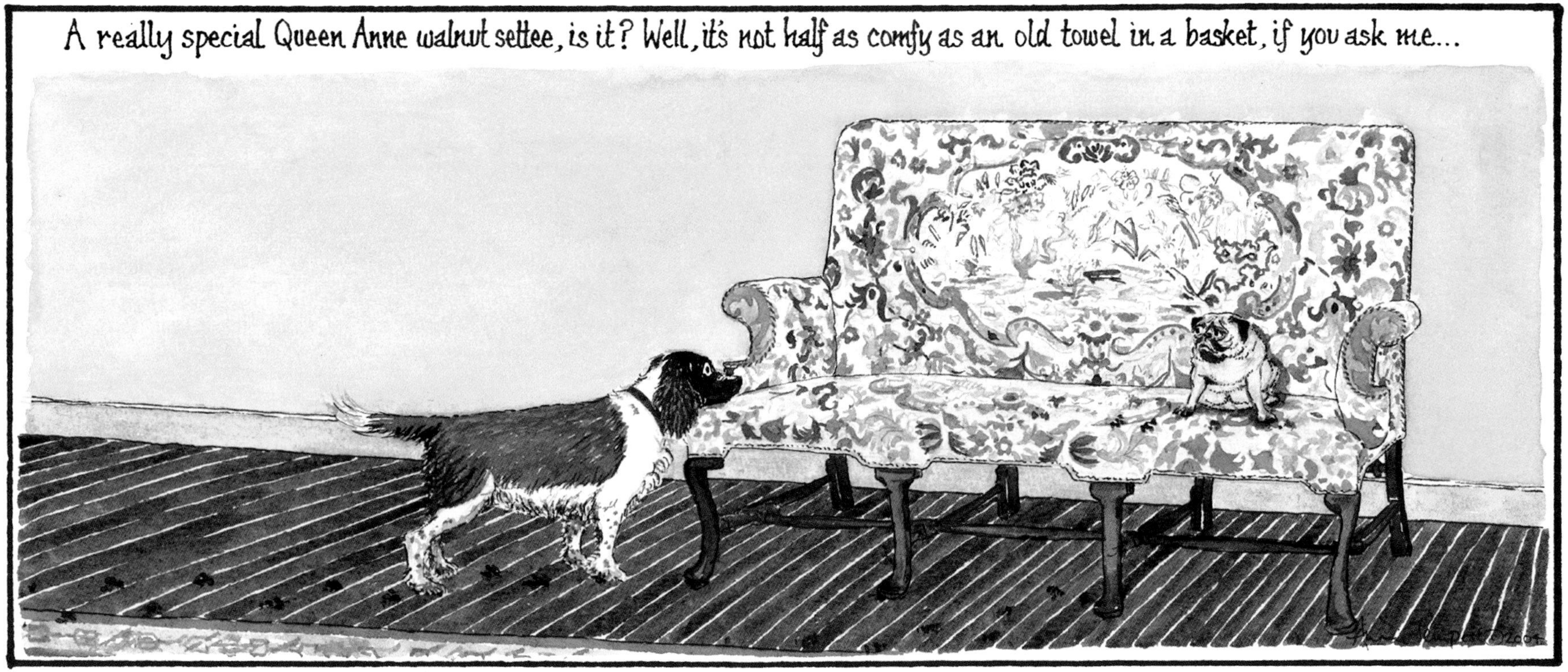
A really special Queen Anne walnut settee, is it? Well, it's not half as comfy as an old towel in a basket, if you ask me...

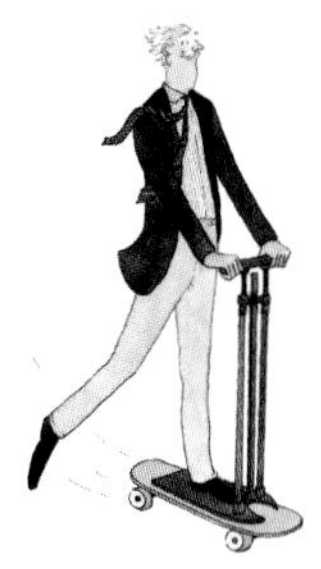

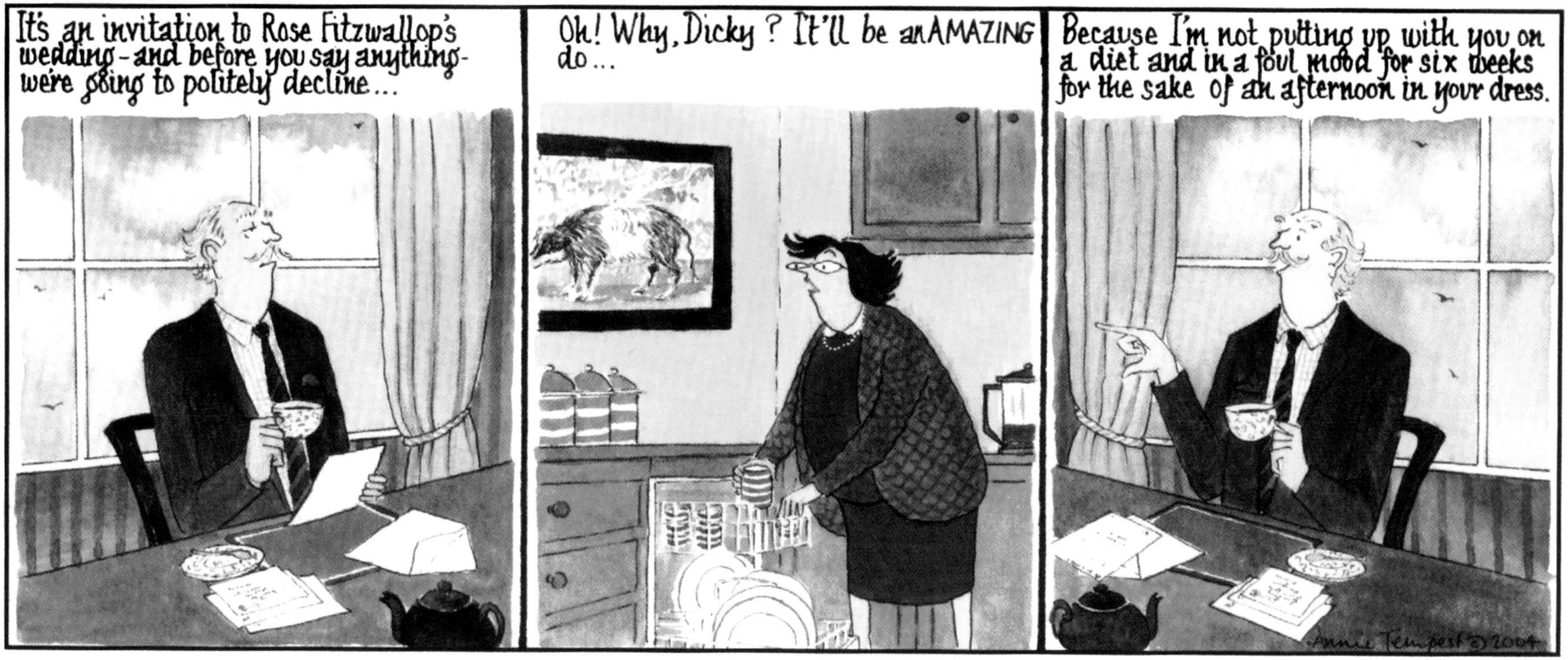
It's an invitation to Rose Fitzwallop's wedding - and before you say anything - we're going to politely decline...
Oh! Why, Dicky? It'll be an AMAZING do...
Because I'm not putting up with you on a diet and in a foul mood for six weeks for the sake of an afternoon in your dress.
Annie Tempest © 2004

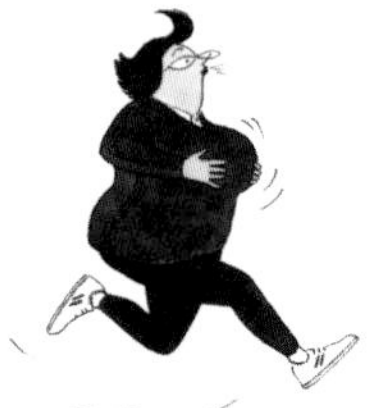

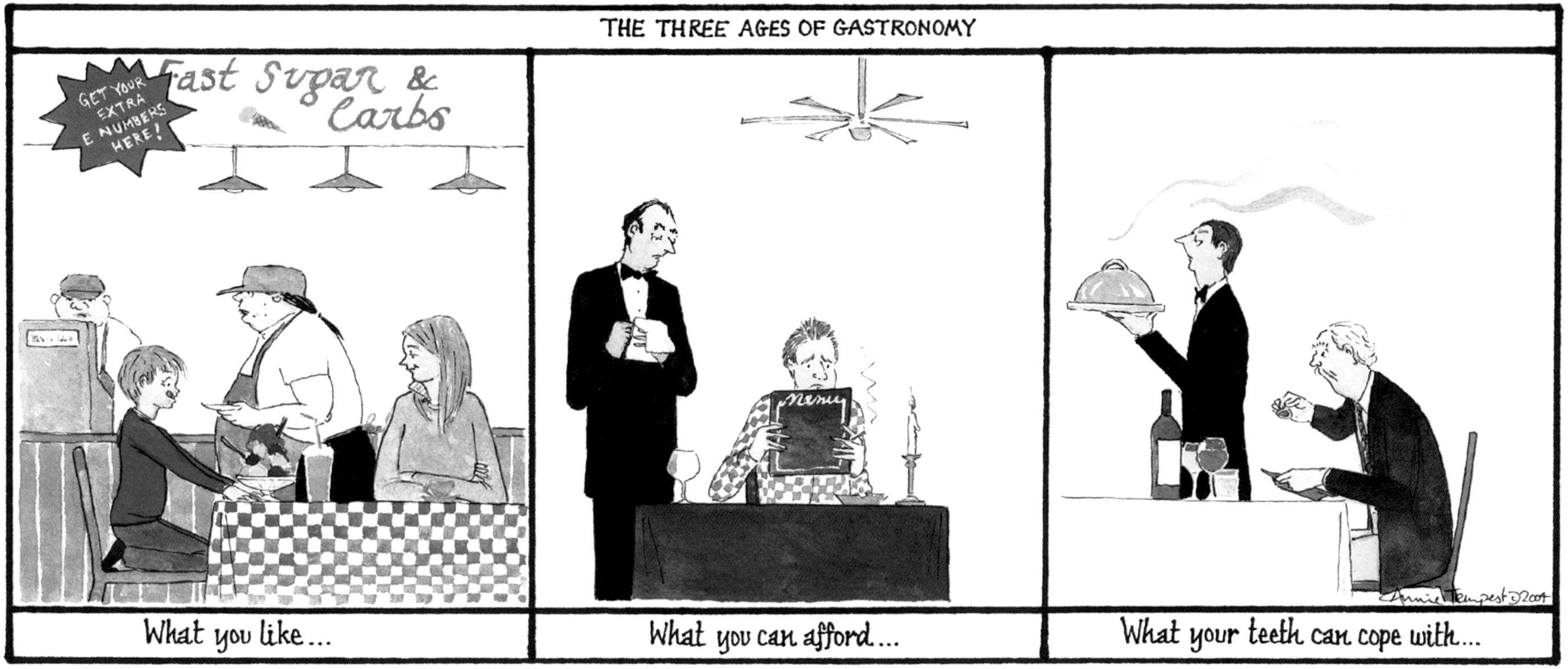
THE THREE AGES OF GASTRONOMY
GET YOUR EXTRA E NUMBERS HERE!
Fast Sugar & Carbs
Menu
Annie Tempest ©2004

What you like... What you can afford... What your teeth can cope with...

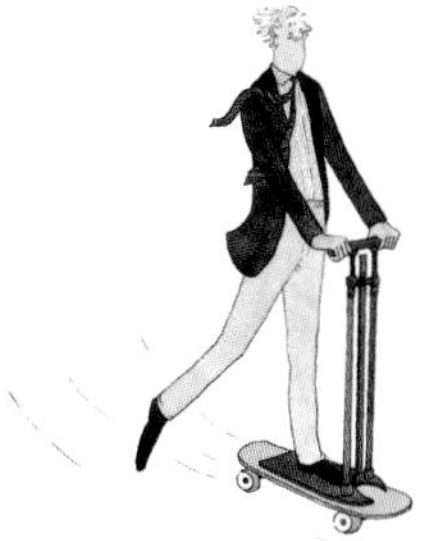

November 11th, 2004

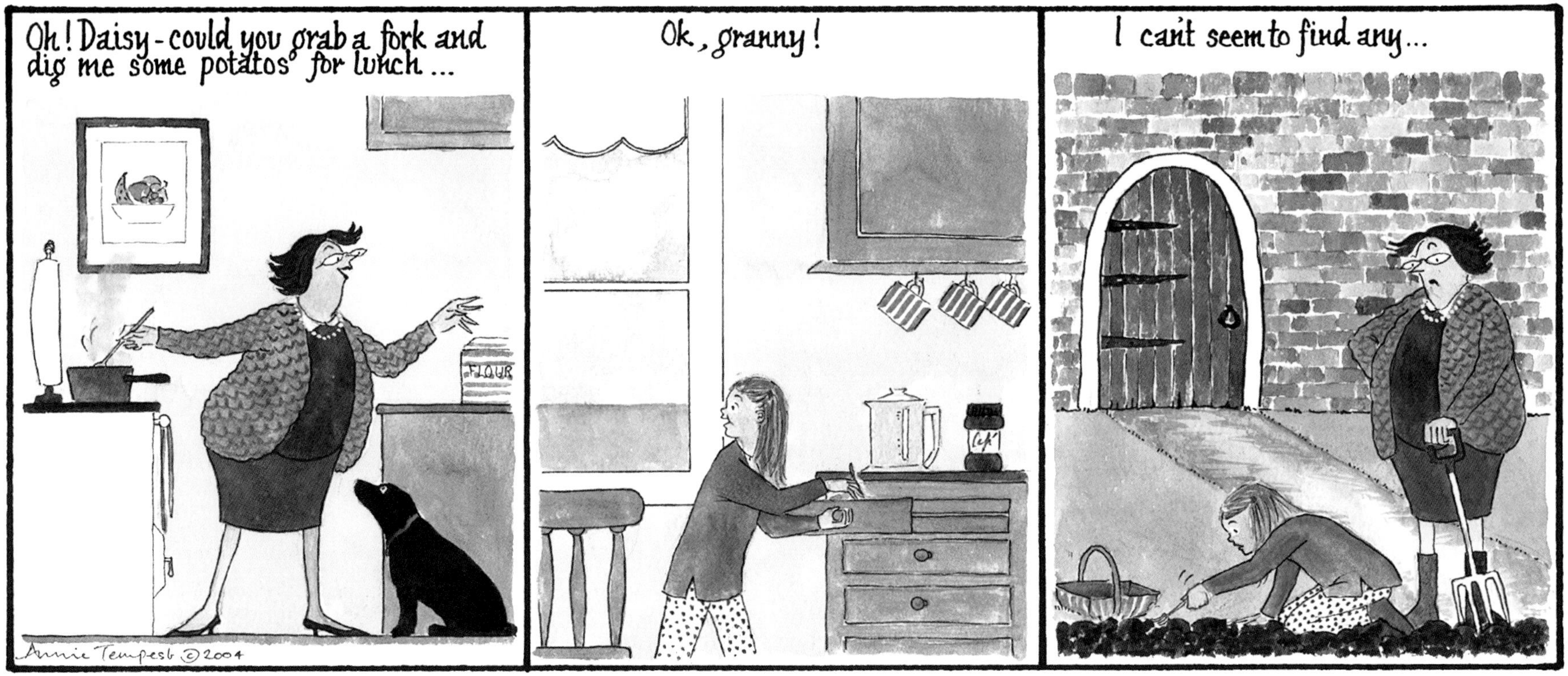
Oh! Daisy - could you grab a fork and dig me some potatos for lunch ...
Ok, granny!
I can't seem to find any...
FLOUR
Annie Tempest ©2004

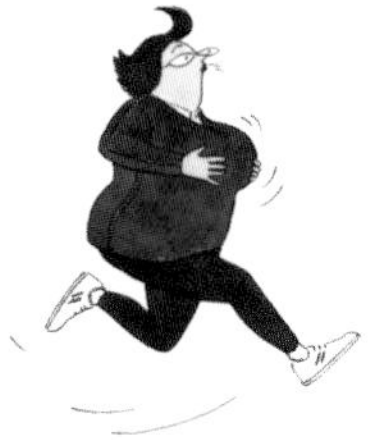

November 18th, 2004

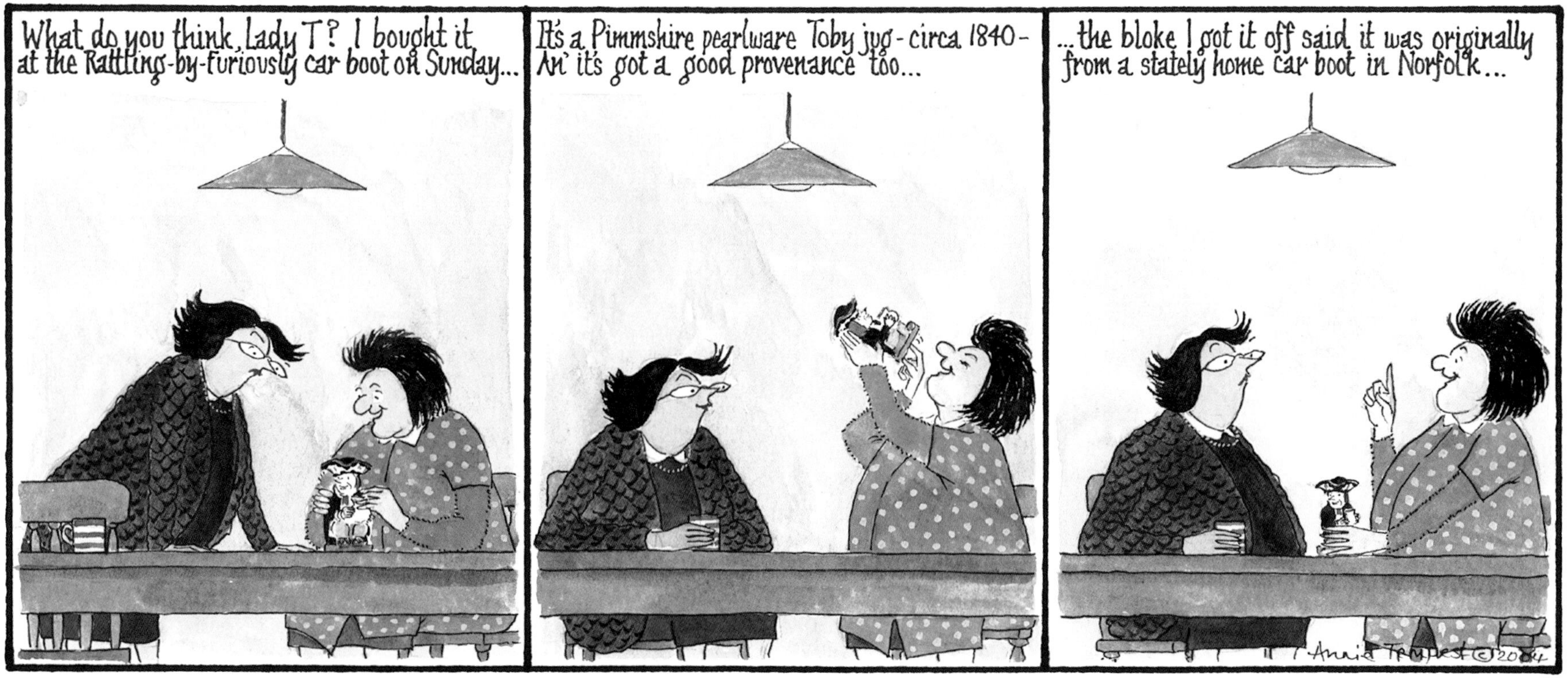
What do you think, Lady T? I bought it at the Rattling-by-Furiously car boot on Sunday...
It's a Pimmshire pearlware Toby jug - circa 1840 - An' it's got a good provenance too...
...the bloke I got it off said it was originally from a stately home car boot in Norfolk...
Annie Tempest © 2004

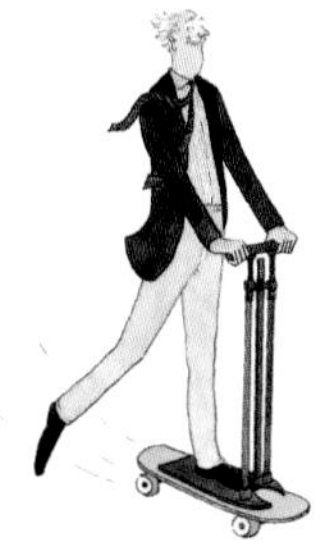

November 25th, 2004

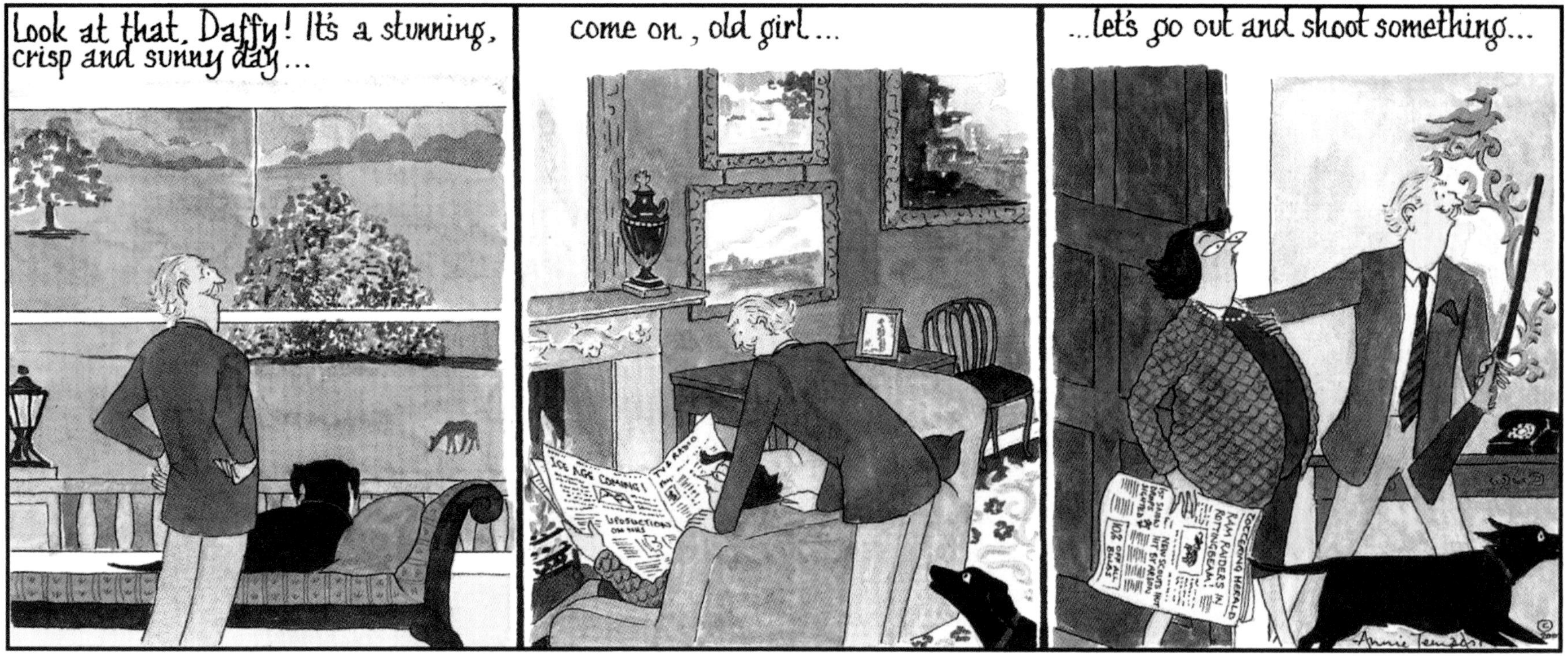
Look at that, Daffy! It's a stunning, crisp and sunny day...
come on, old girl...
...let's go out and shoot something...

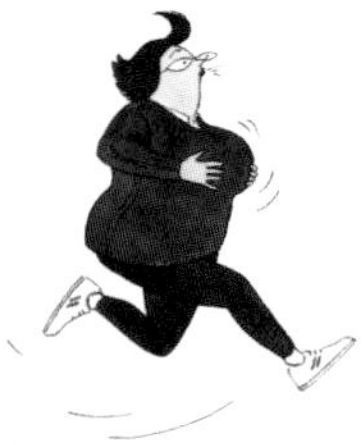

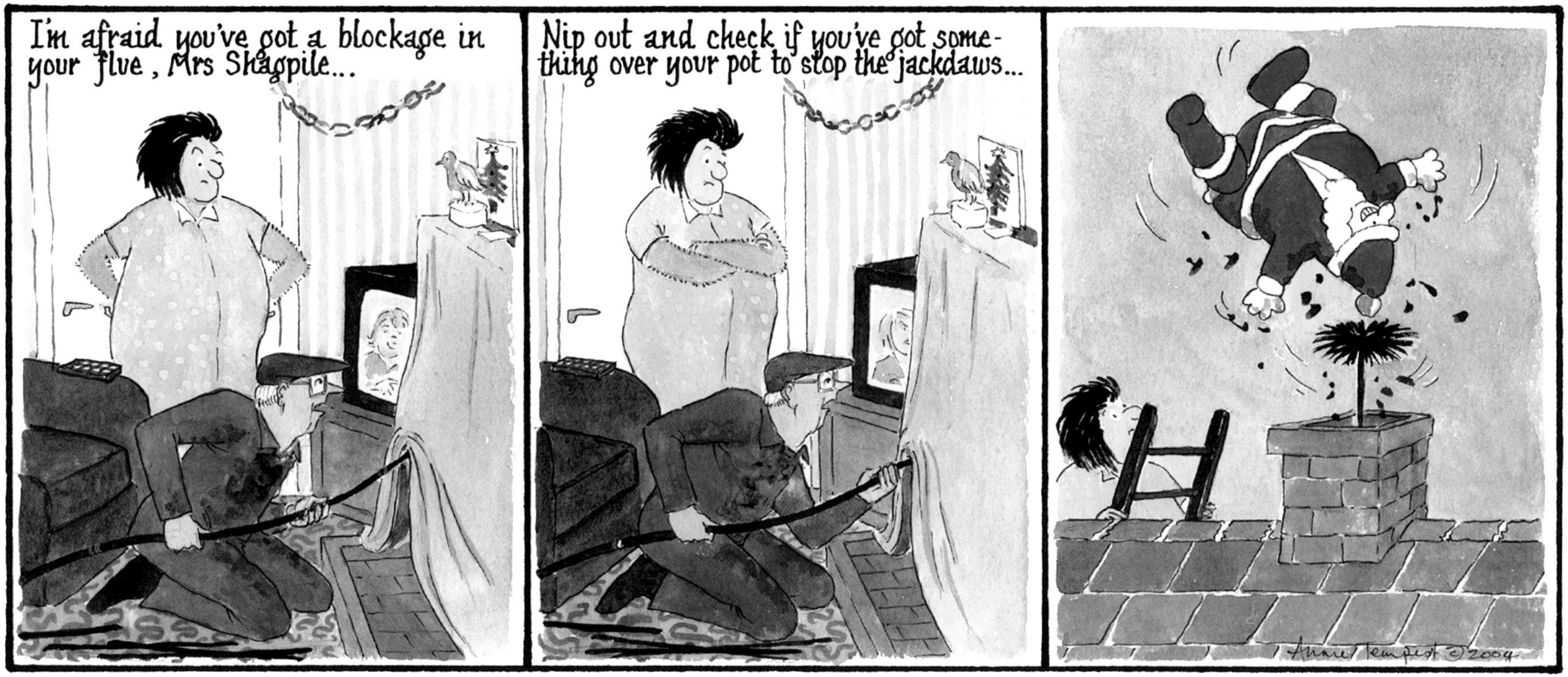
I'm afraid you've got a blockage in
your flue, Mrs Shagpile...
Nip out and check if you've got something over your pot to stop the jackdaws...

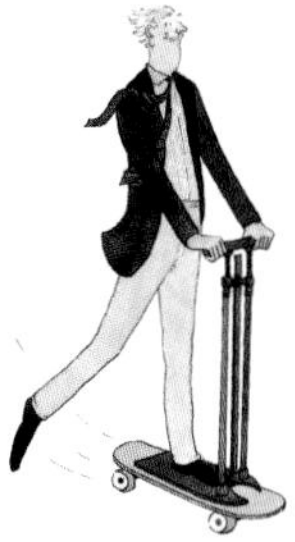

December 9th, 2004

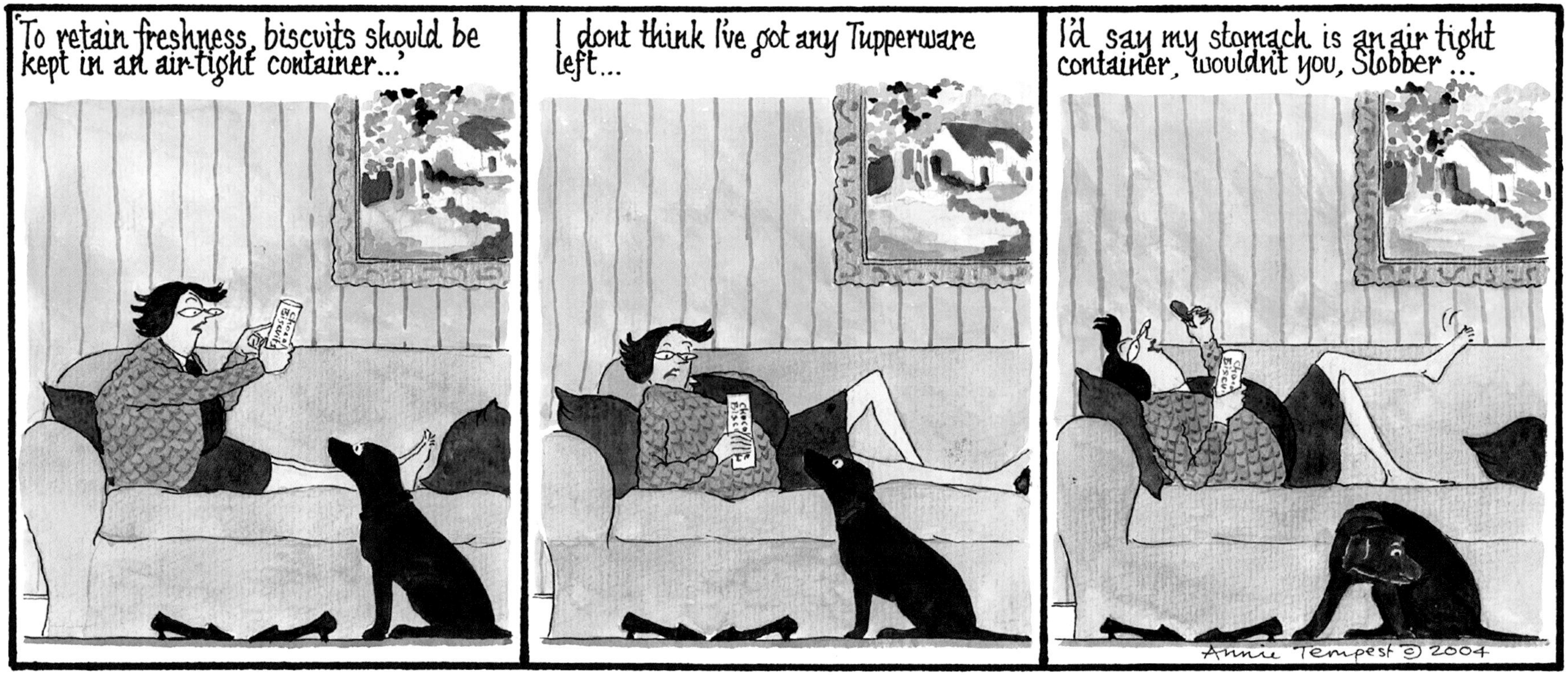
'To retain freshness, biscuits should be kept in an air-tight container...'
I dont think I've got any Tupperware left...
I'd say my stomach is an air tight container, wouldn't you, Slobber ...
Annie Tempest © 2004

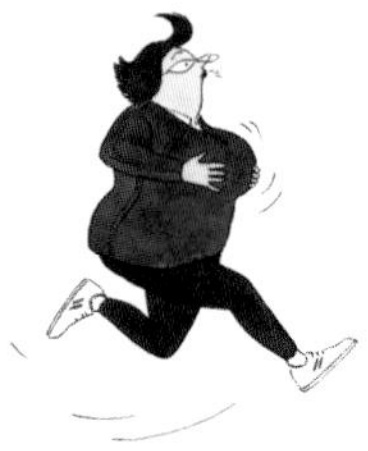

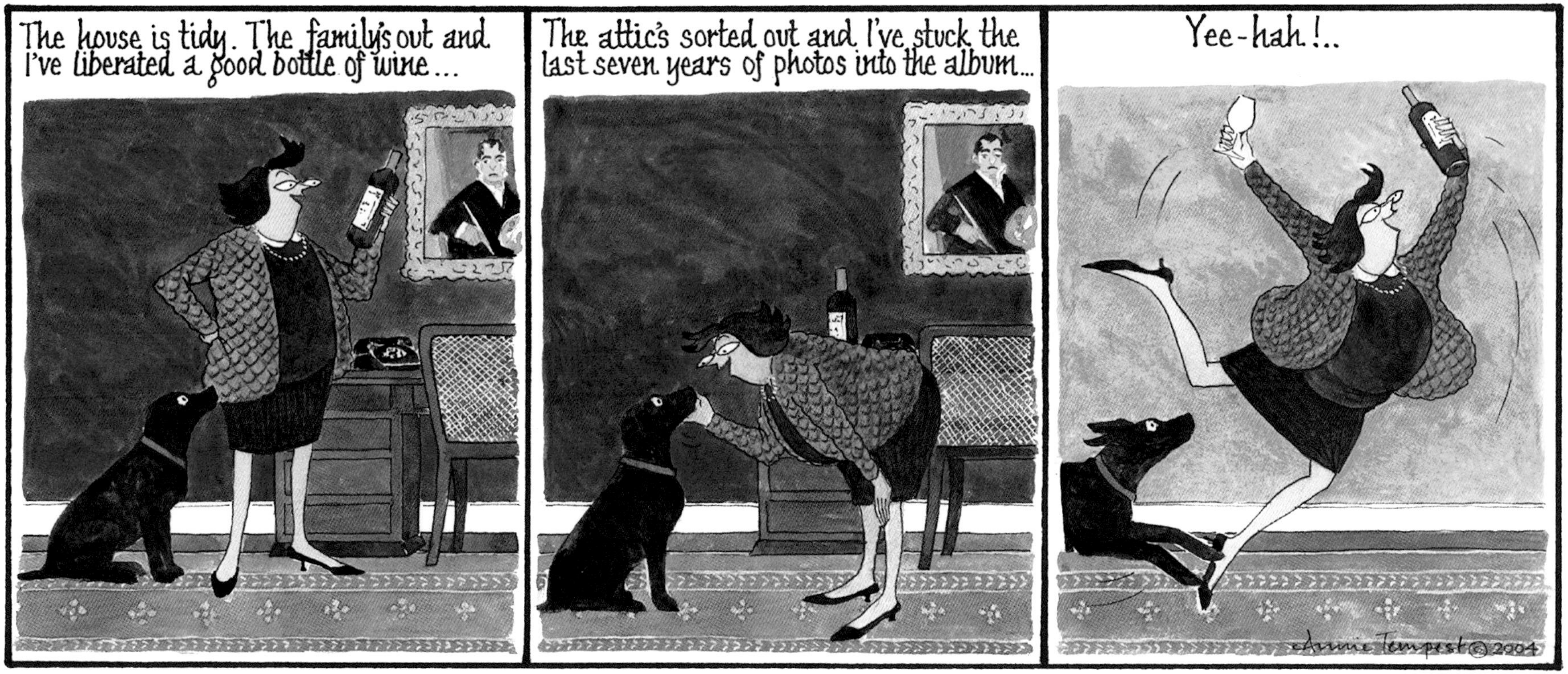
The house is tidy. The family's out and I've liberated a good bottle of wine...
The attic's sorted out and I've stuck the last seven years of photos into the album...
Yee-hah!..
Annie Tempest © 2004

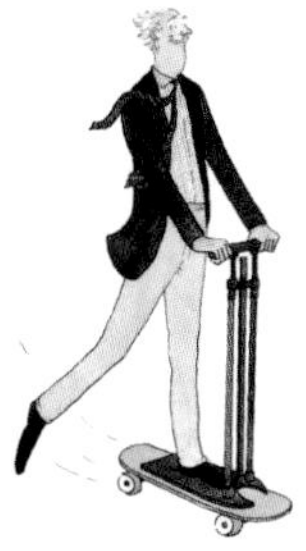

December 30th, 2004

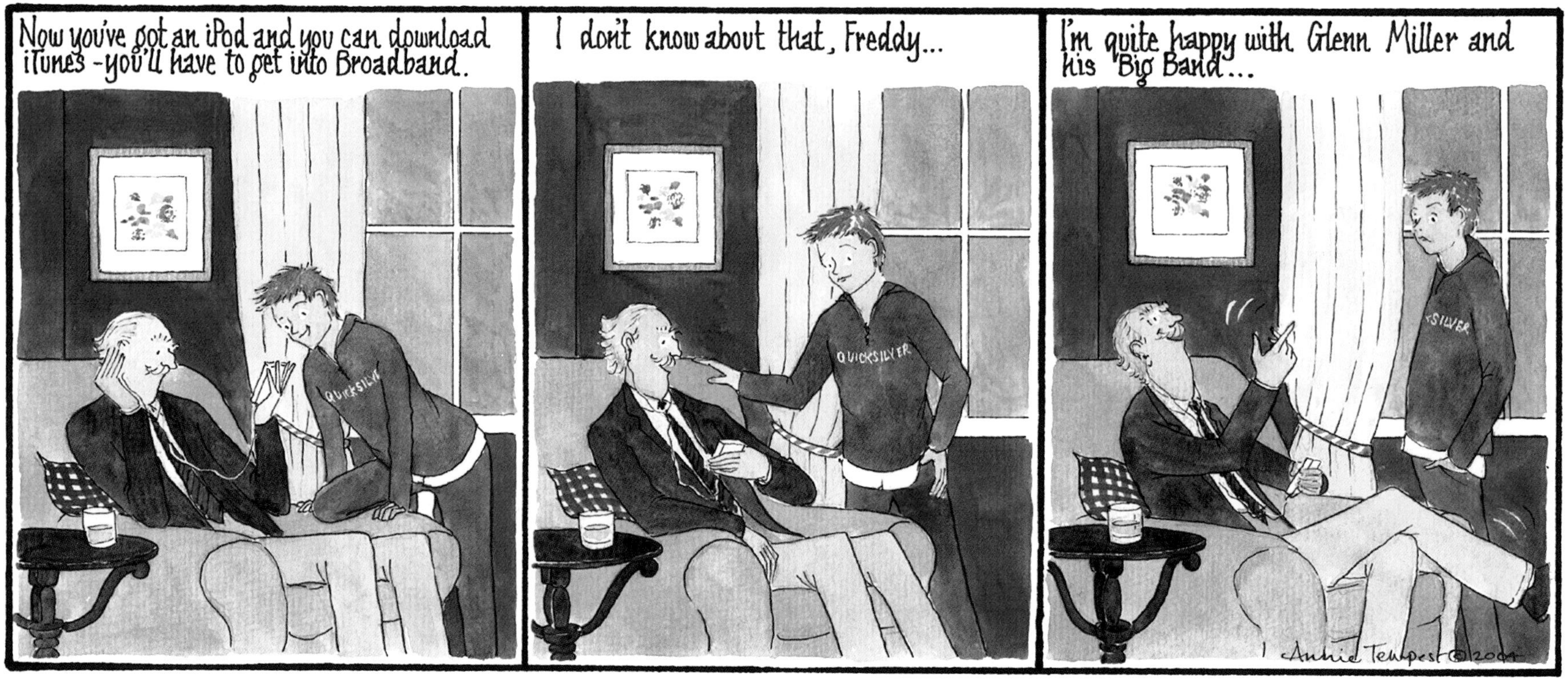
Now you've got an iPod and you can download iTunes - you'll have to get into Broadband.
QUICKSILVER
I don't know about that, Freddy...
QUICKSILVER
I'm quite happy with Glenn Miller and his 'Big Band'...
SILVER
Annie Tempest ©2004

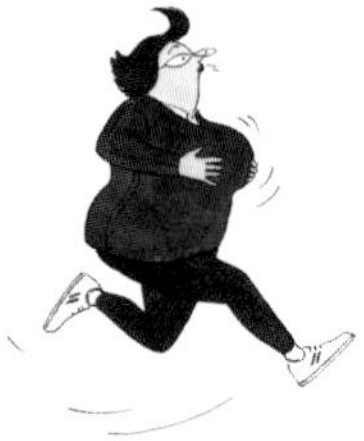

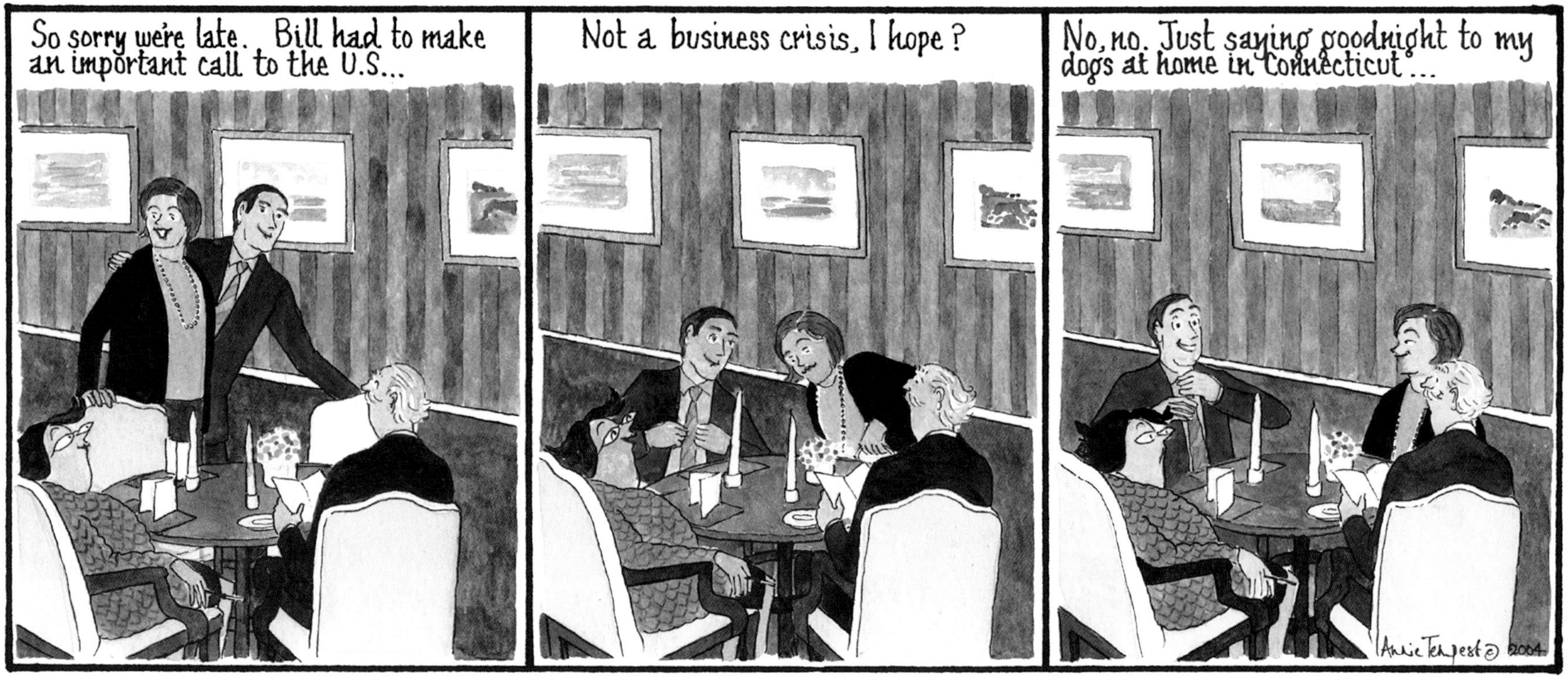
So sorry we're late. Bill had to make an important call to the U.S...
Not a business crisis, I hope?
No, no. Just saying goodnight to my dogs at home in Connecticut...
Annie Tempest © 2004

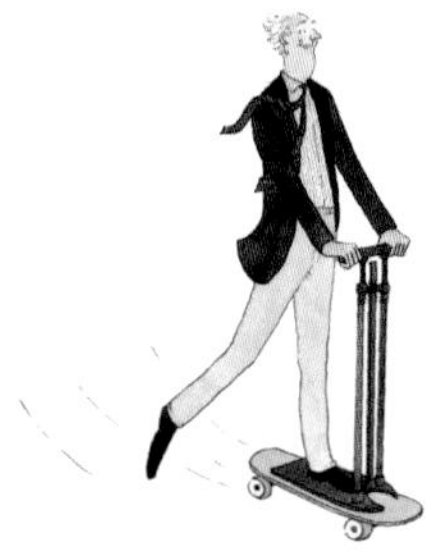

January 13th, 2005

THE LABRADOR CHARACTER: A strong drive to please its master...

"Quick! Jump up here - you're getting muddy paws all over the carpet..."

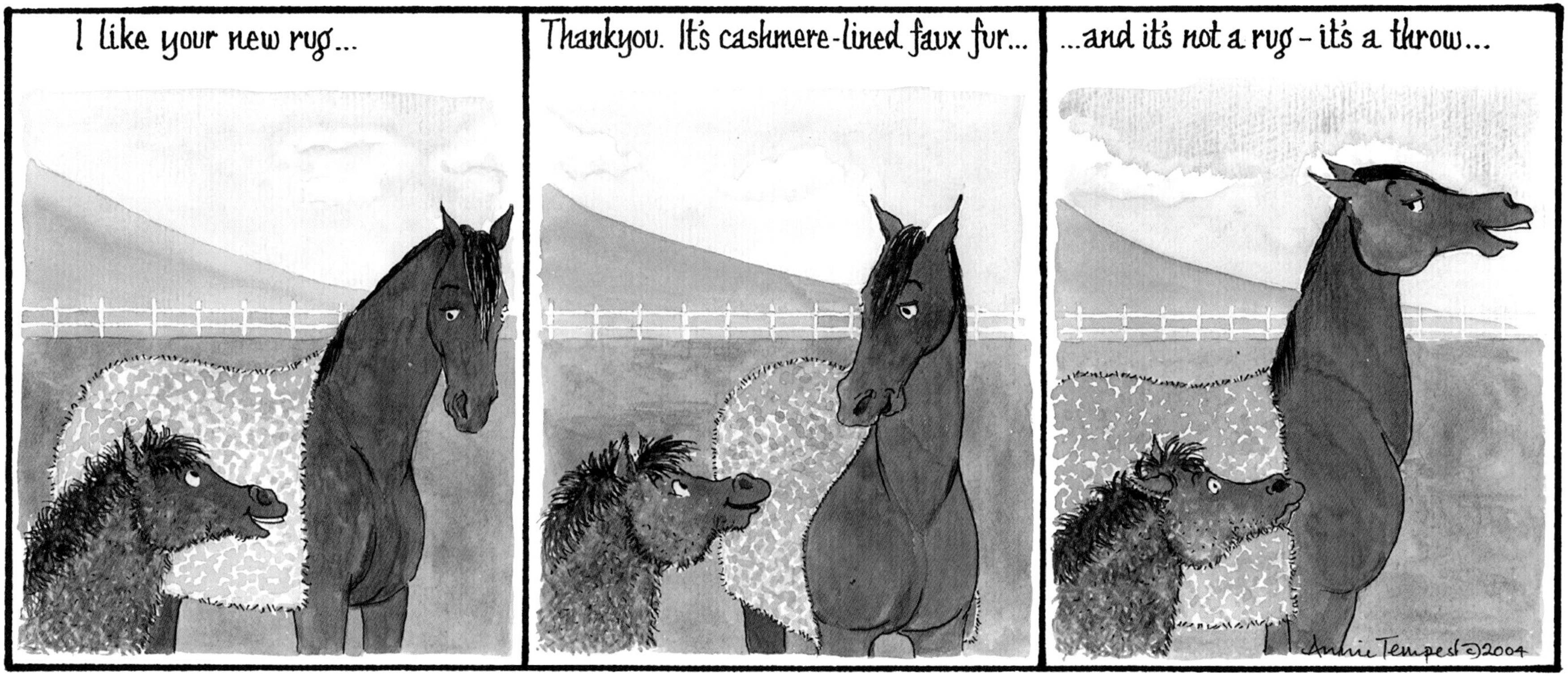
I like your new rug...
Thankyou. It's cashmere-lined faux fur...
...and it's not a rug – it's a throw...
Annie Tempest ©2004

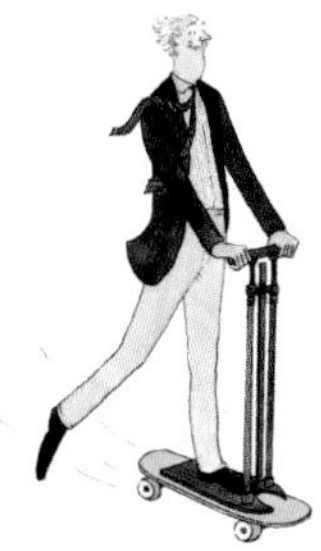

January 27th, 2005

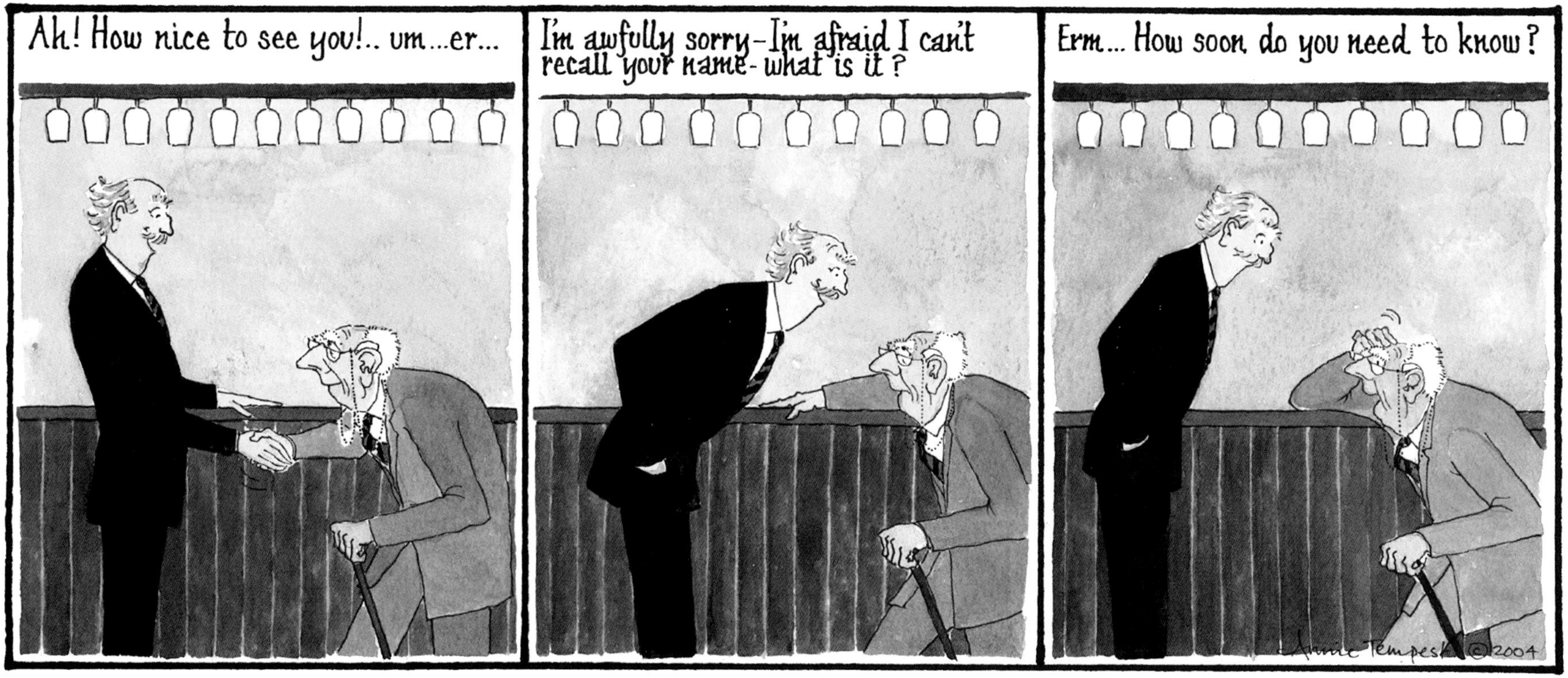
Ah! How nice to see you!.. um...er...
I'm awfully sorry – I'm afraid I can't recall your name – what is it?
Erm... How soon do you need to know?
Annie Tempest ©2004

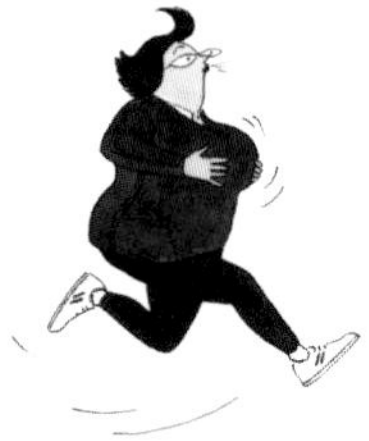

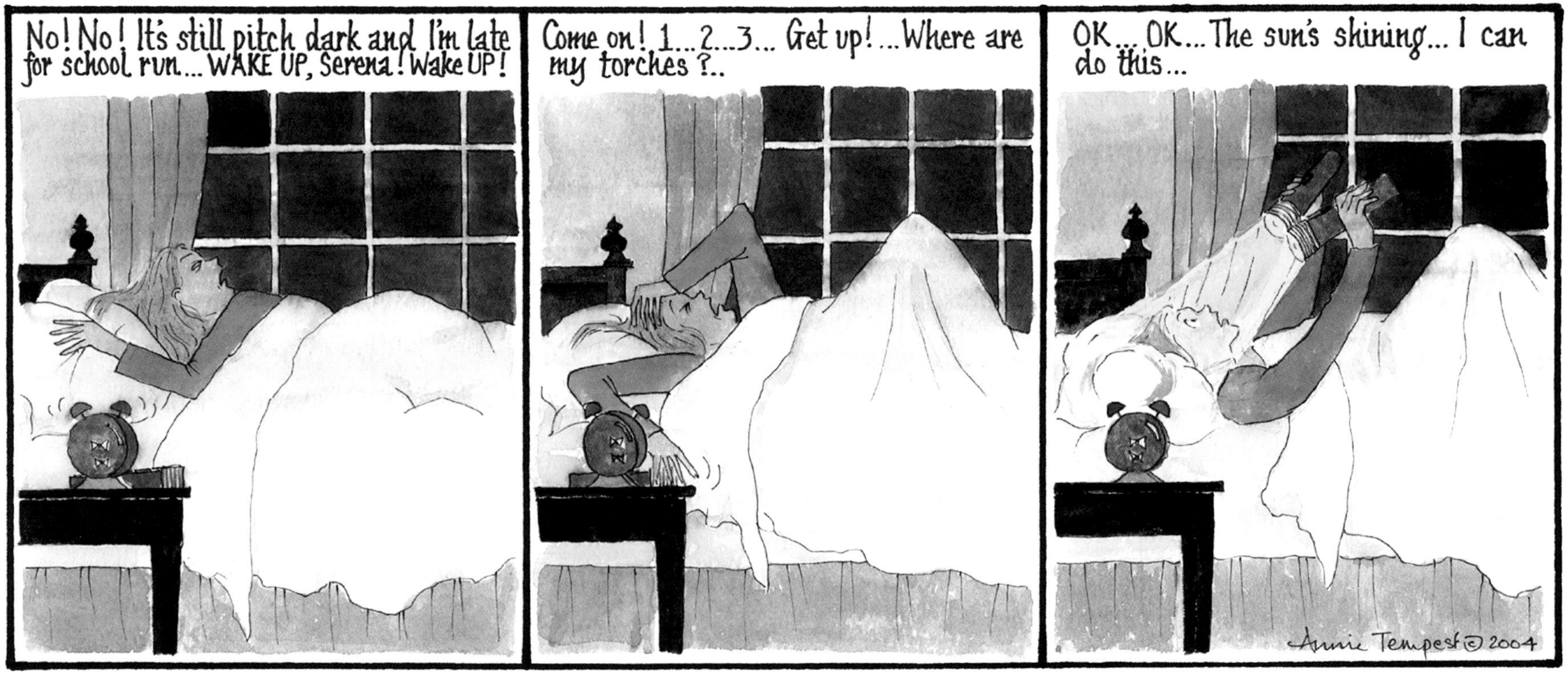
No! No! It's still pitch dark and I'm late for school run... WAKE UP, Serena! Wake UP!
Come on! 1...2...3... Get up! ...Where are my torches?..
OK... OK... The sun's shining... I can do this...
Annie Tempest © 2004

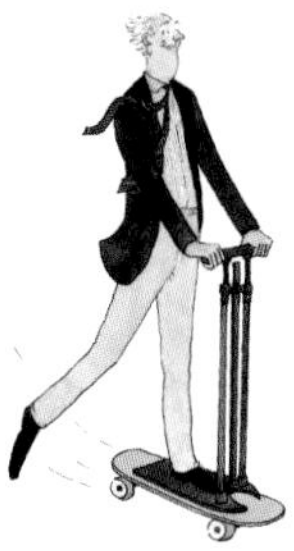

February 10th, 2005

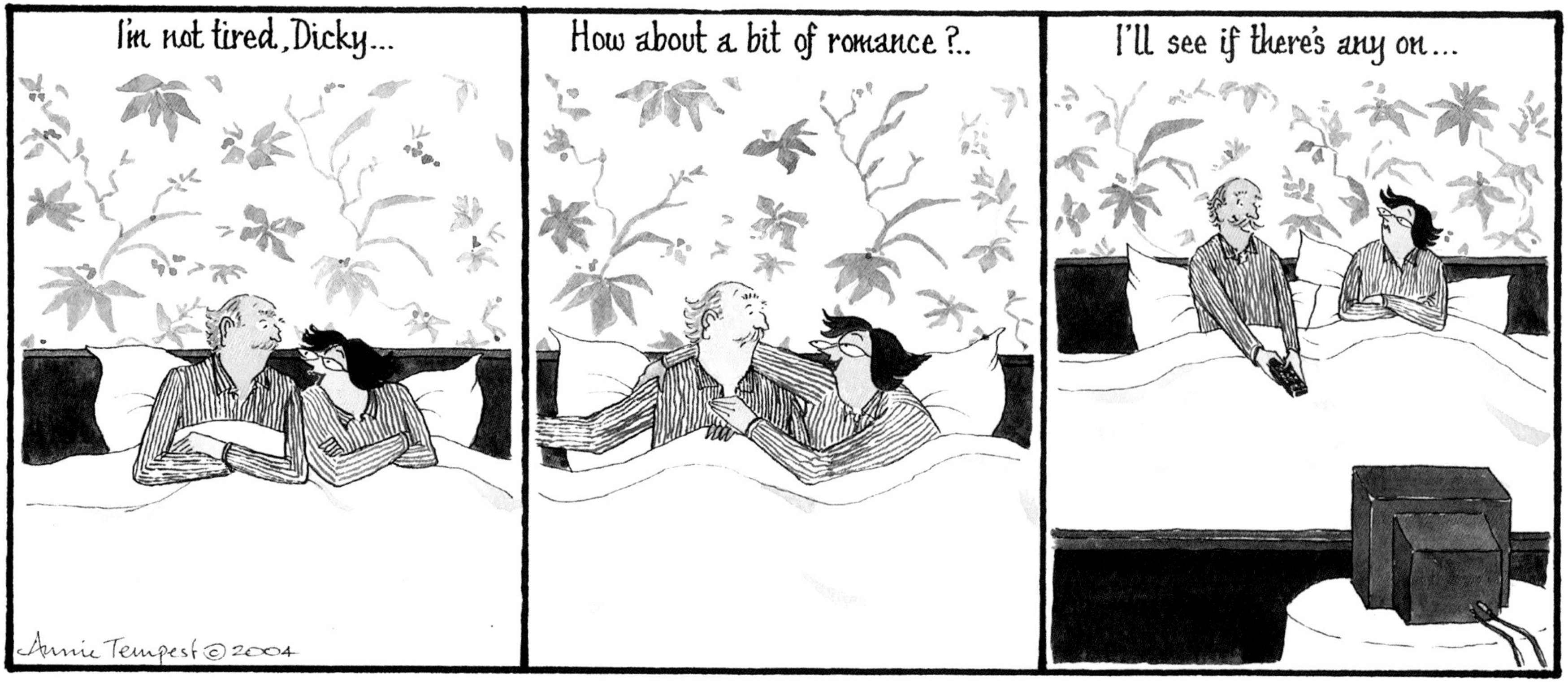
I'm not tired, Dicky...
How about a bit of romance?..
I'll see if there's any on...
Annie Tempest © 2004

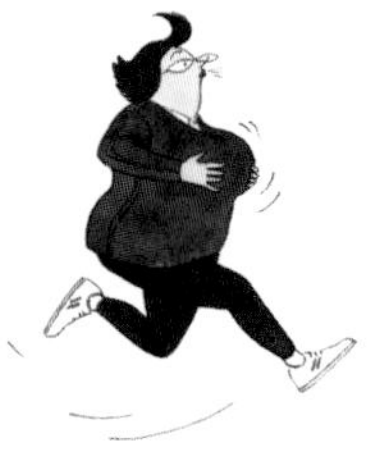

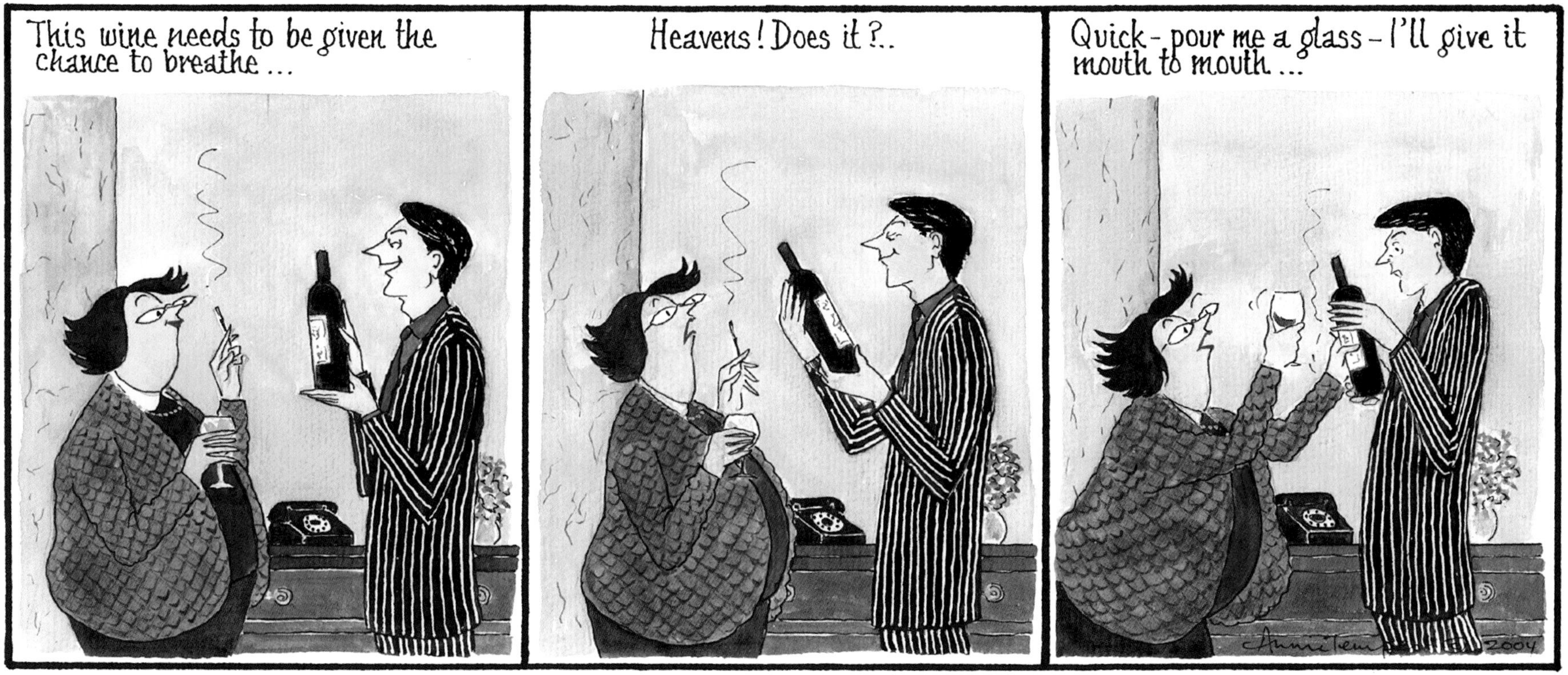
This wine needs to be given the chance to breathe ...
Heavens! Does it?..
Quick - pour me a glass - I'll give it mouth to mouth ...

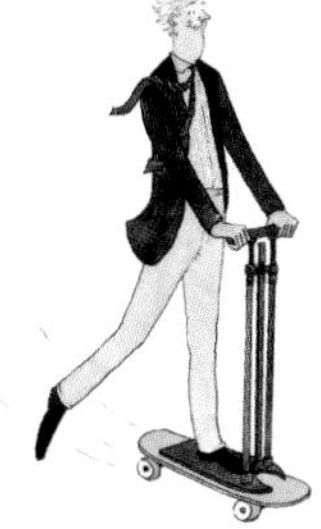

February 24th, 2005

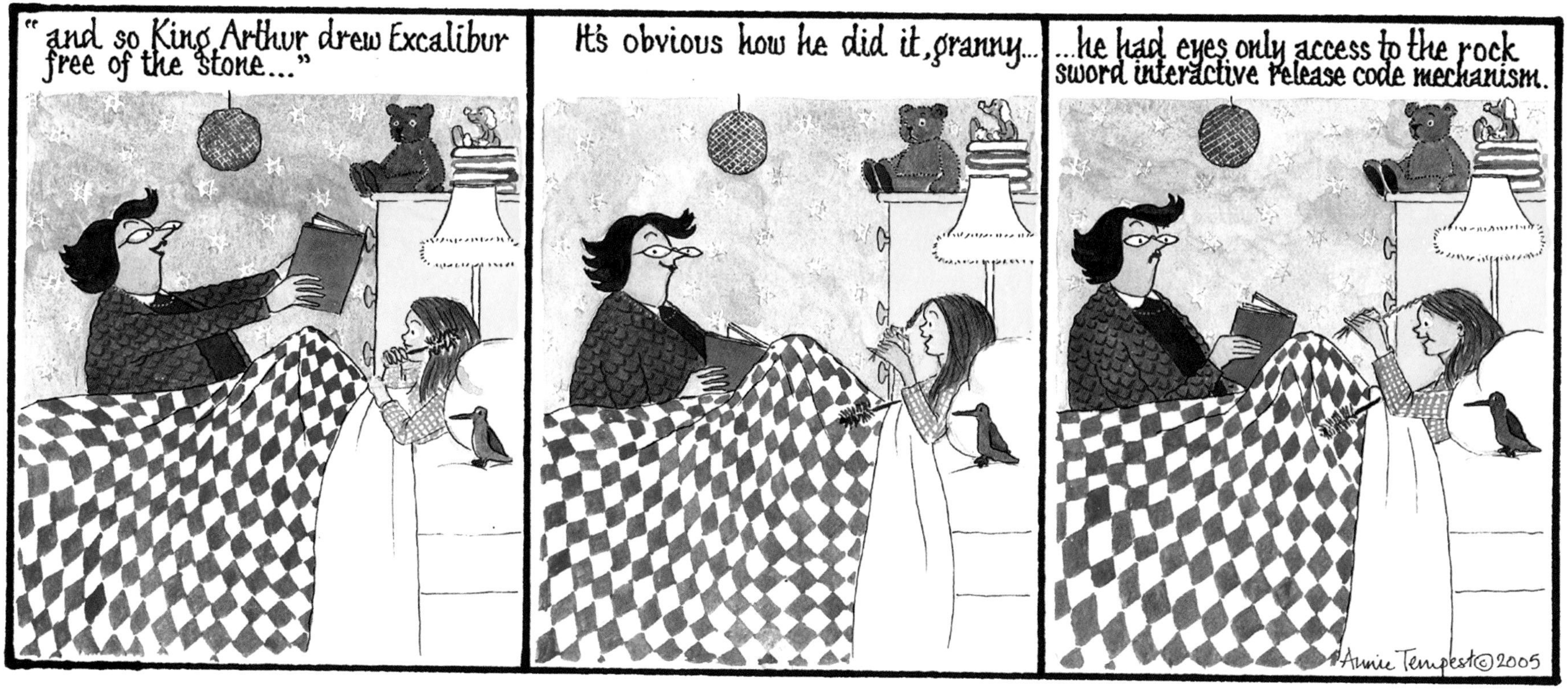
"and so King Arthur drew Excalibur free of the stone..."
It's obvious how he did it, granny...
...he had eyes only access to the rock sword interactive release code mechanism.
Annie Tempest © 2005

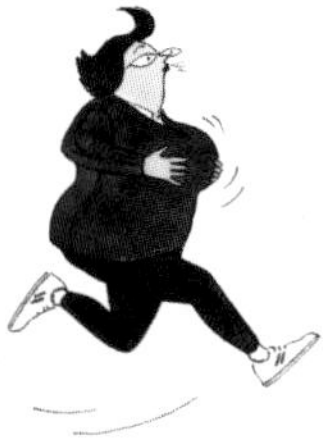

March 3rd, 2005

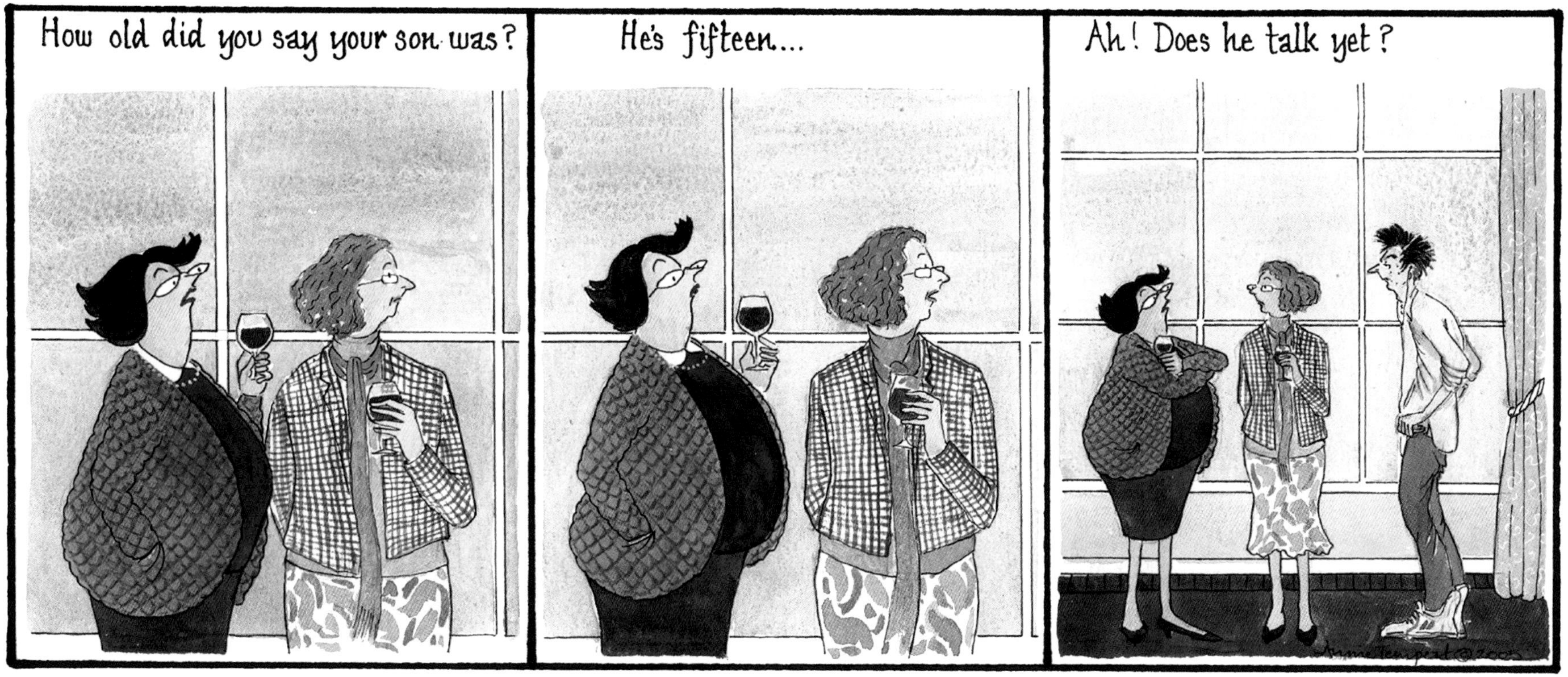
How old did you say your son was?
He's fifteen...
Ah! Does he talk yet?

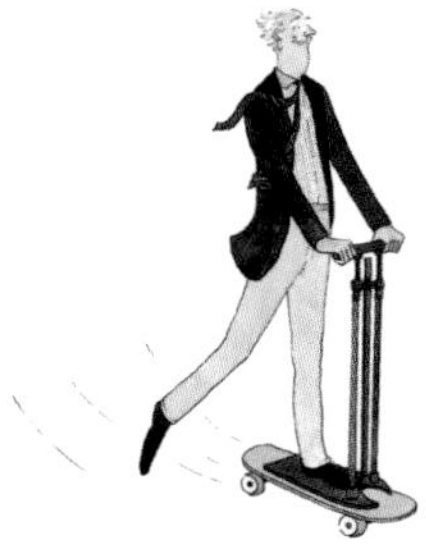

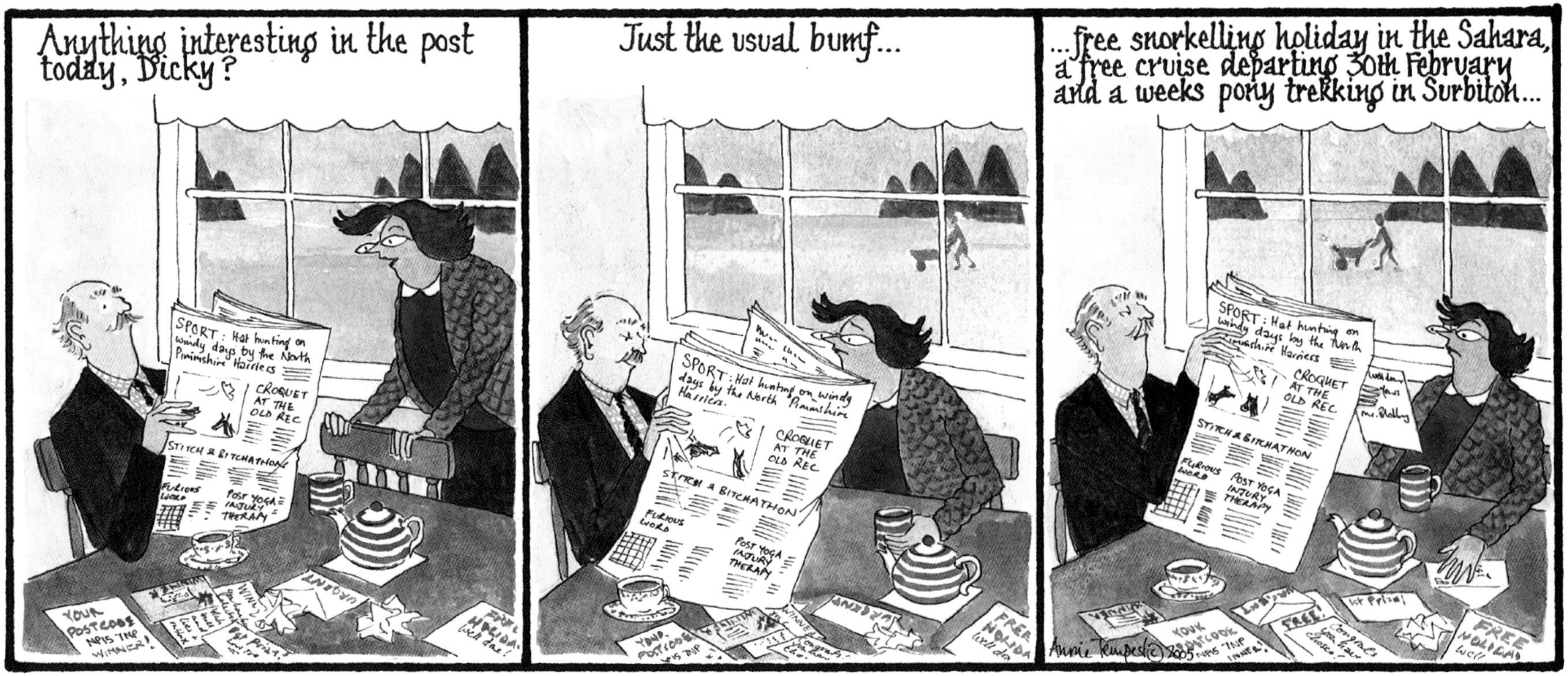
Anything interesting in the post today, Dicky?
SPORT: Hat hunting on windy days by the North Pimmshire Harriers
CROQUET AT THE OLD REC
STITCH & BITCHATHON
FURIOUS WORD
POST YOGA INJURY THERAPY
Just the usual bumf...
...free snorkelling holiday in the Sahara, a free cruise departing 30th February and a weeks pony trekking in Surbiton...
Annie Tempest (c) 2005

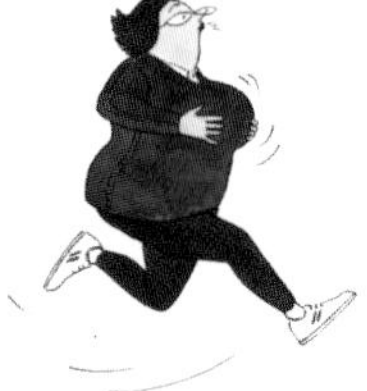

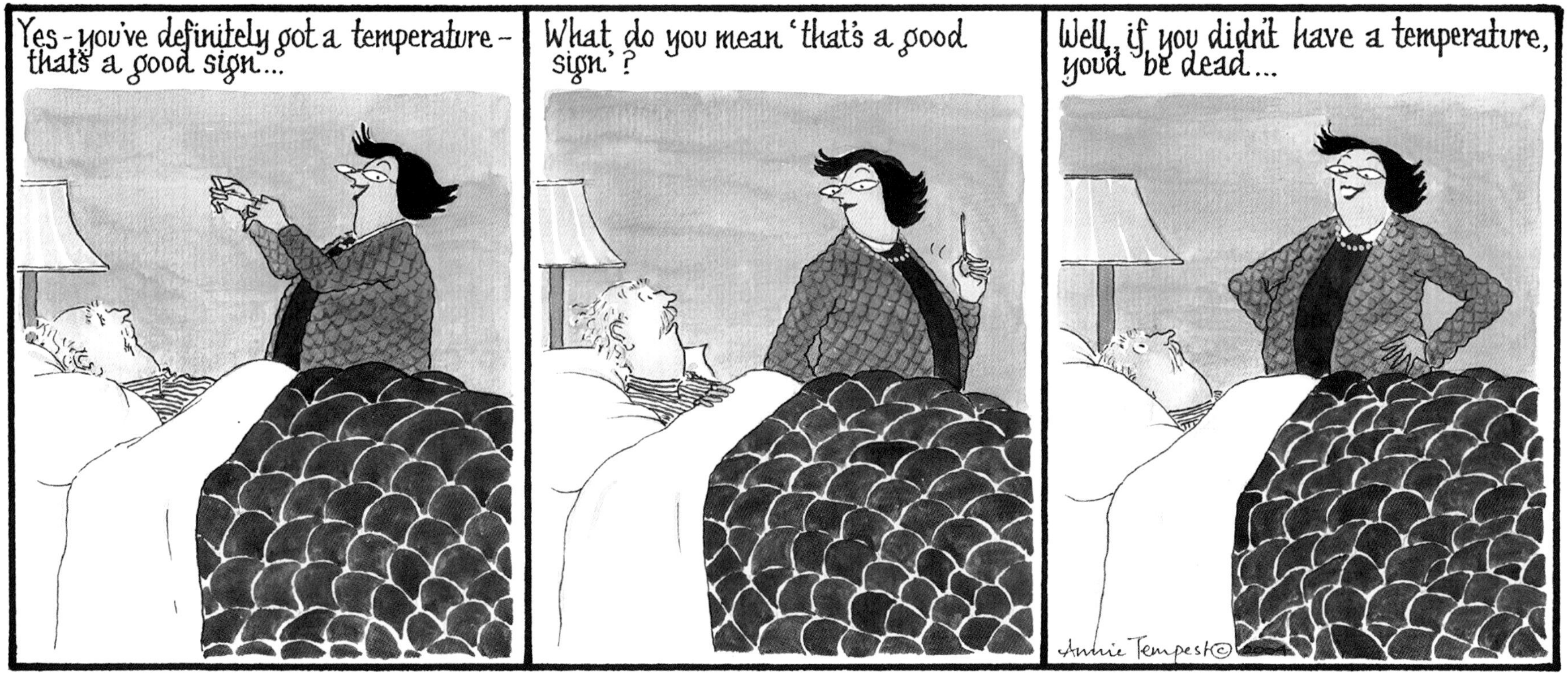
Yes - you've definitely got a temperature - that's a good sign...
What do you mean 'that's a good sign'?
Well, if you didn't have a temperature, you'd be dead...
Annie Tempest©

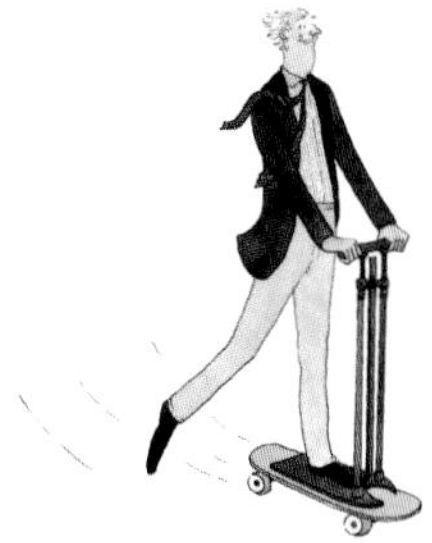

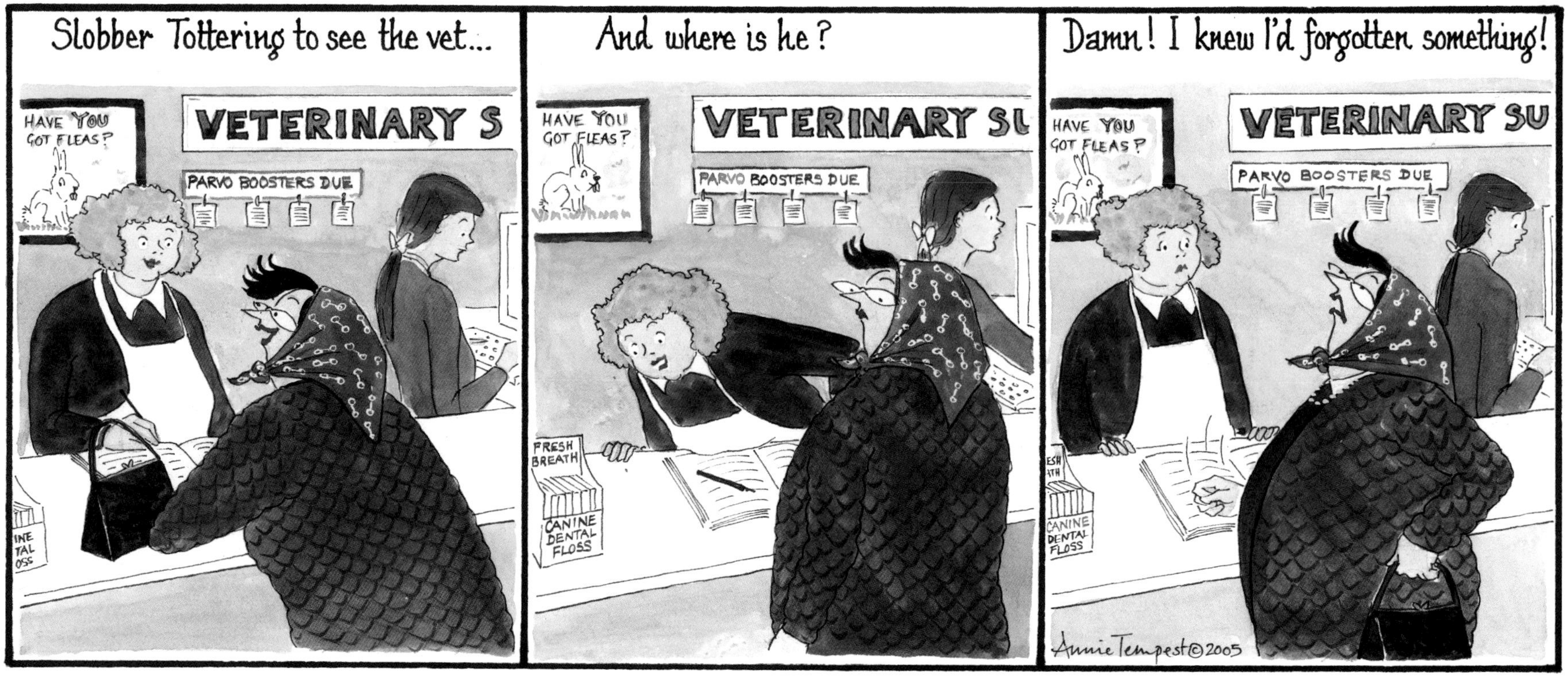
Slobber Tottering to see the vet...
HAVE YOU GOT FLEAS?
VETERINARY S
PARVO BOOSTERS DUE
And where is he?
HAVE YOU GOT FLEAS?
VETERINARY SU
PARVO BOOSTERS DUE
FRESH BREATH
CANINE DENTAL FLOSS
Damn! I knew I'd forgotten something!
HAVE YOU GOT FLEAS?
VETERINARY SU
PARVO BOOSTERS DUE
CANINE DENTAL FLOSS
Annie Tempest © 2005

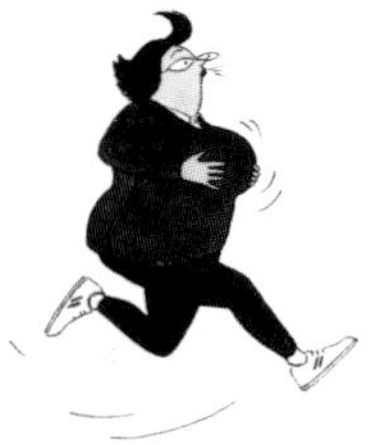

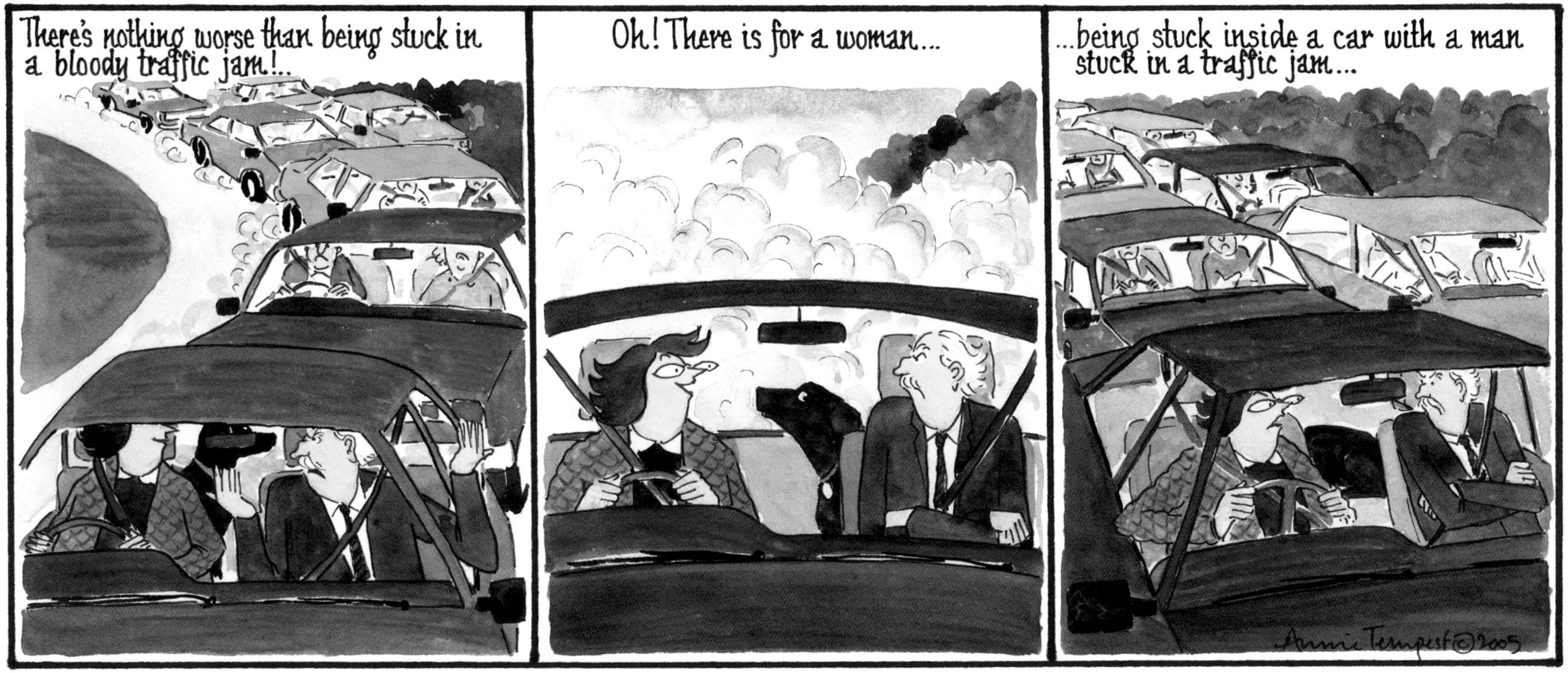
There's nothing worse than being stuck in a bloody traffic jam!..
Oh! There is for a woman....
...being stuck inside a car with a man stuck in a traffic jam...
Annie Tempest © 2005

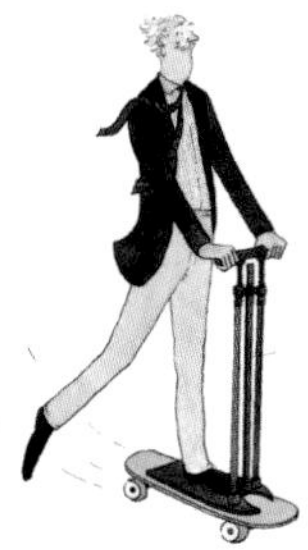

April 7th, 2005

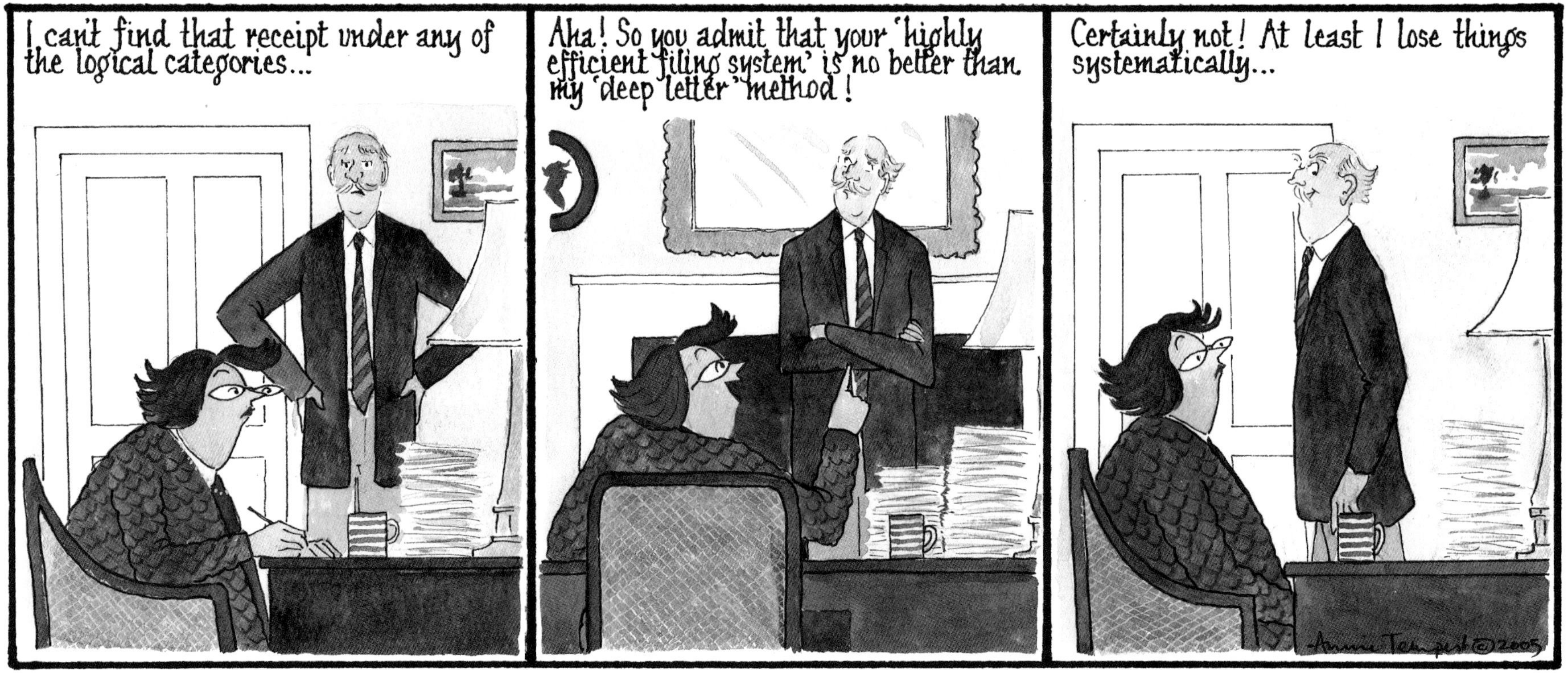
I can't find that receipt under any of the logical categories...
Aha! So you admit that your 'highly efficient filing system' is no better than my 'deep letter' method!
Certainly not! At least I lose things systematically...
Annie Tempest © 2005

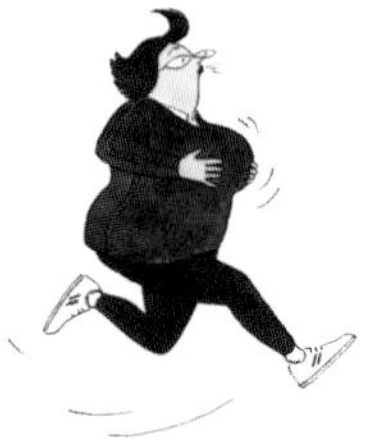

April 14th, 2005

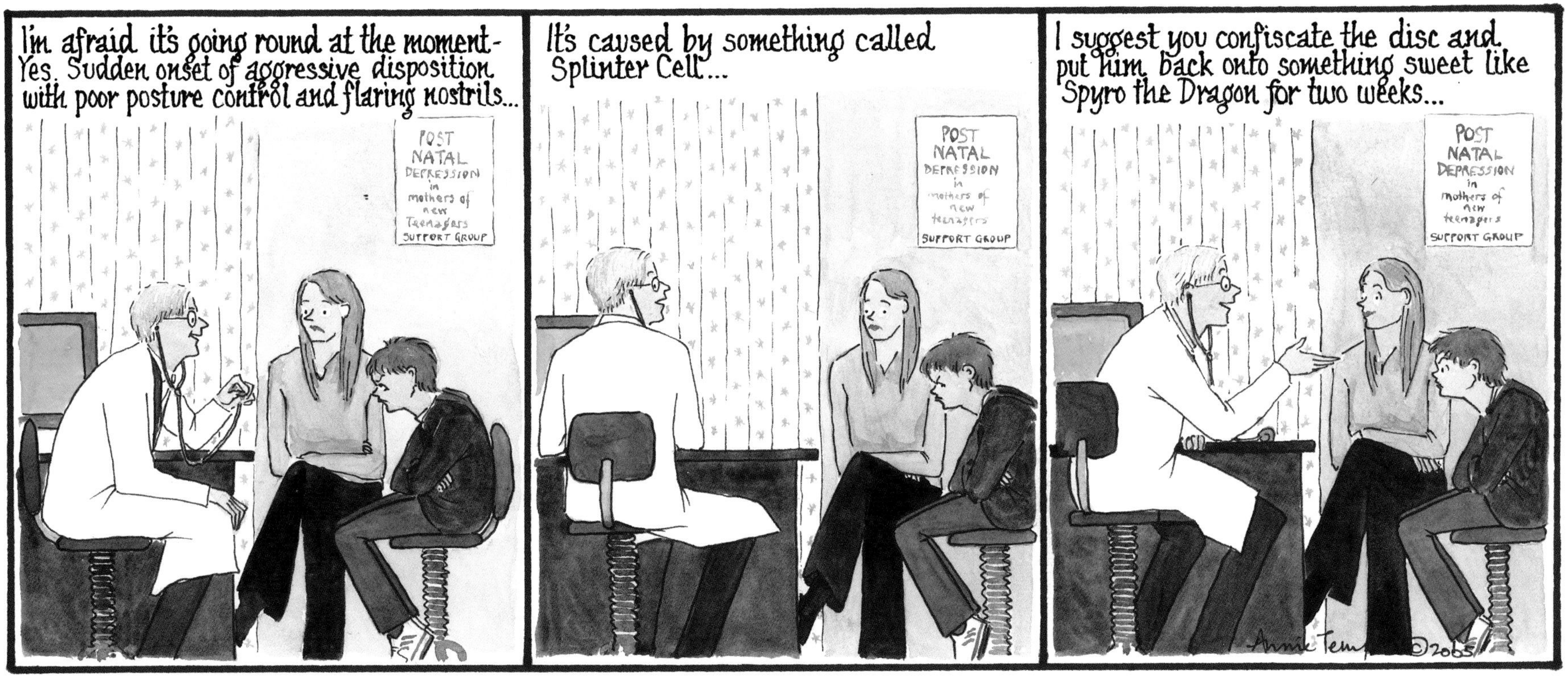
I'm afraid it's going round at the moment- Yes. Sudden onset of aggressive disposition with poor posture control and flaring nostrils...
POST NATAL DEPRESSION in mothers of new Teenagers SUPPORT GROUP
It's caused by something called Splinter Cell...
I suggest you confiscate the disc and put him back onto something sweet like Spyro the Dragon for two weeks...

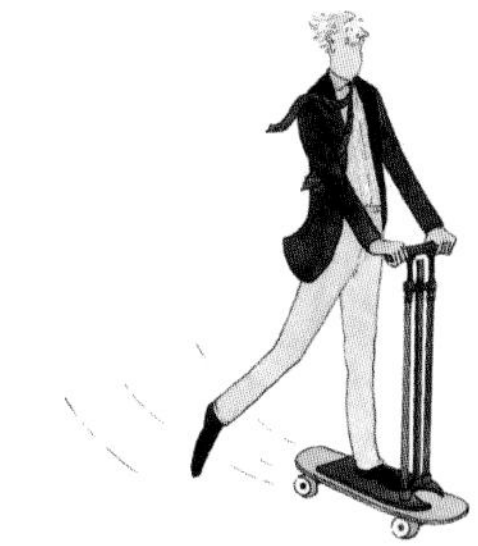

April 21st, 2005

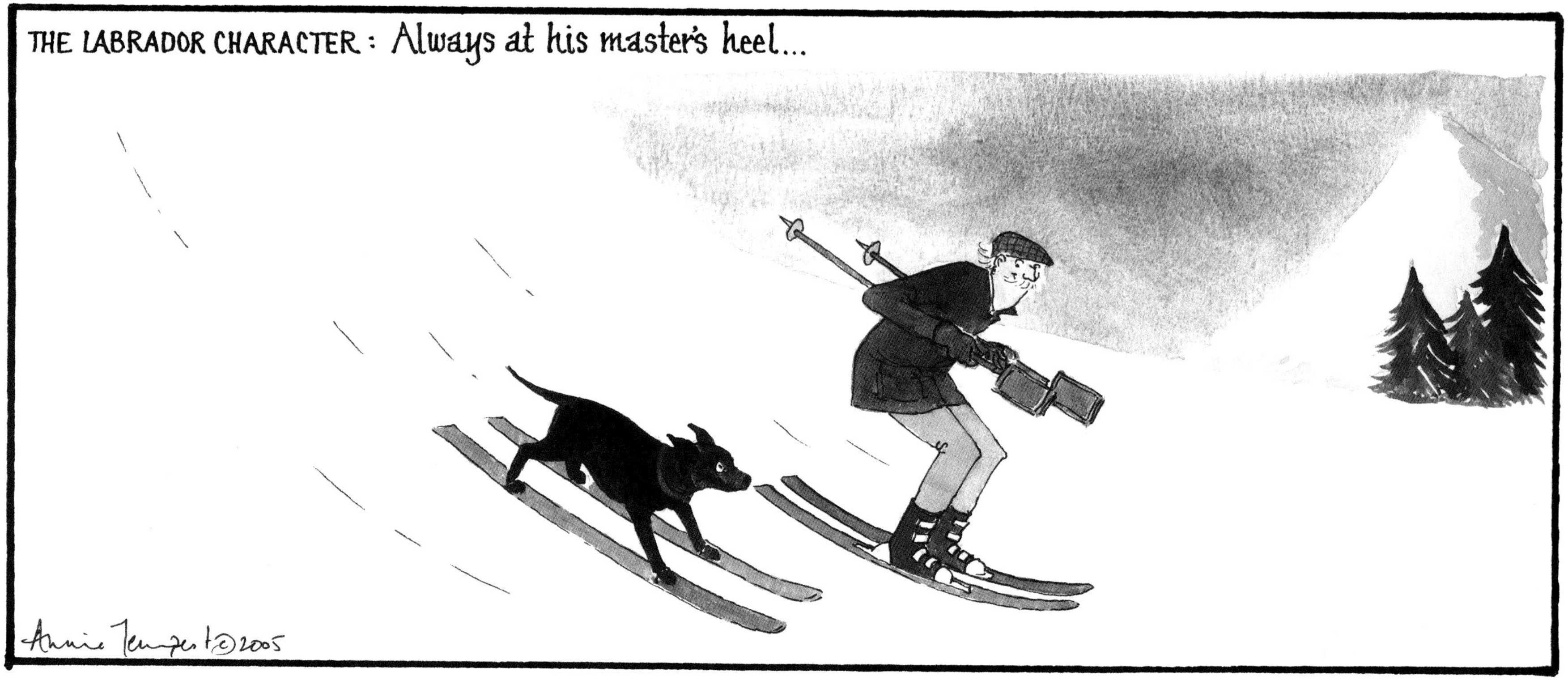
THE LABRADOR CHARACTER : Always at his master's heel...
Annie Tempest © 2005

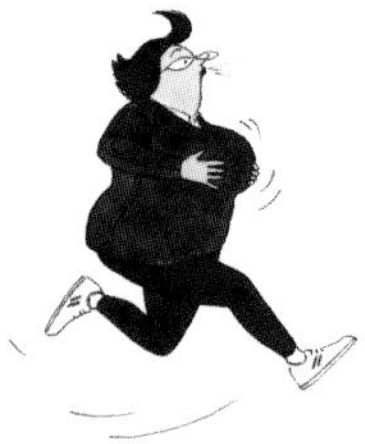

Don't look now – but Charles and Cynthia Snafflegirth are here...

...She looks more like a horse every time I see her...

...I'm positive I saw her ears go back...

May 5th, 2005

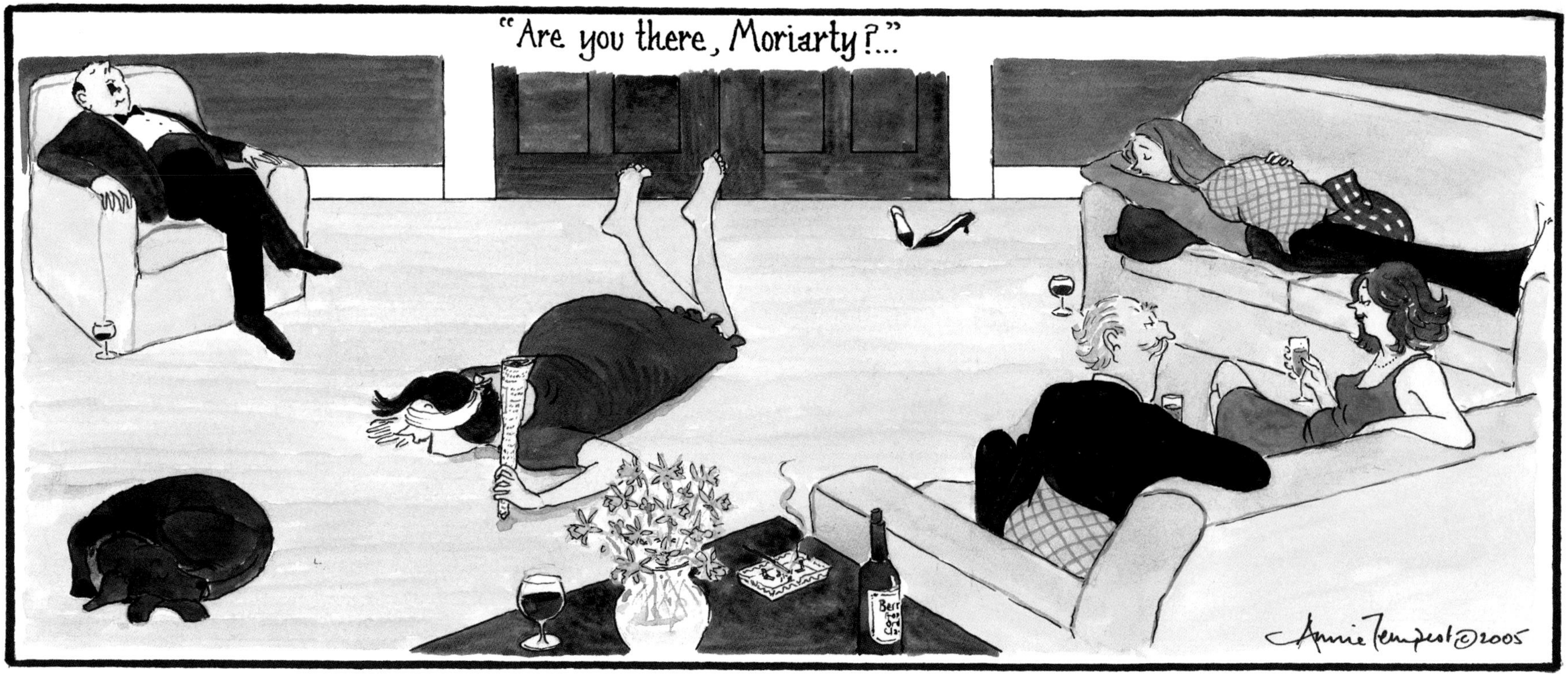
Annie Tempest ©2005

"Are you there, Moriarty?..."

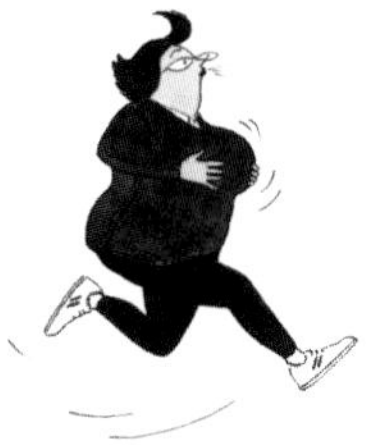

May 12th, 2005

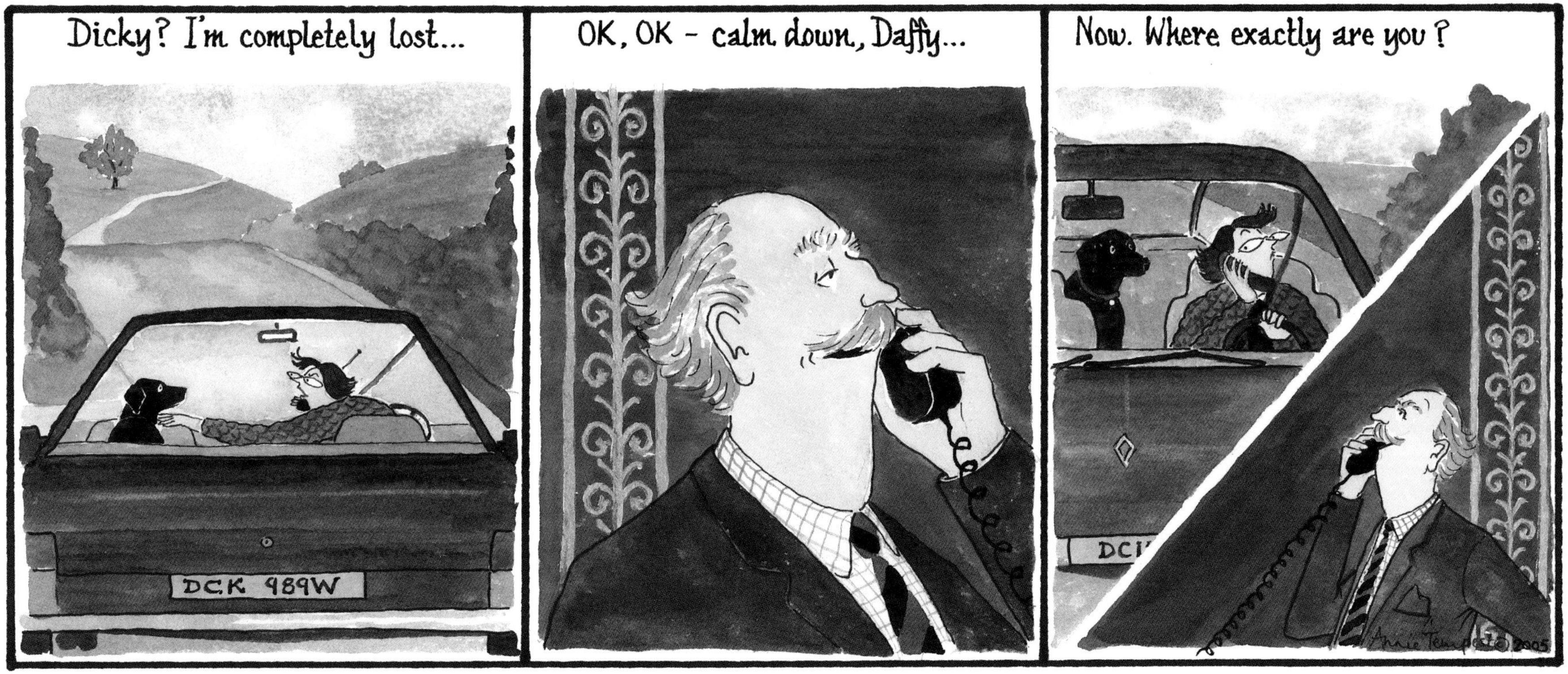
Dicky? I'm completely lost...
OK, OK - calm down, Daffy...
Now. Where exactly are you?
DC.K 989W

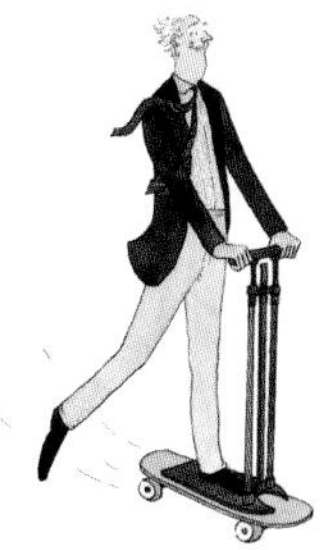

May 19th, 2005

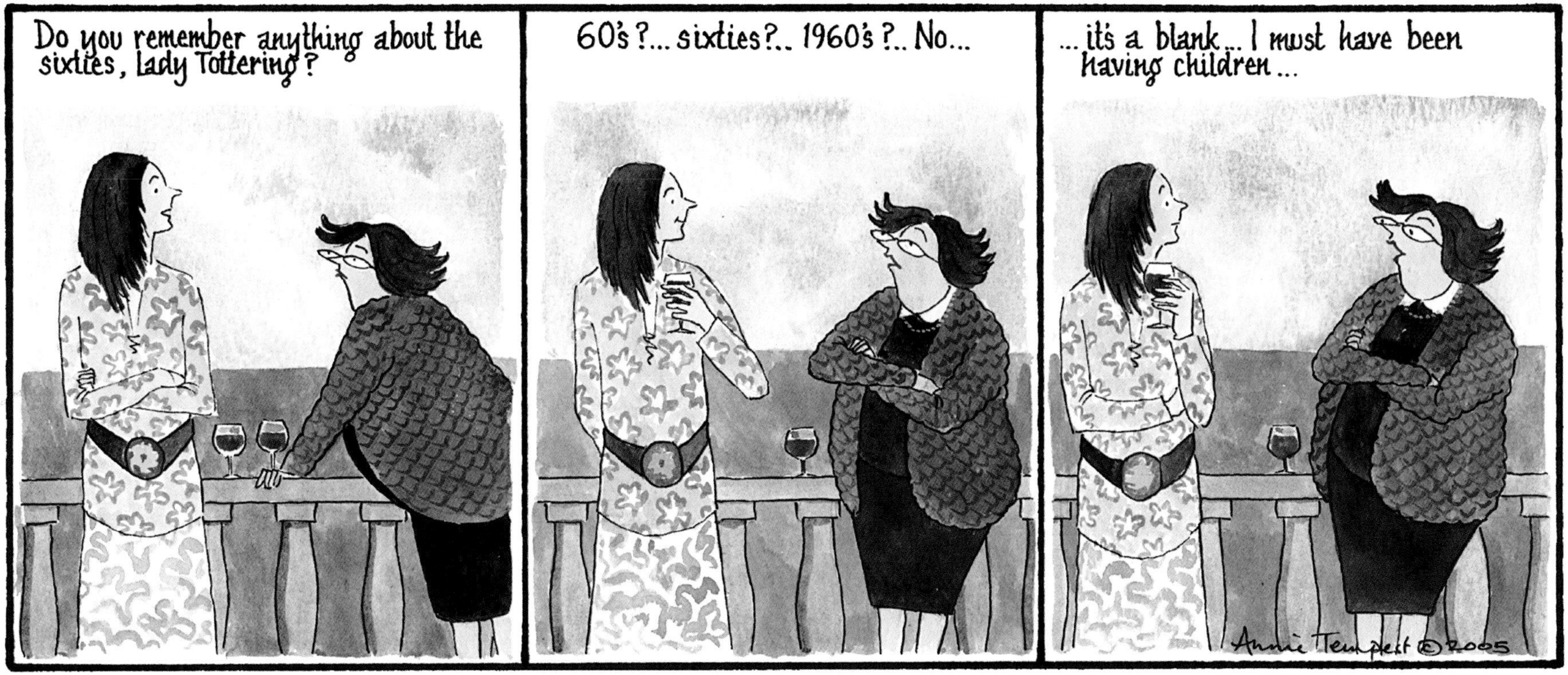
Do you remember anything about the sixties, Lady Tottering?
60's?... sixties?.. 1960's?.. No...
...it's a blank... I must have been having children...
Annie Tempest © 2005

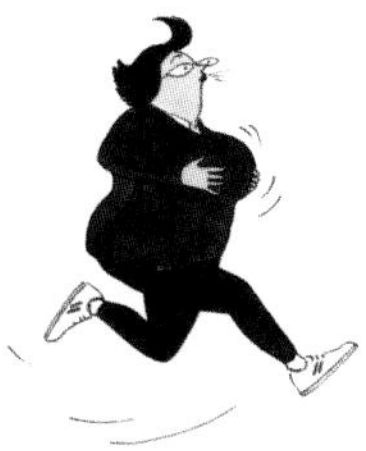

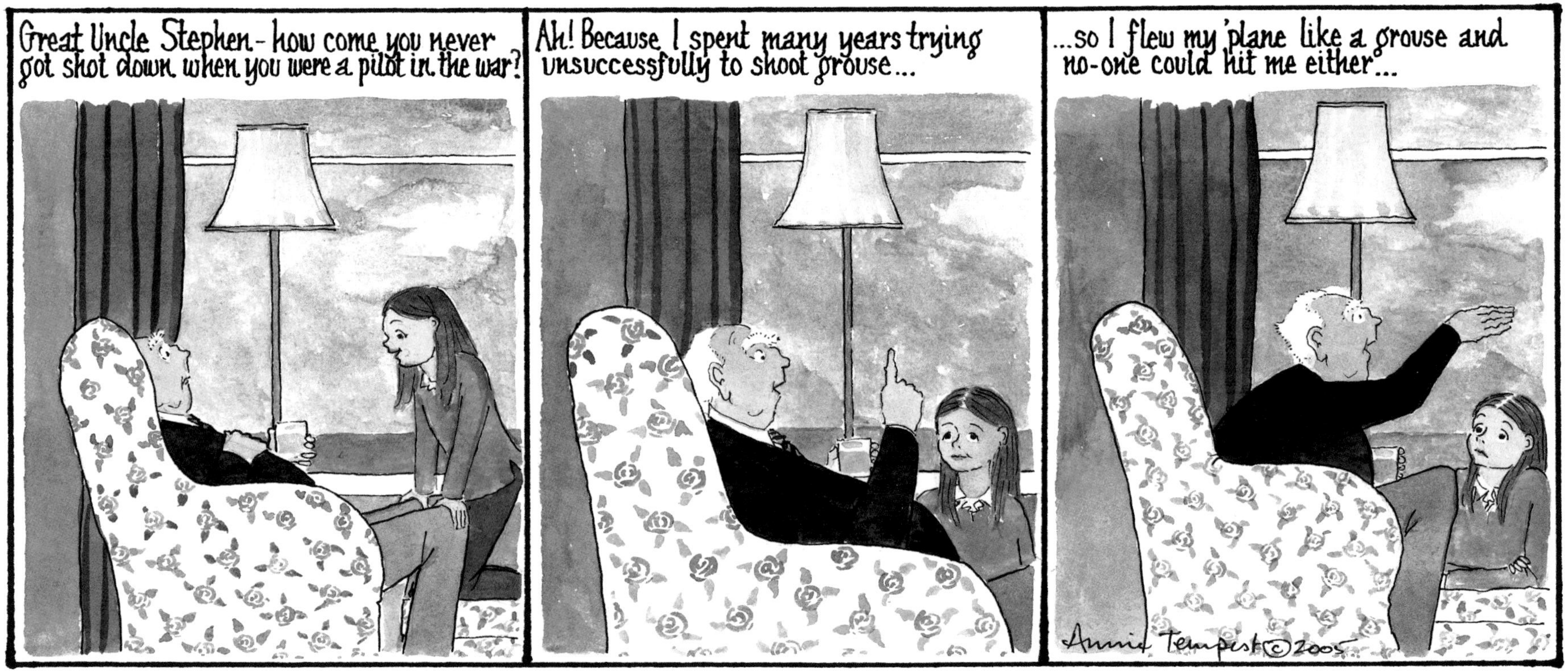
Great Uncle Stephen - how come you never got shot down when you were a pilot in the war?
Ah! Because I spent many years trying unsuccessfully to shoot grouse...
...so I flew my 'plane like a grouse and no-one could hit me either...
Annie Tempest © 2005

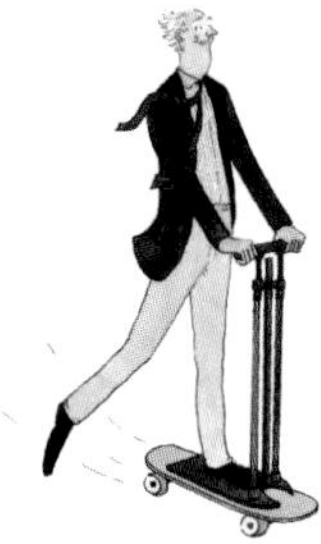

June 2nd, 2005

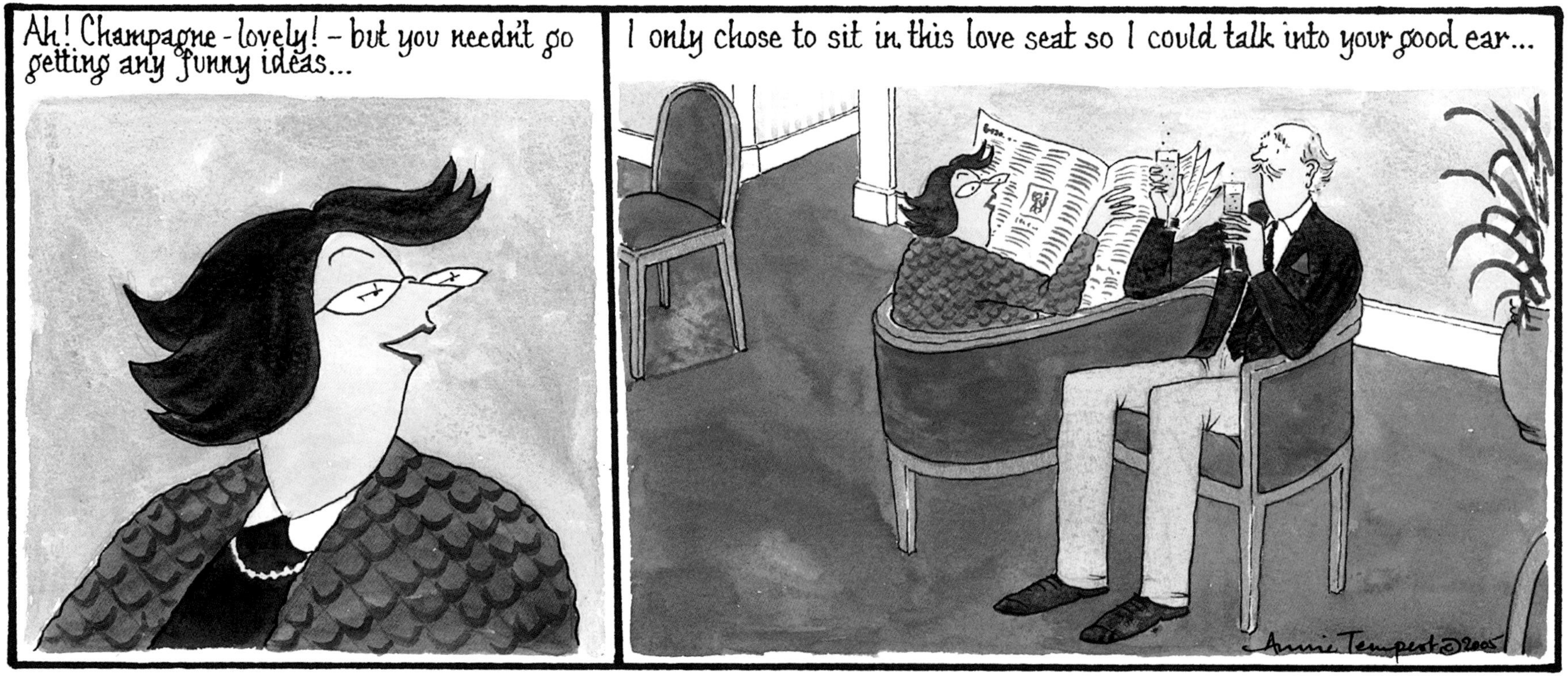
Ah! Champagne - lovely! - but you needn't go getting any funny ideas...
I only chose to sit in this love seat so I could talk into your good ear...
Annie Tempest ©2005

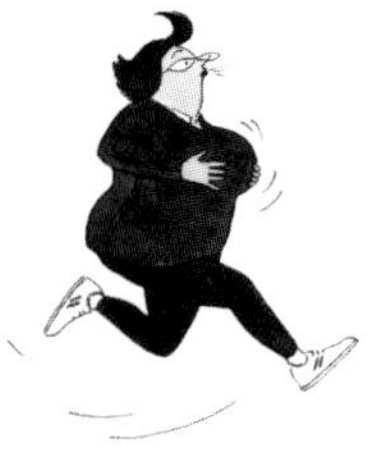

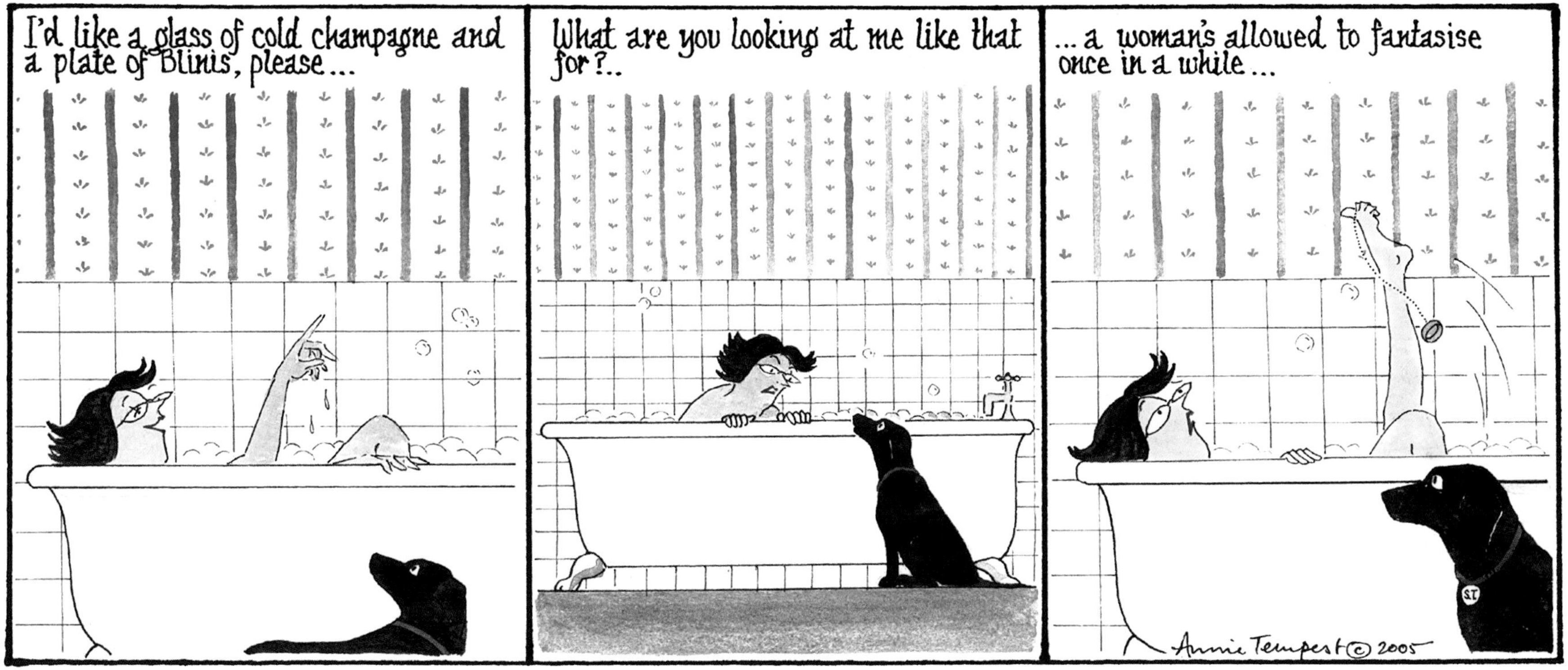
I'd like a glass of cold champagne and a plate of Blinis, please...
What are you looking at me like that for?..
...a woman's allowed to fantasise once in a while...
S.T.
Annie Tempest © 2005

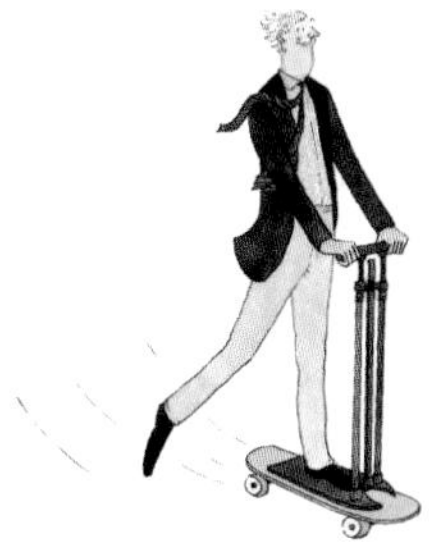

June 16th, 2005

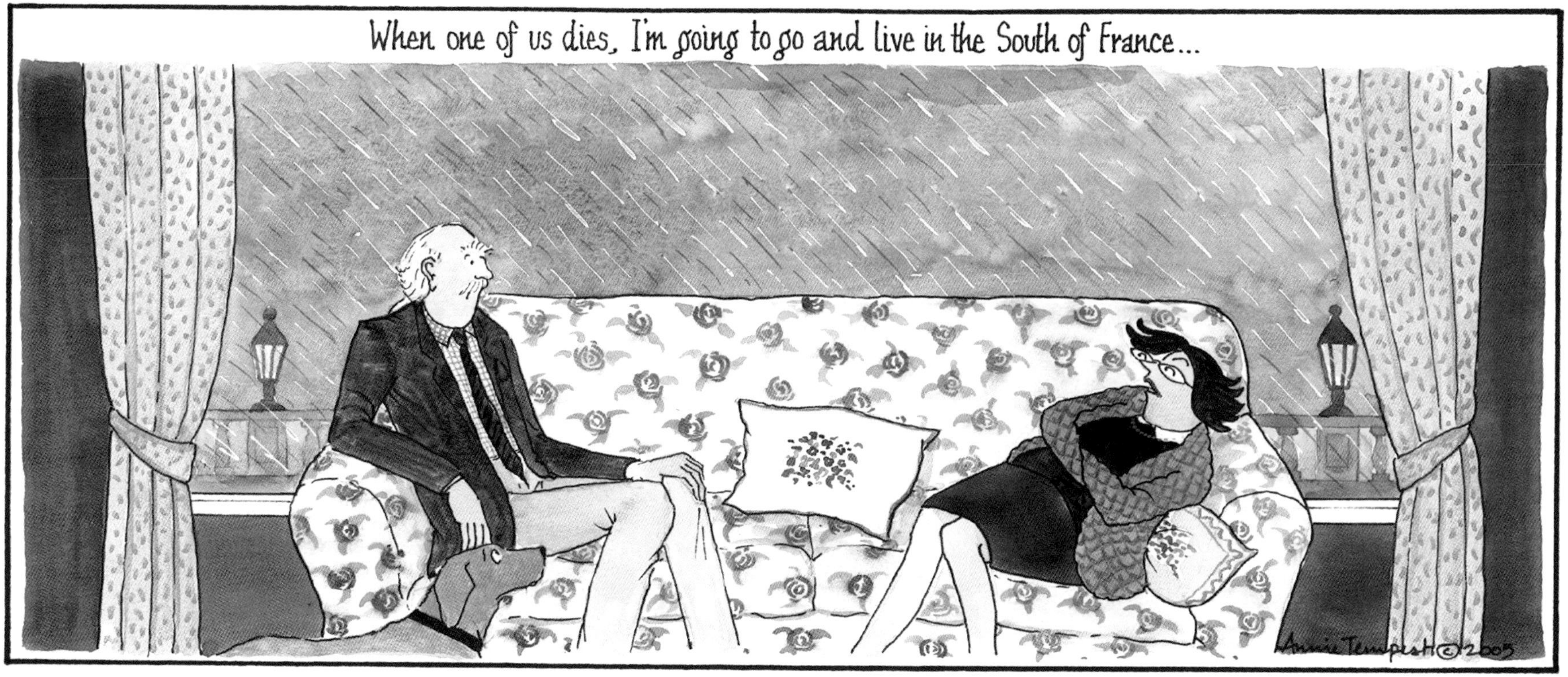
Annie Tempest © 2005
When one of us dies, I'm going to go and live in the South of France...

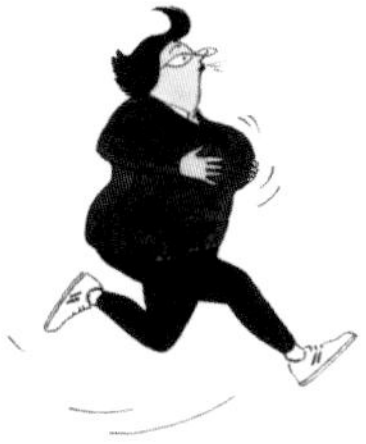

June 23rd, 2005

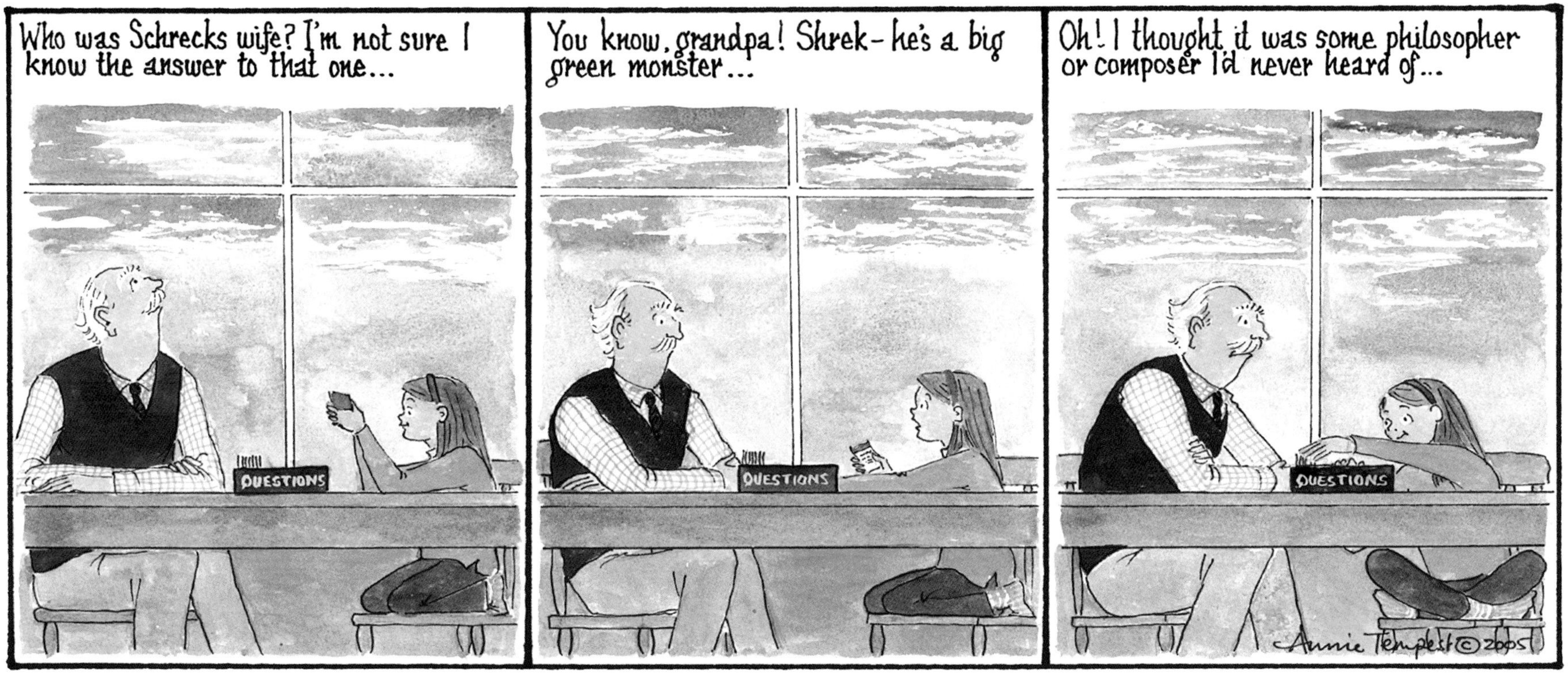
Who was Schrecks wife? I'm not sure I know the answer to that one...
QUESTIONS
You know, grandpa! Shrek - he's a big green monster...
QUESTIONS
Oh! I thought it was some philosopher or composer I'd never heard of...
QUESTIONS
Annie Tempest © 2005

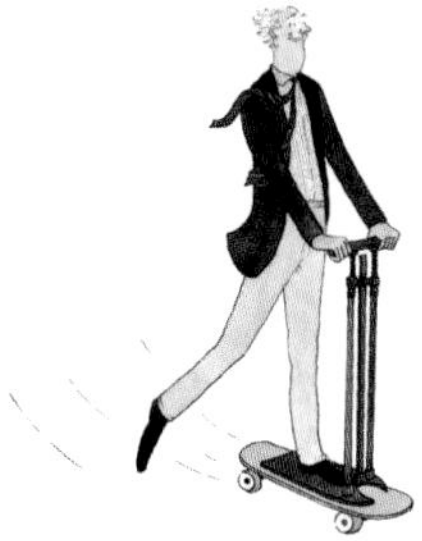

June 30th, 2005

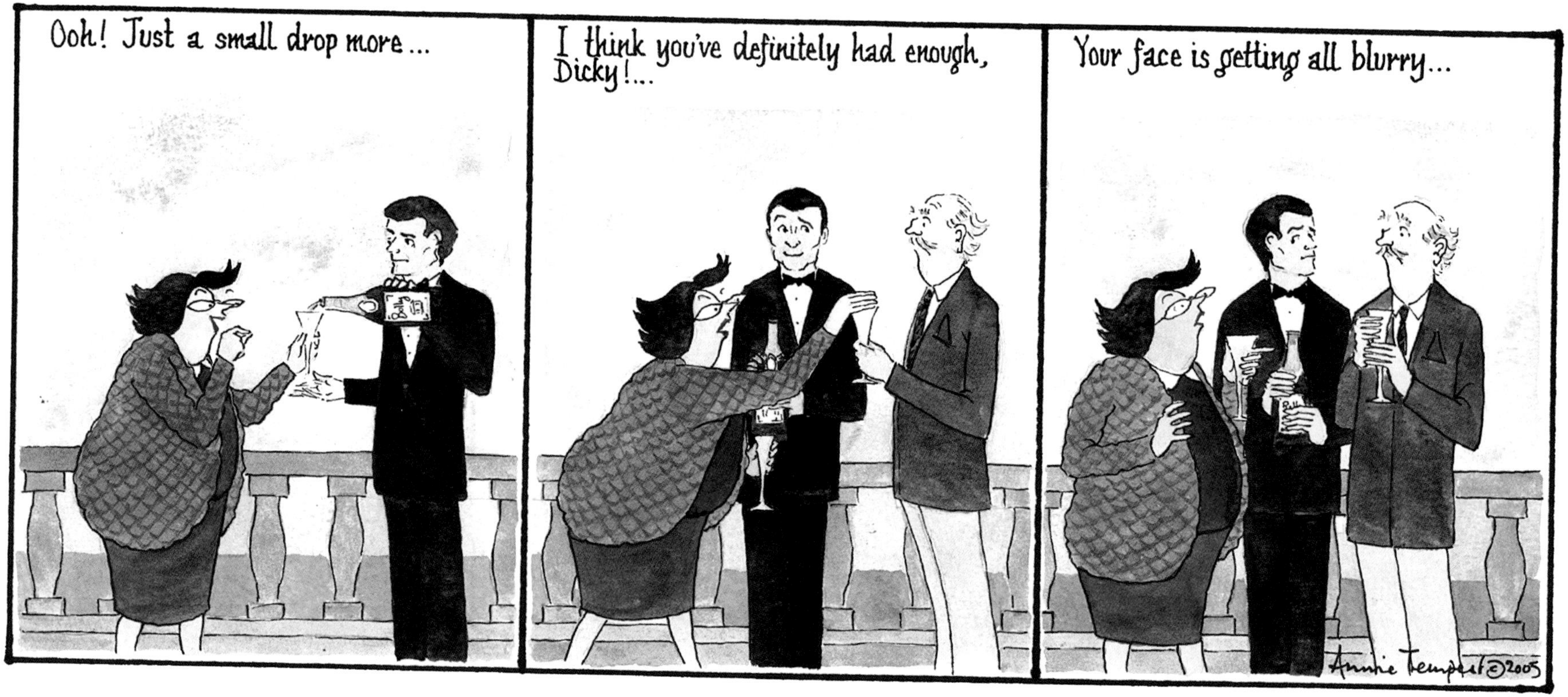
Ooh! Just a small drop more...
I think you've definitely had enough, Dicky!...
Your face is getting all blurry...
Annie Tempest ©2005

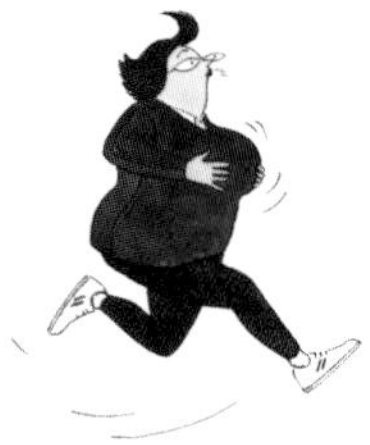

July 7th, 2005

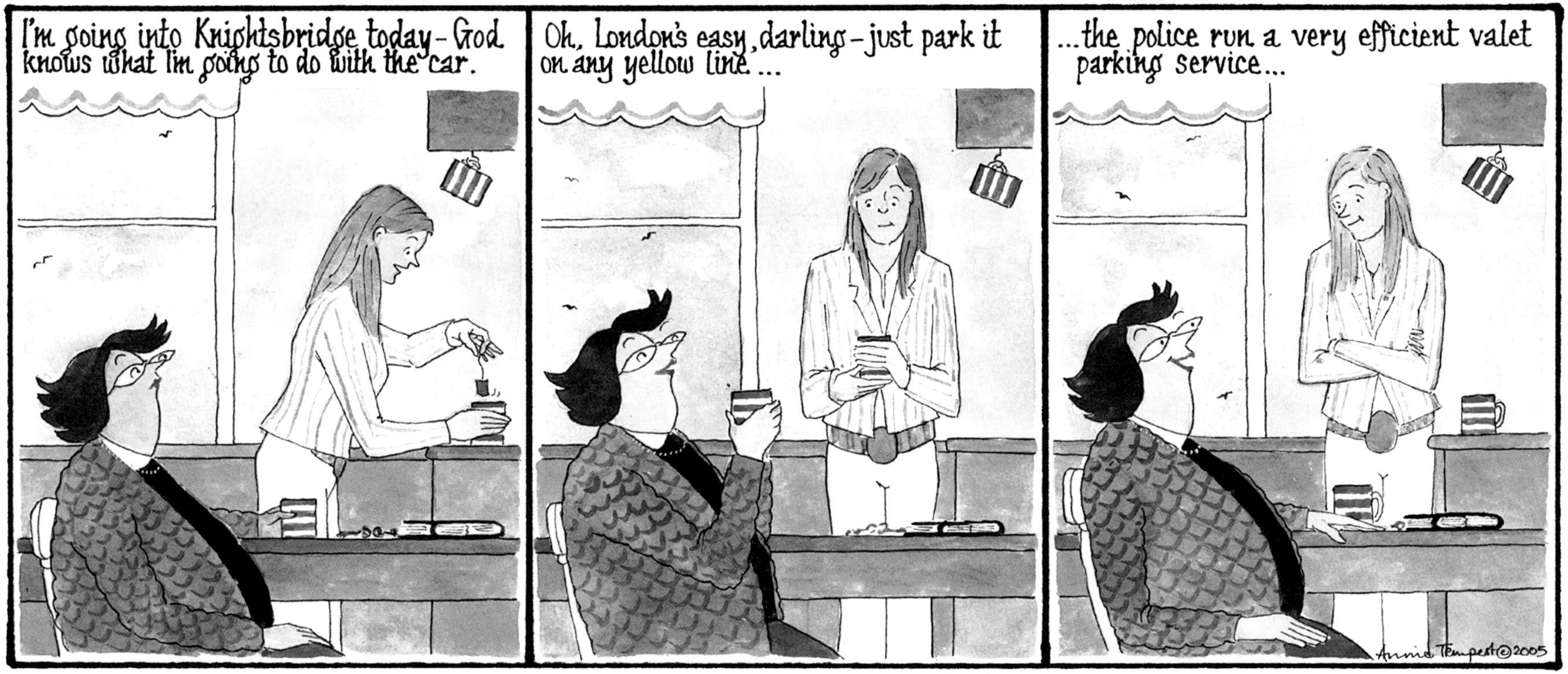
I'm going into Knightsbridge today - God knows what I'm going to do with the car.
Oh, London's easy, darling - just park it on any yellow line...
...the police run a very efficient valet parking service...
Annie Tempest © 2005

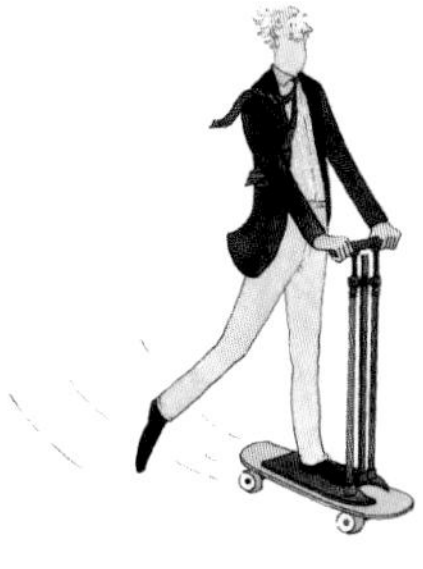

July 14th, 2005

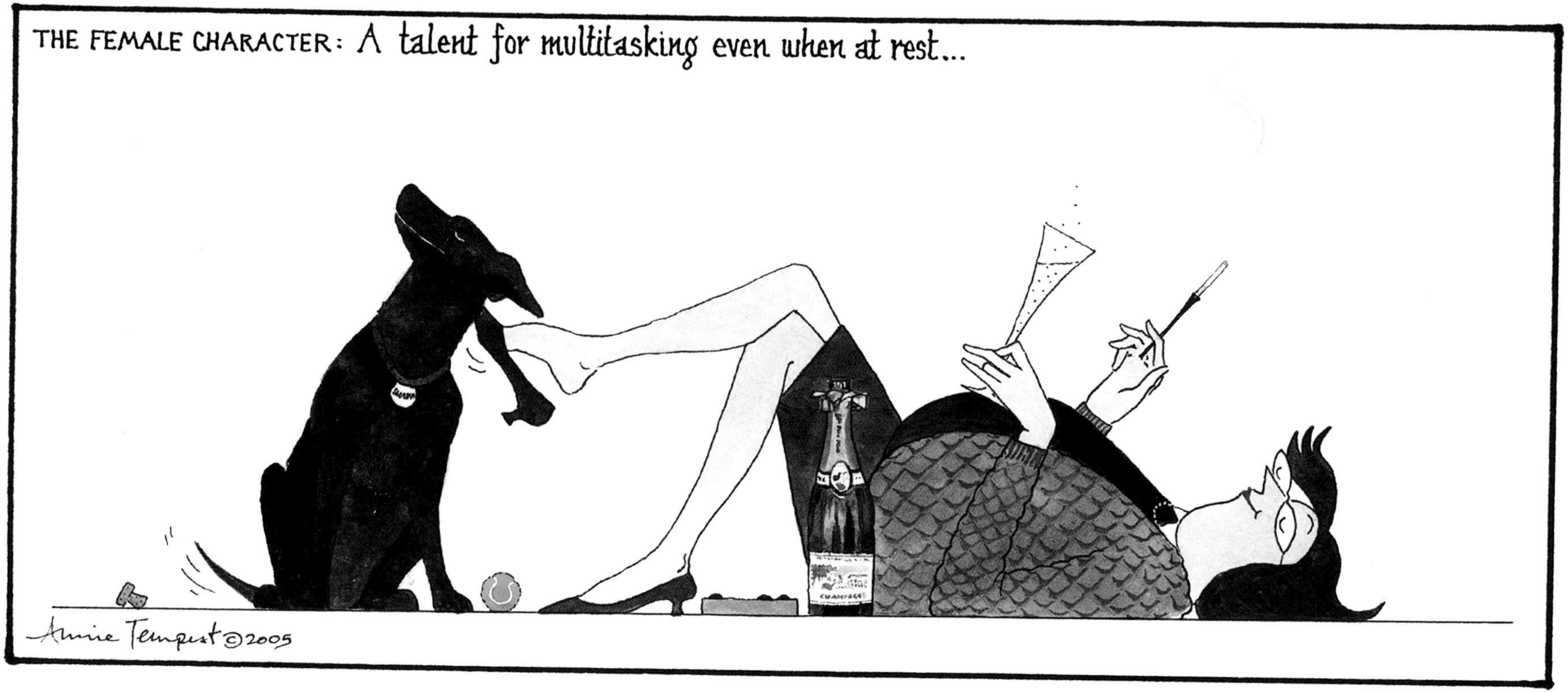
THE FEMALE CHARACTER: A talent for multitasking even when at rest...
Annie Tempest ©2005

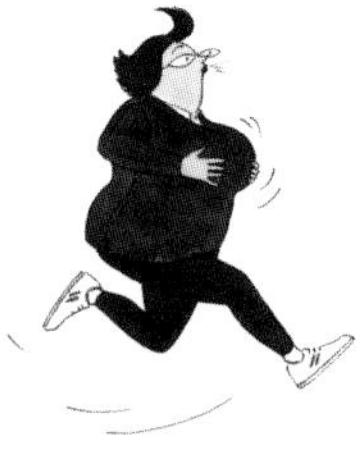

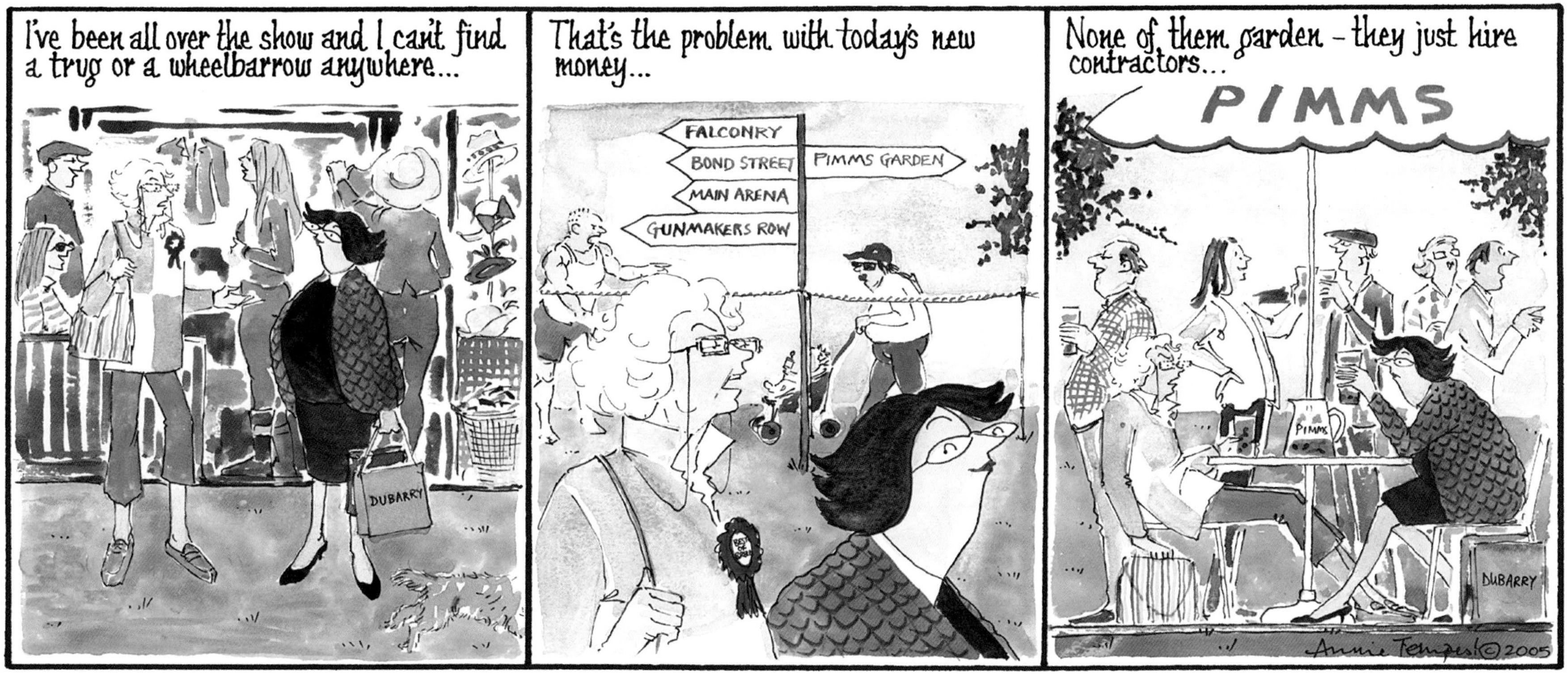
I've been all over the show and I can't find a trug or a wheelbarrow anywhere...
DUBARRY
That's the problem with today's new money...
FALCONRY
BOND STREET
PIMMS GARDEN
MAIN ARENA
GUNMAKERS ROW
None of them garden – they just hire contractors...
PIMMS
PIMMS
DUBARRY
Annie Tempest © 2005

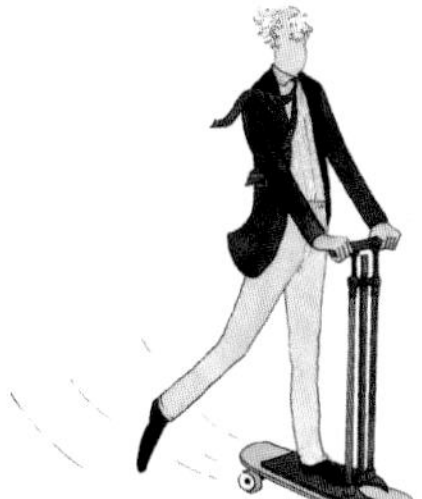

July 28th, 2005

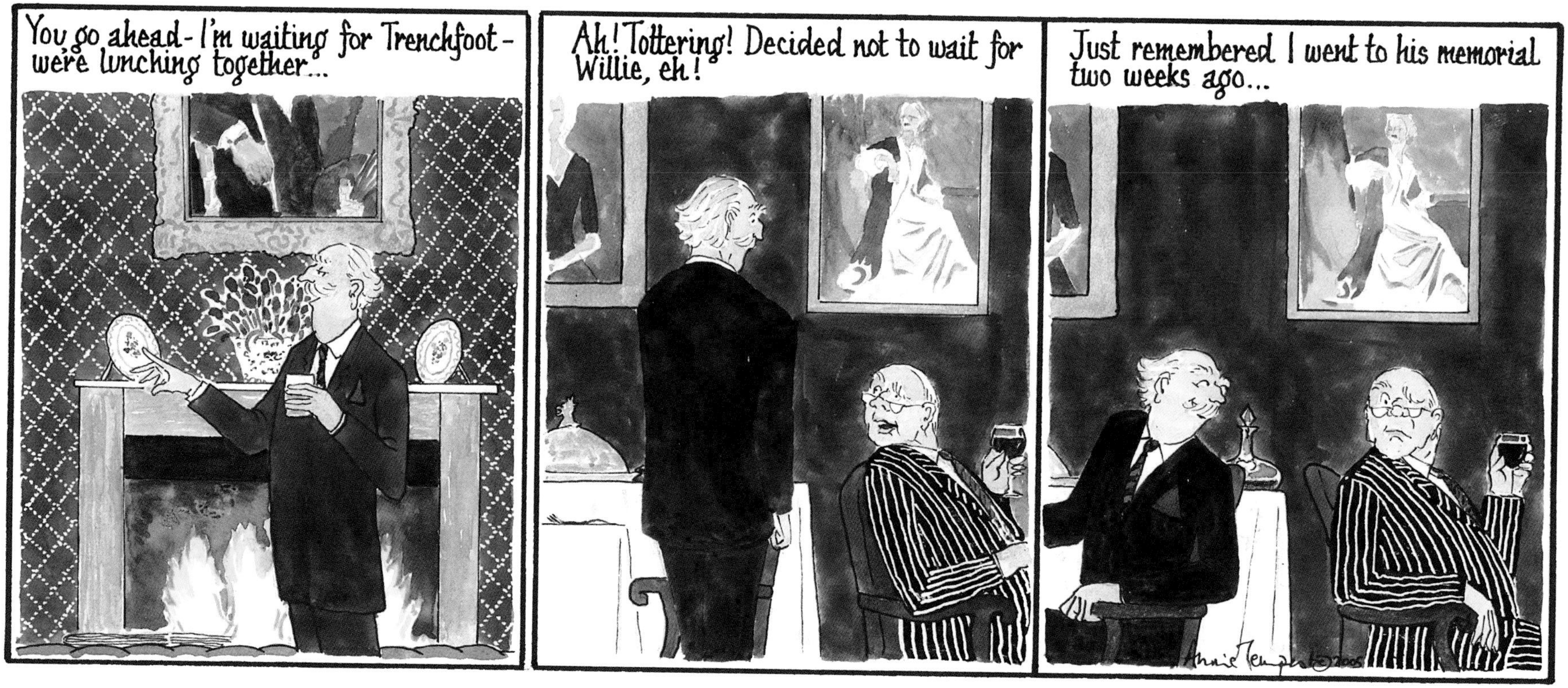
You go ahead - I'm waiting for Trenchfoot - we're lunching together...
Ah! Tottering! Decided not to wait for Willie, eh!
Just remembered I went to his memorial two weeks ago...

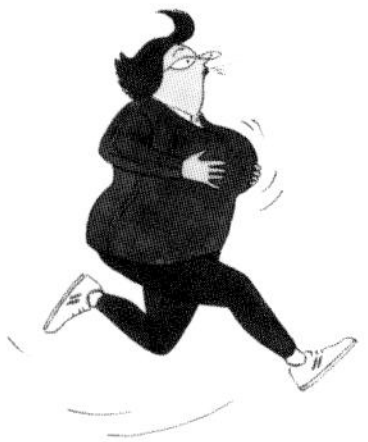

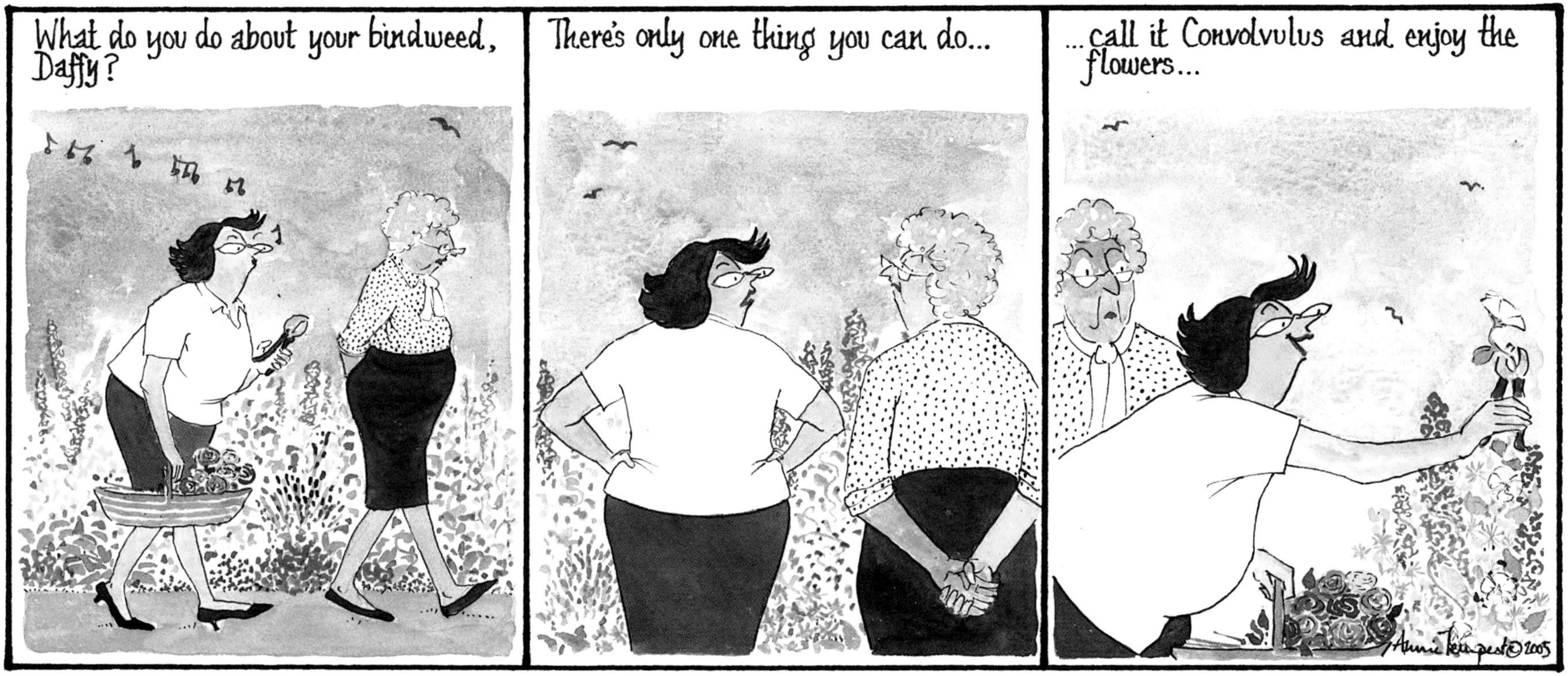
What do you do about your bindweed, Daffy?
There's only one thing you can do...
...call it Convolvulus and enjoy the flowers...
Annie Tempest © 2005

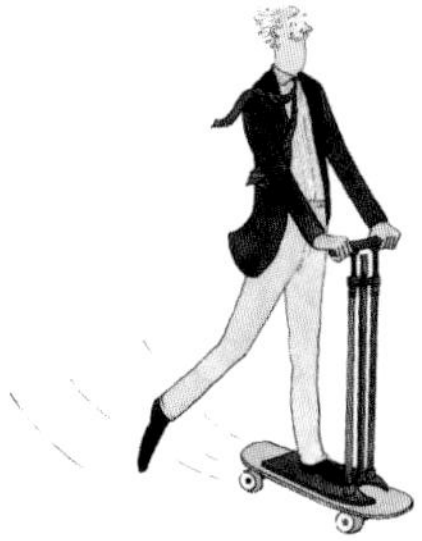

August 11th, 2005

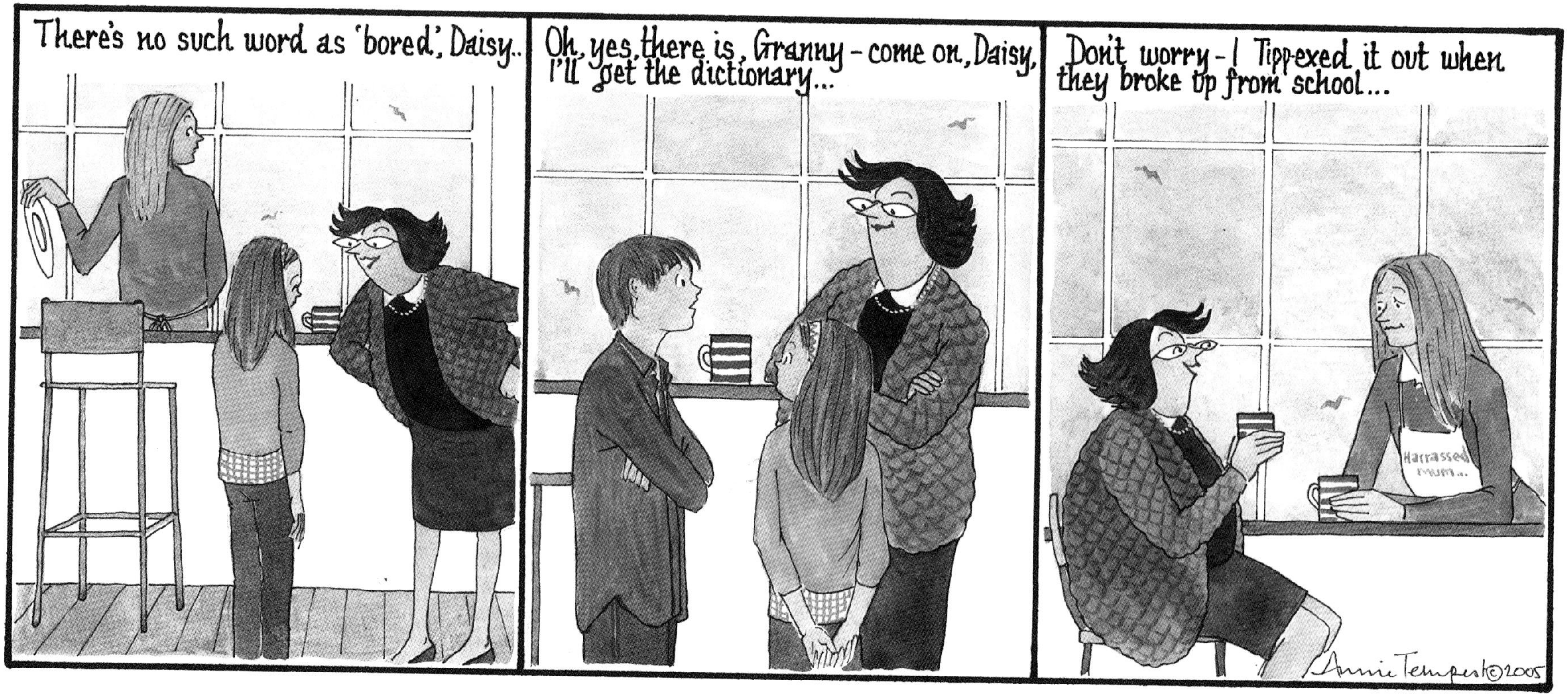

There's no such word as 'bored', Daisy..
Oh, yes, there is, Granny – come on, Daisy, I'll get the dictionary...
Don't worry – I Tipp-exed it out when they broke up from school...
Harrassed Mum..
Annie Tempest©2005

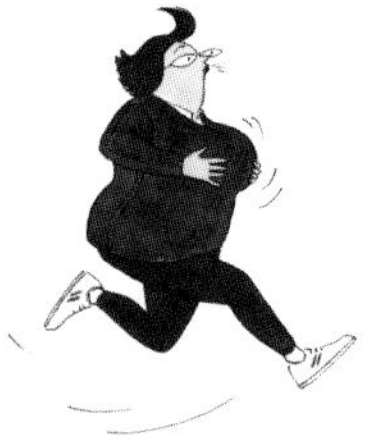

August 18th, 2005

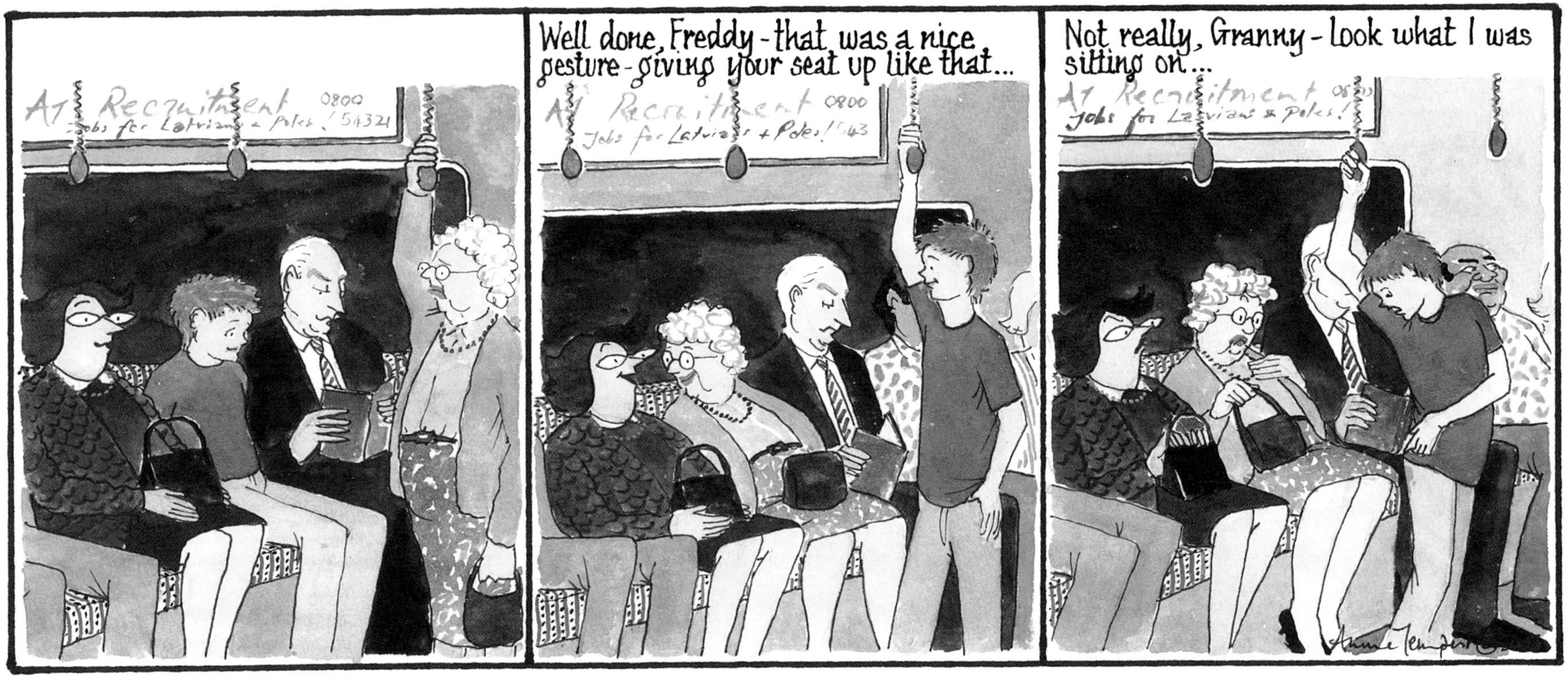
A1 Recruitment 0800
Jobs for Latvians & Poles! 54321
Well done, Freddy - that was a nice gesture - giving your seat up like that...
Not really, Granny - look what I was sitting on...

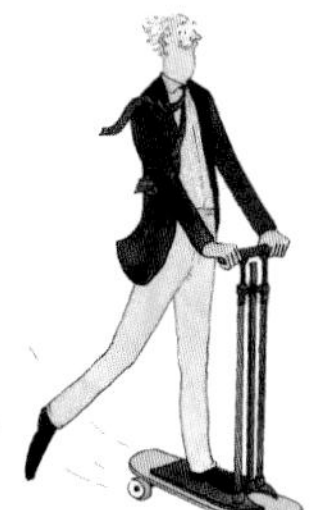

August 25th, 2005

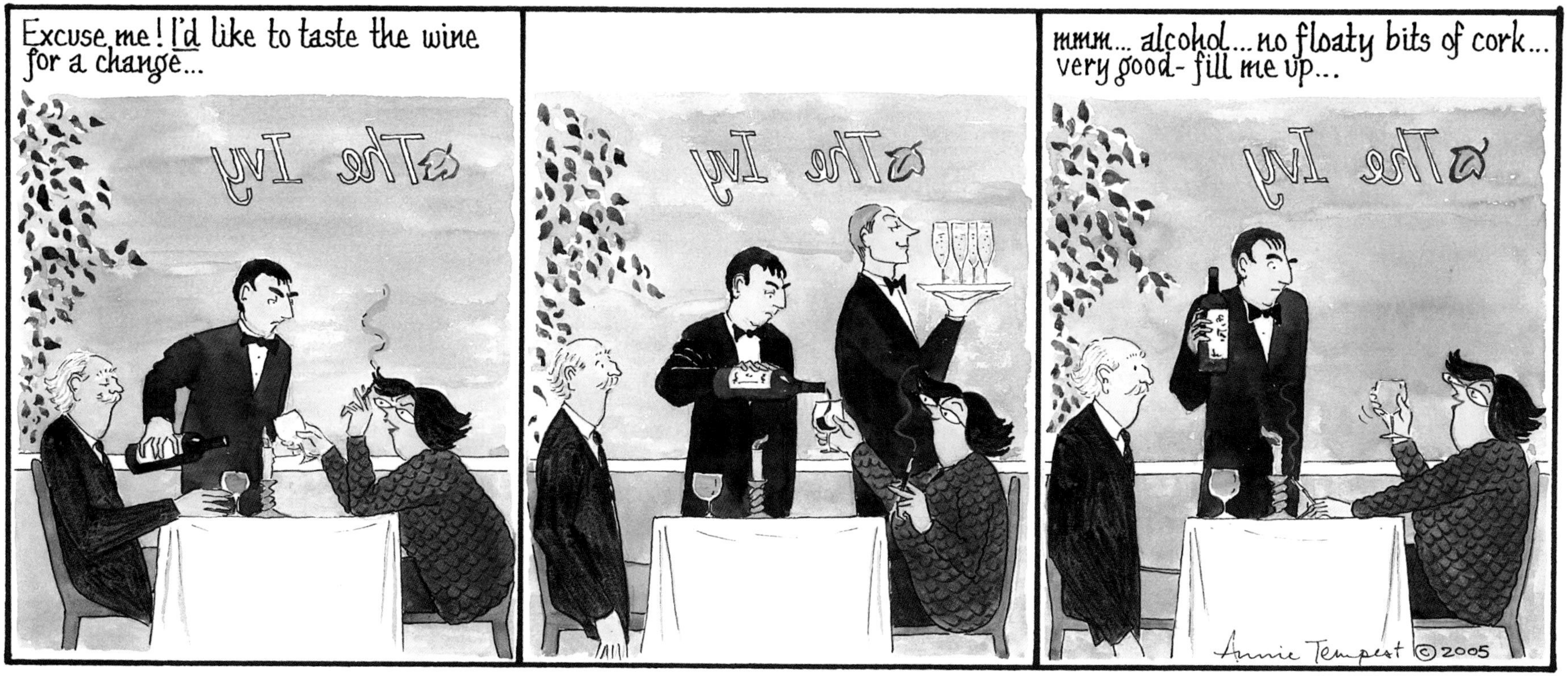

Excuse me! I'd like to taste the wine for a change...
mmm... alcohol... no floaty bits of cork... very good- fill me up...
Annie Tempest © 2005

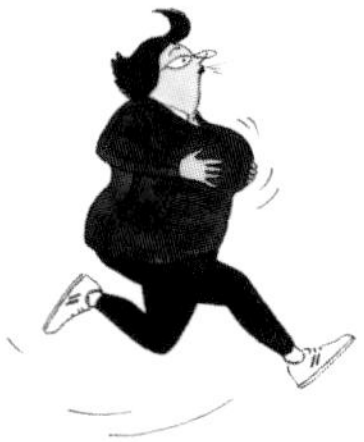

September 1st, 2005

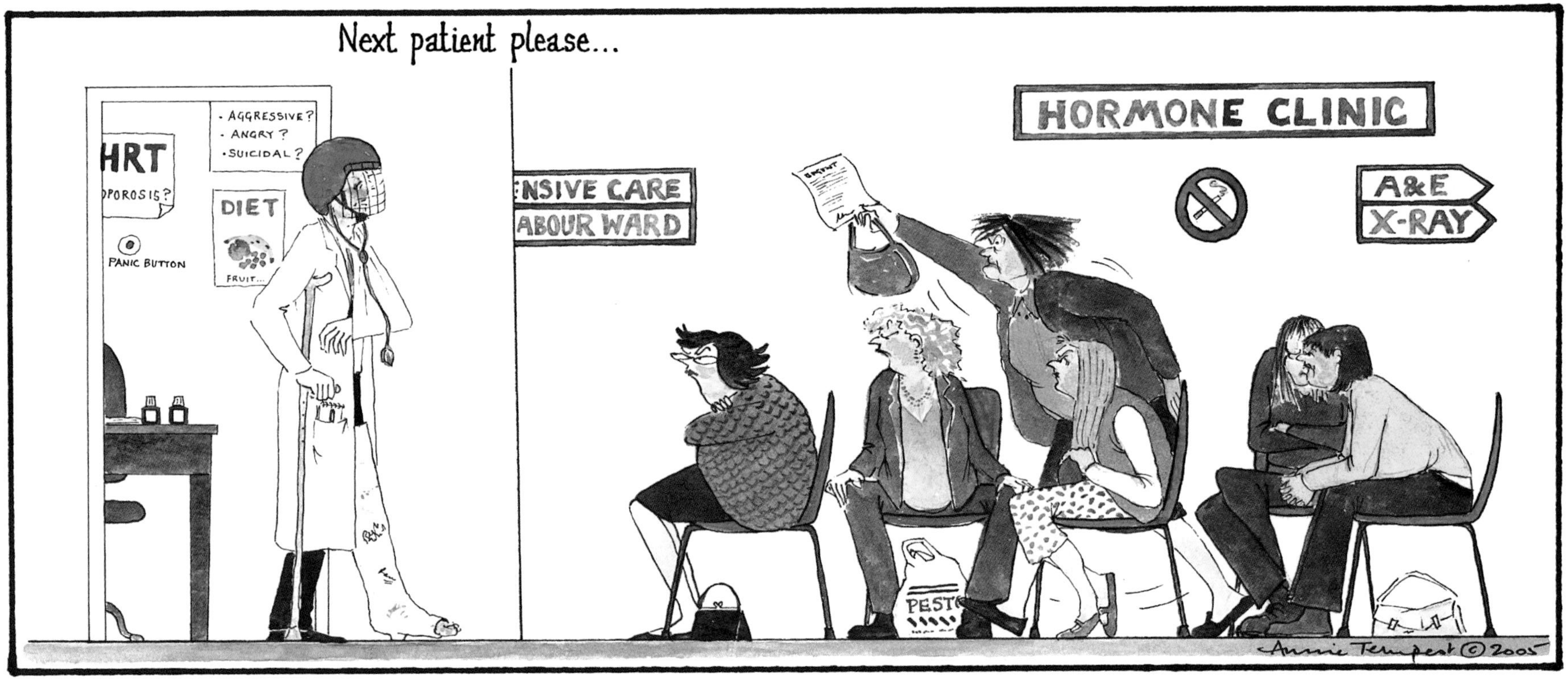

Next patient please...
HRT
PPOROSIS?
PANIC BUTTON
· AGGRESSIVE?
· ANGRY?
· SUICIDAL?
DIET
FRUIT...
NSIVE CARE
ABOUR WARD
HORMONE CLINIC
A&E
X-RAY
Annie Tempest © 2005

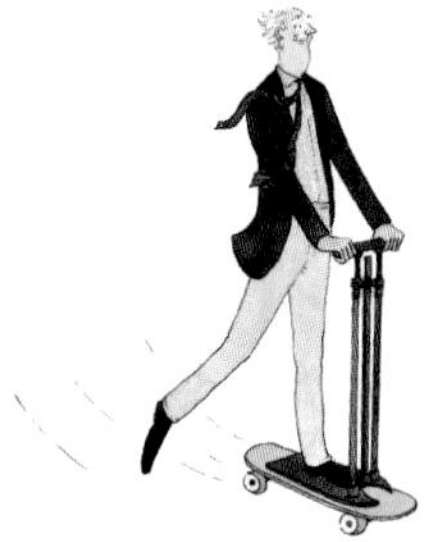

September 8th, 2005

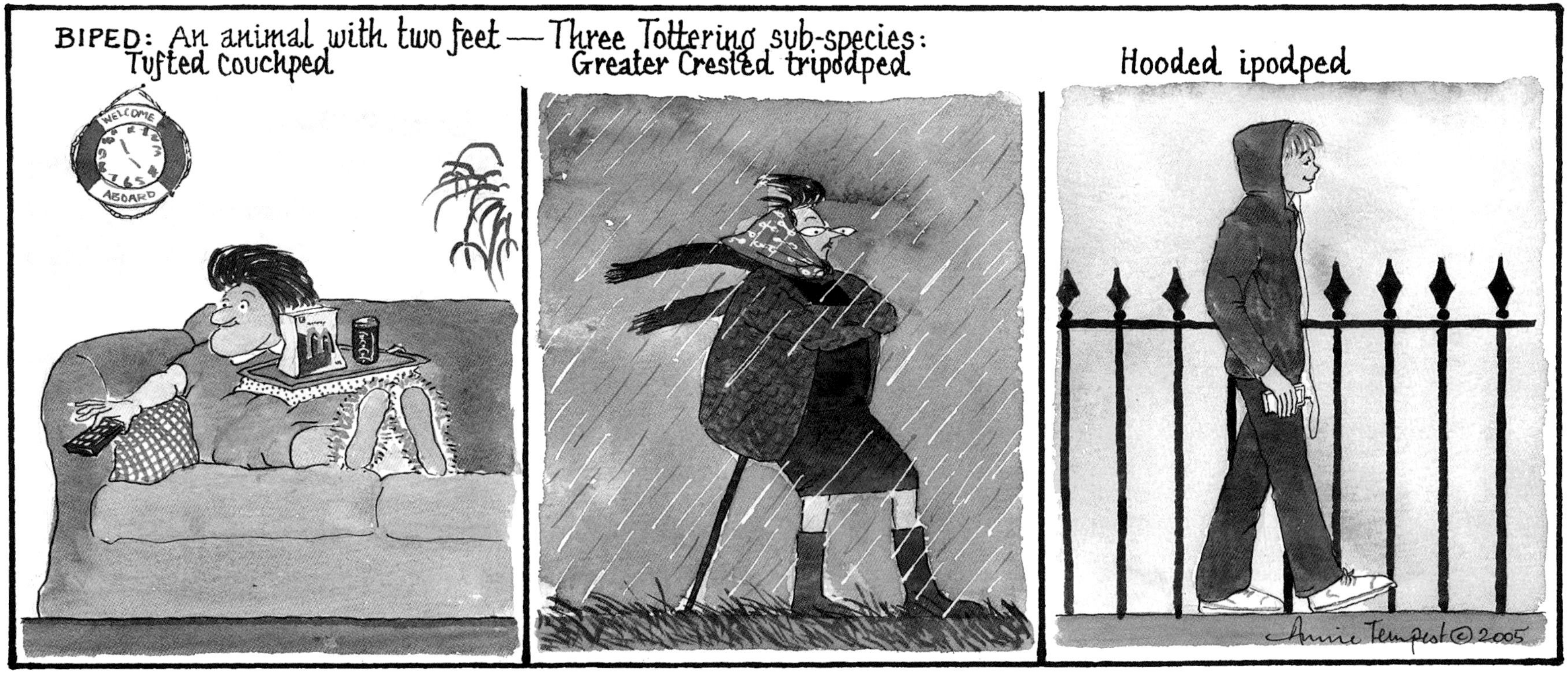
BIPED: An animal with two feet — Three Tottering sub-species:
Tufted couchped
WELCOME
ABOARD
Greater Crested tripodped
Hooded ipodped
Annie Tempest © 2005

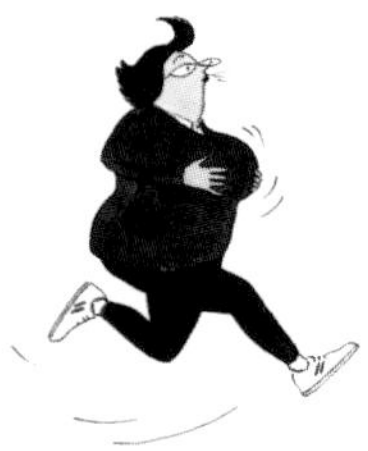

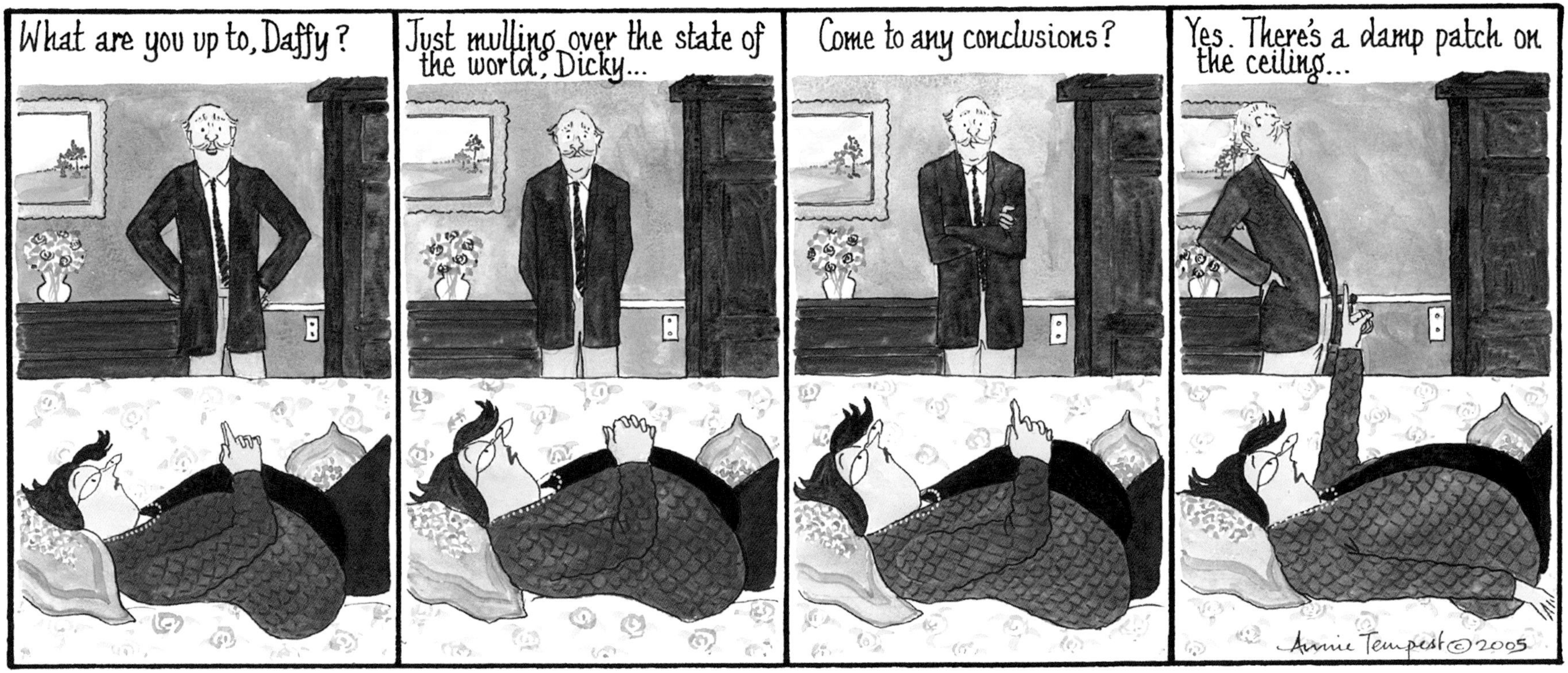
What are you up to, Daffy?
Just mulling over the state of the world, Dicky...
Come to any conclusions?
Yes. There's a damp patch on the ceiling...
Annie Tempest © 2005

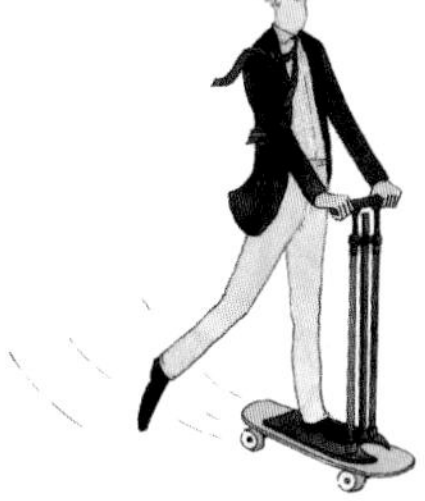

September 22nd, 2005

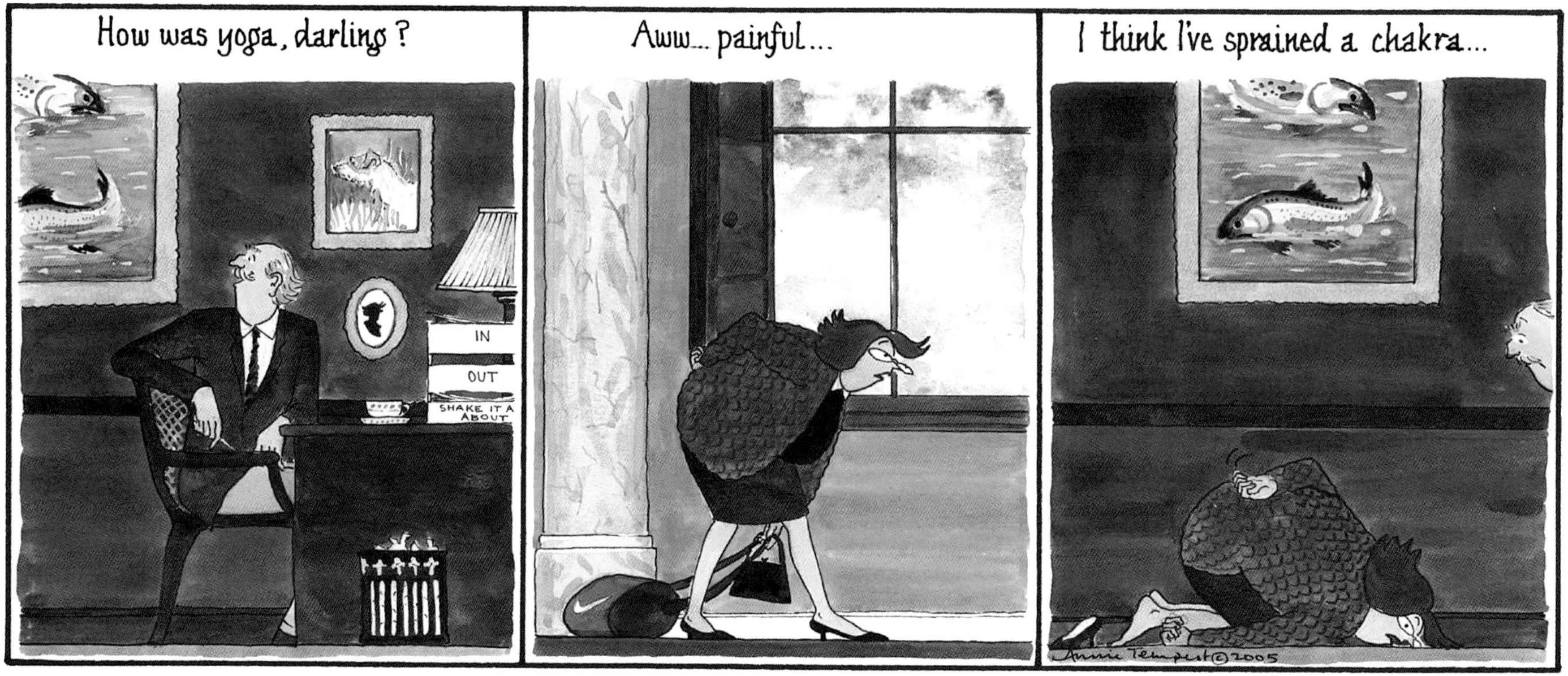

How was yoga, darling?
IN
OUT
SHAKE IT ABOUT
Aww... painful...
I think I've sprained a chakra...

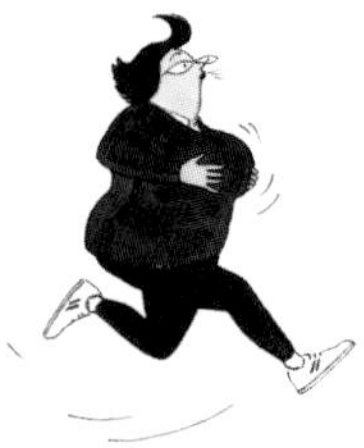

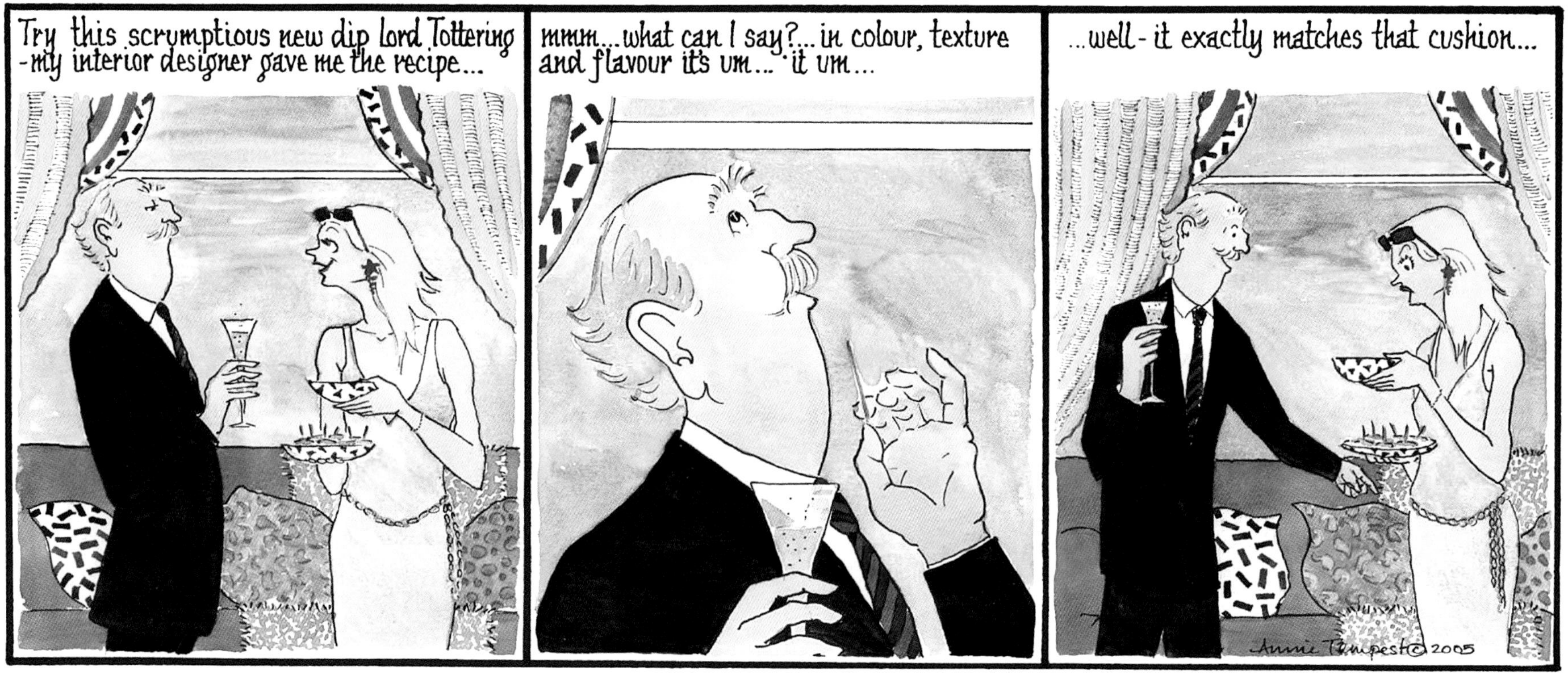
Try this scrumptious new dip lord Tottering -my interior designer gave me the recipe...
mmm... what can I say?... in colour, texture and flavour it's um... it um...
...well - it exactly matches that cushion...
Annie Tempest © 2005

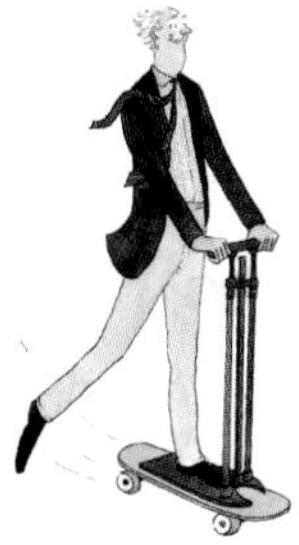

October 6th, 2005

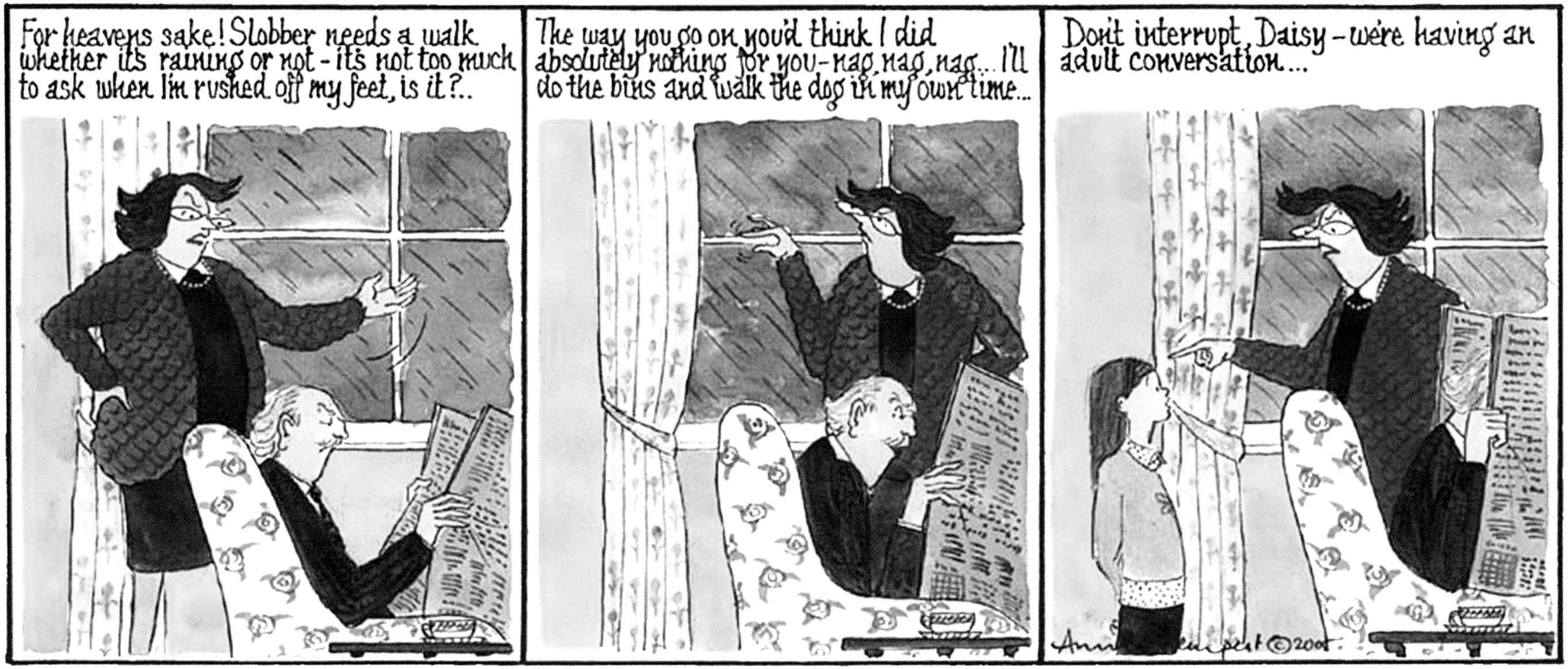
For heavens sake! Slobber needs a walk whether its raining or not - its not too much to ask when Im rushed off my feet, is it?..
The way you go on you'd think I did absolutely nothing for you - nag, nag, nag... I'll do the bins and walk the dog in my own time...
Don't interrupt, Daisy - we're having an adult conversation...

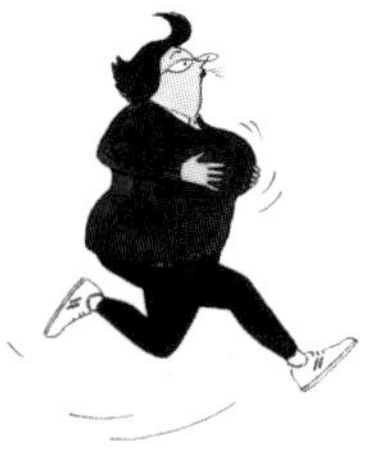

October 13th, 2005

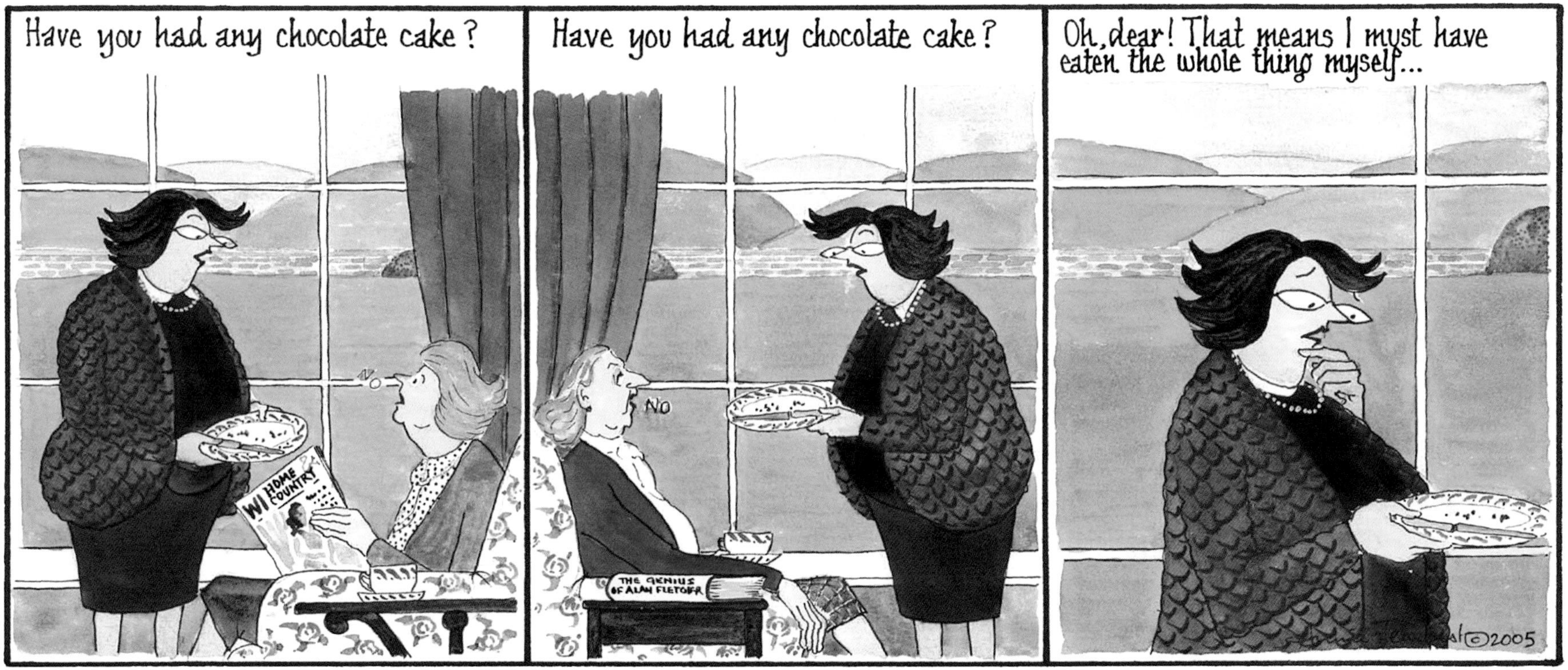
Have you had any chocolate cake?
NO
WI HOME COUNTRY
Have you had any chocolate cake?
NO
THE GENIUS OF ALAN FLETCHER
Oh, dear! That means I must have eaten the whole thing myself...
©2005

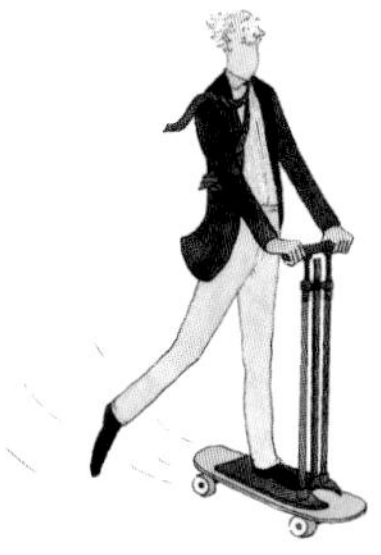

October 20th, 2005 and November 10th, 2005
(This cartoon was repeated due to a mistake at *Country Life* magazine.)

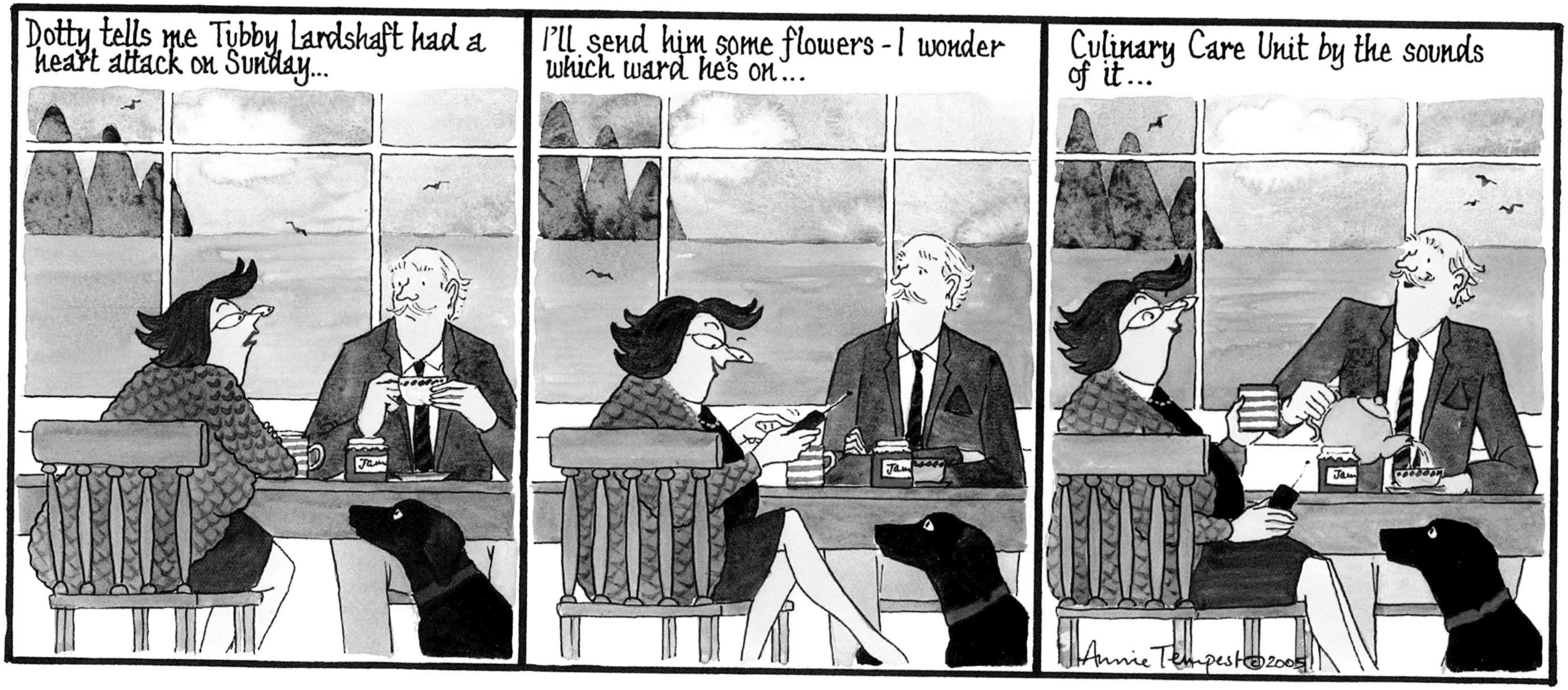

Dotty tells me Tubby Lardshaft had a heart attack on Sunday...
I'll send him some flowers - I wonder which ward he's on...
Culinary Care Unit by the sounds of it...
Annie Tempest © 2005

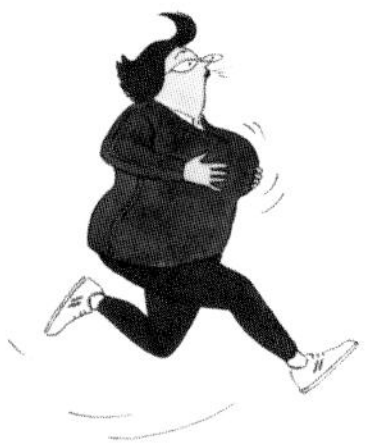

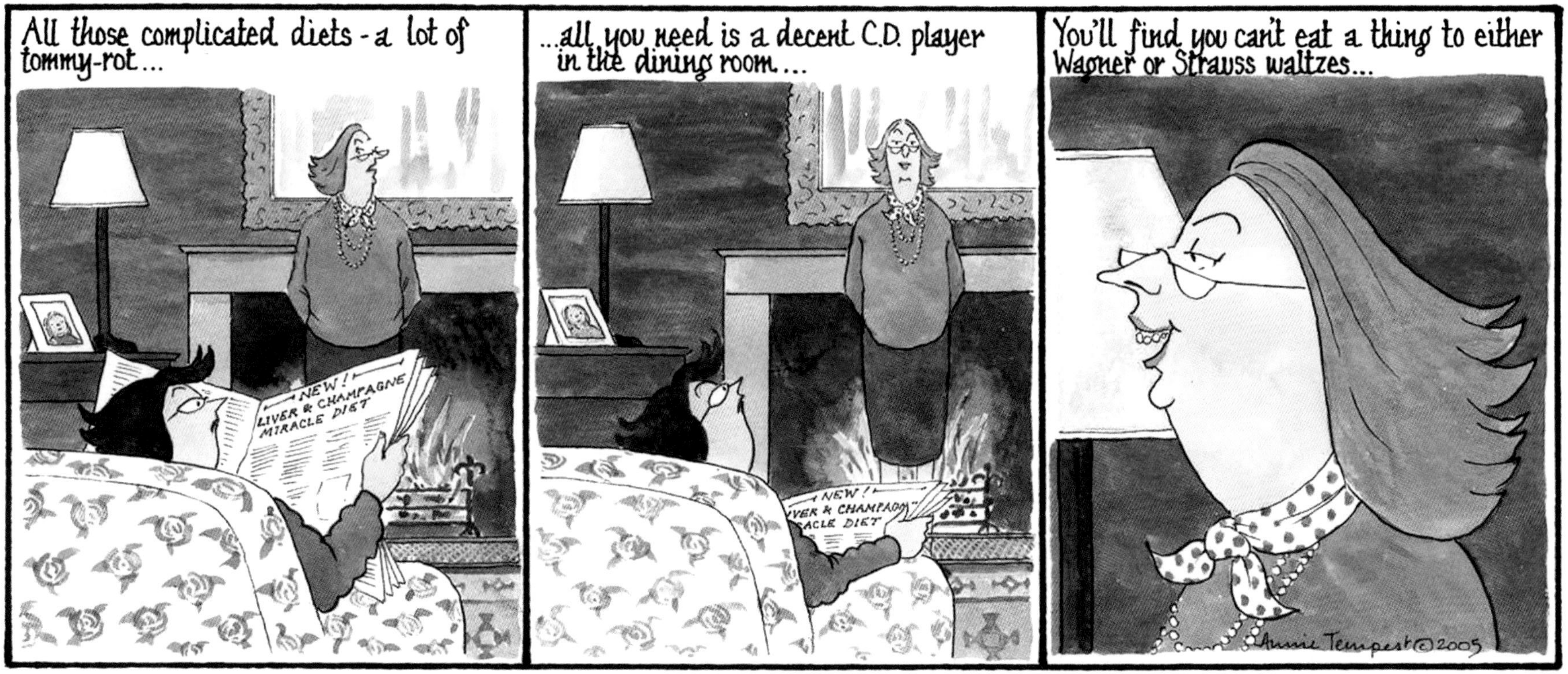
All those complicated diets - a lot of tommy-rot...
NEW! LIVER & CHAMPAGNE MIRACLE DIET
...all you need is a decent C.D. player in the dining room...
NEW! LIVER & CHAMPAGNE MIRACLE DIET
You'll find you can't eat a thing to either Wagner or Strauss waltzes...
Annie Tempest © 2005

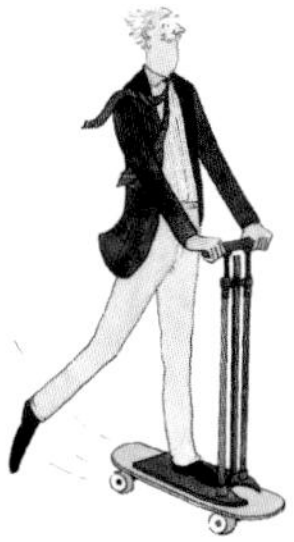

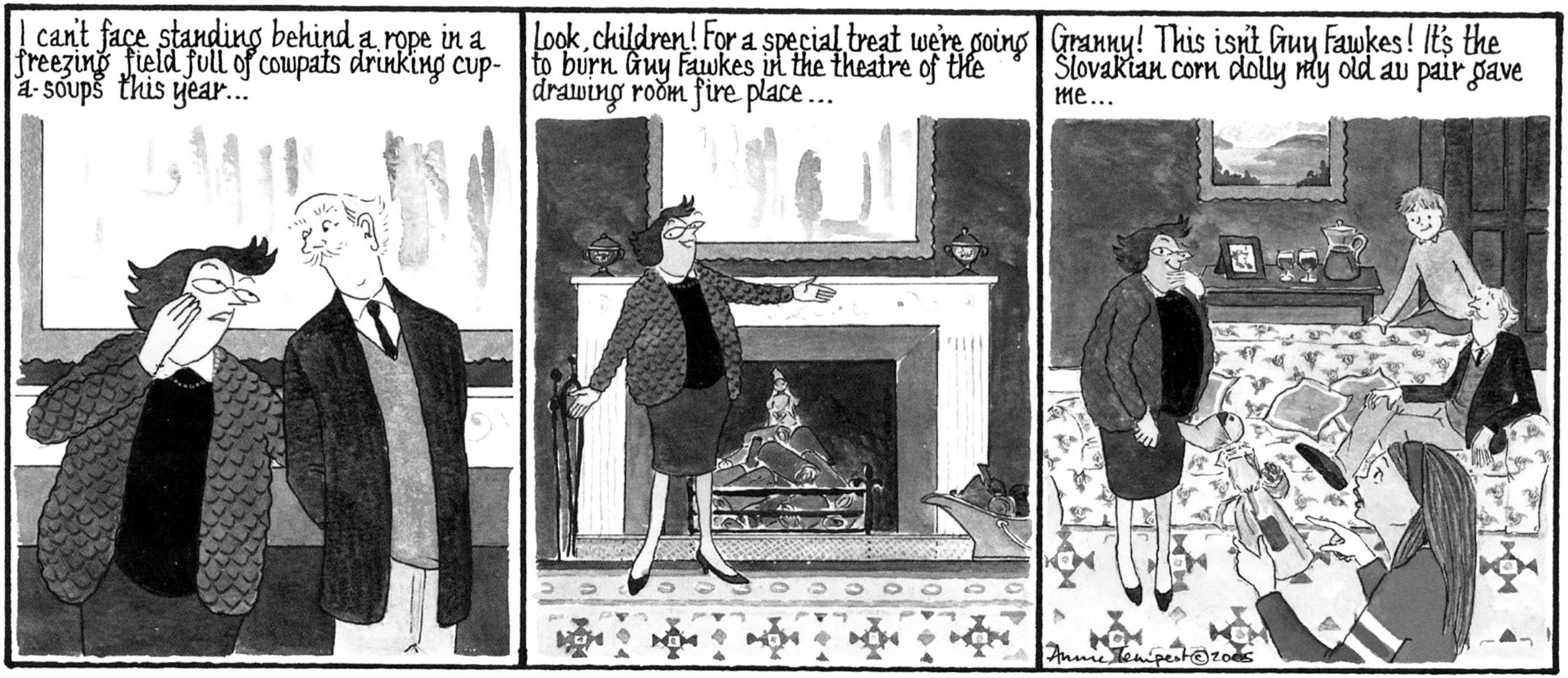
I can't face standing behind a rope in a freezing field full of cowpats drinking cup-a-soups this year...
Look, children! For a special treat we're going to burn Guy Fawkes in the theatre of the drawing room fire place...
Granny! This isn't Guy Fawkes! It's the Slovakian corn dolly my old au pair gave me...
Annie Tempest © 2005

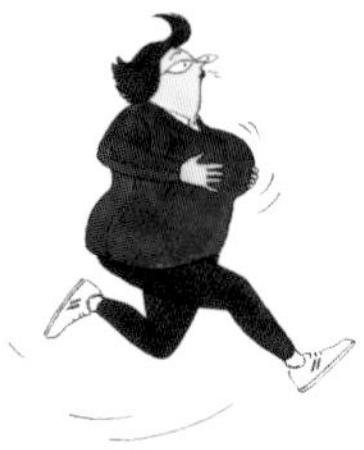

November 17th, 2005

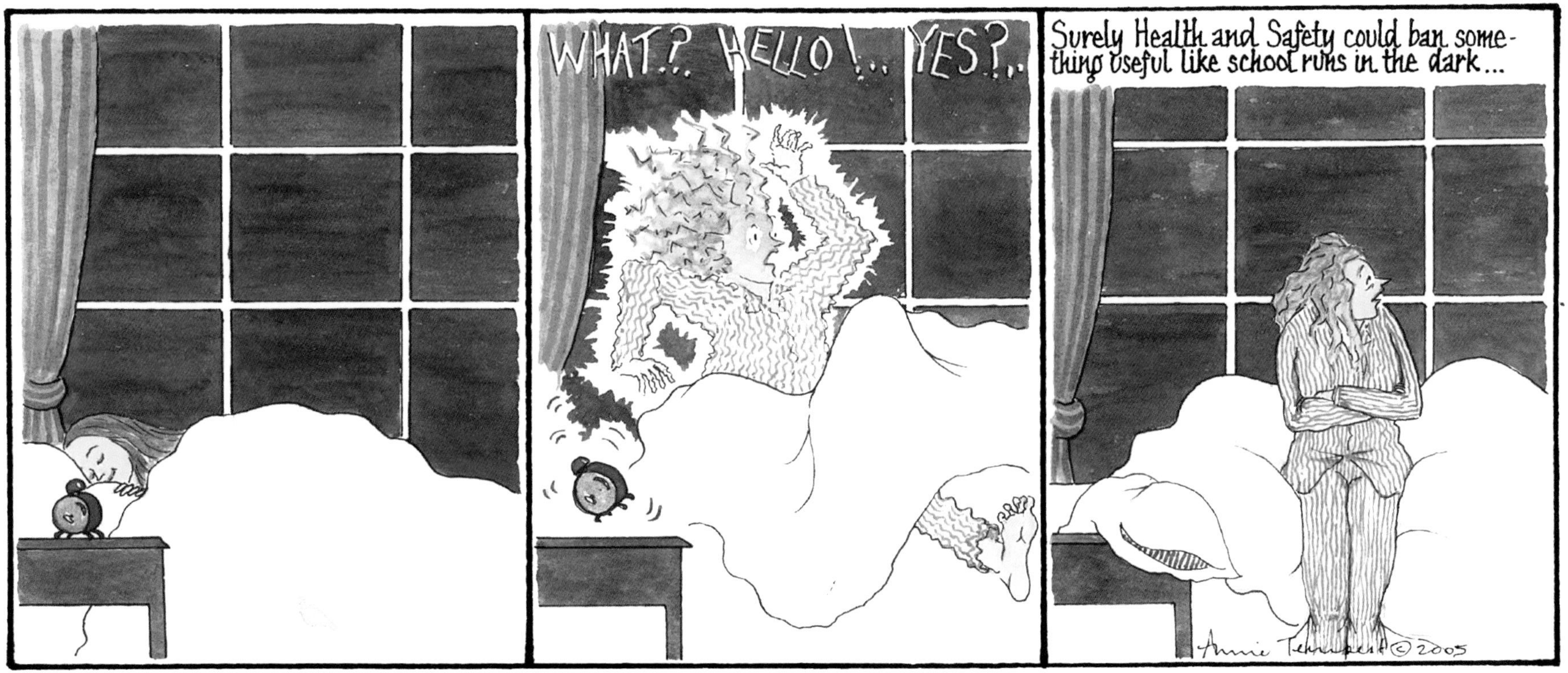
WHAT?.. HELLO!.. YES?..
Surely Health and Safety could ban something useful like school runs in the dark...
Annie Tempest © 2005

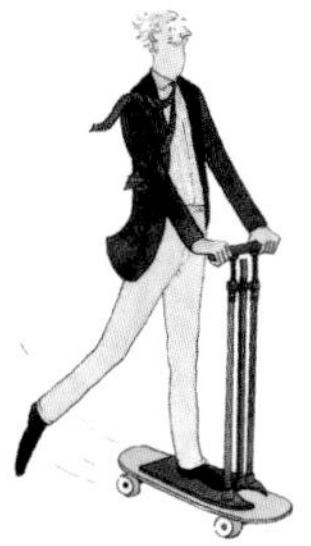

November 24th, 2005

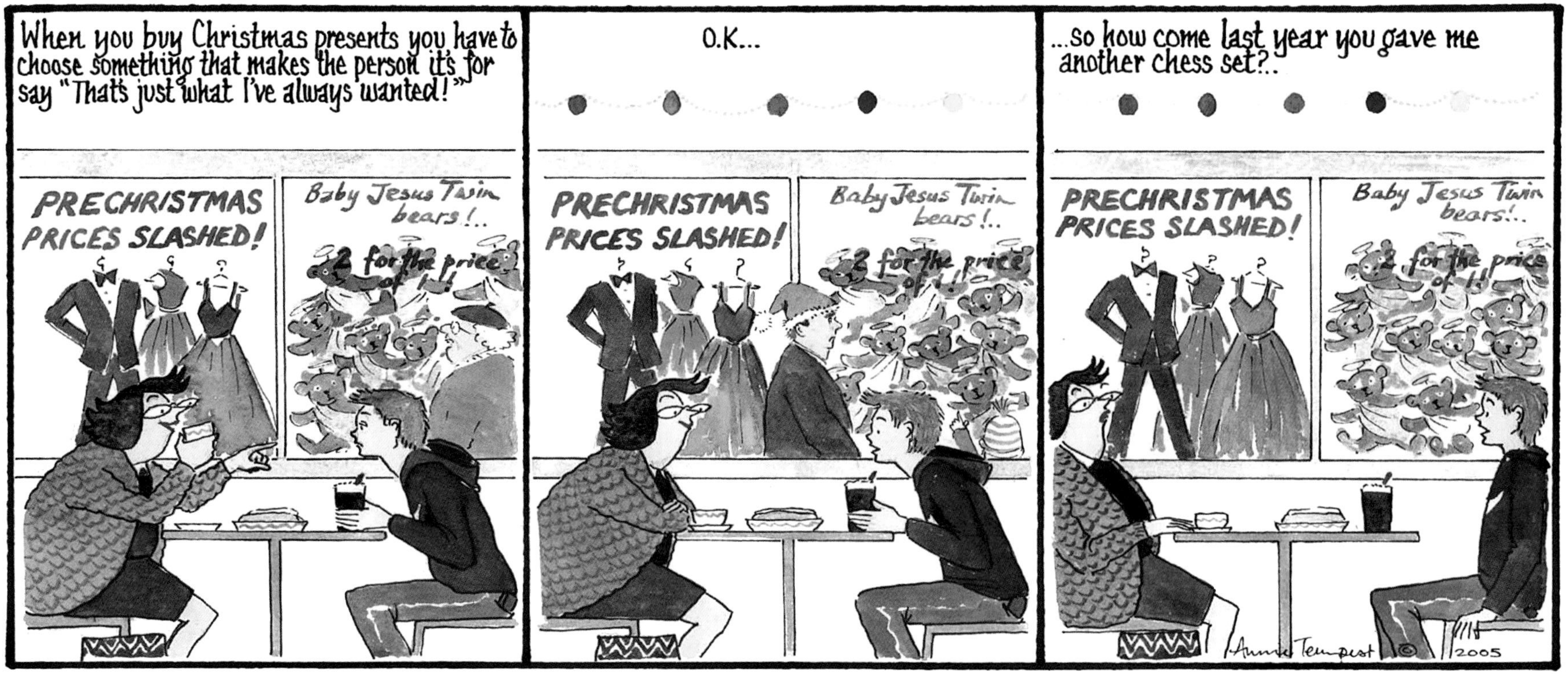
When you buy Christmas presents you have to choose something that makes the person it's for say "That's just what I've always wanted!"
PRECHRISTMAS PRICES SLASHED!
Baby Jesus Twin bears!..
2 for the price of 1!
O.K...
...so how come last year you gave me another chess set?..
Anne Tempest © 2005

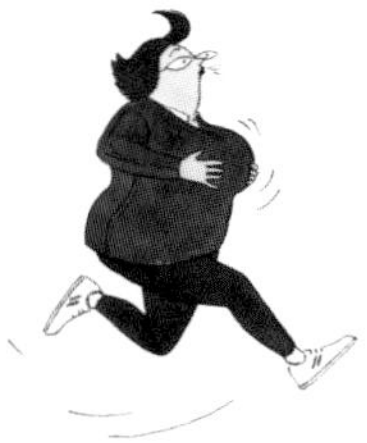

December 1st, 2005

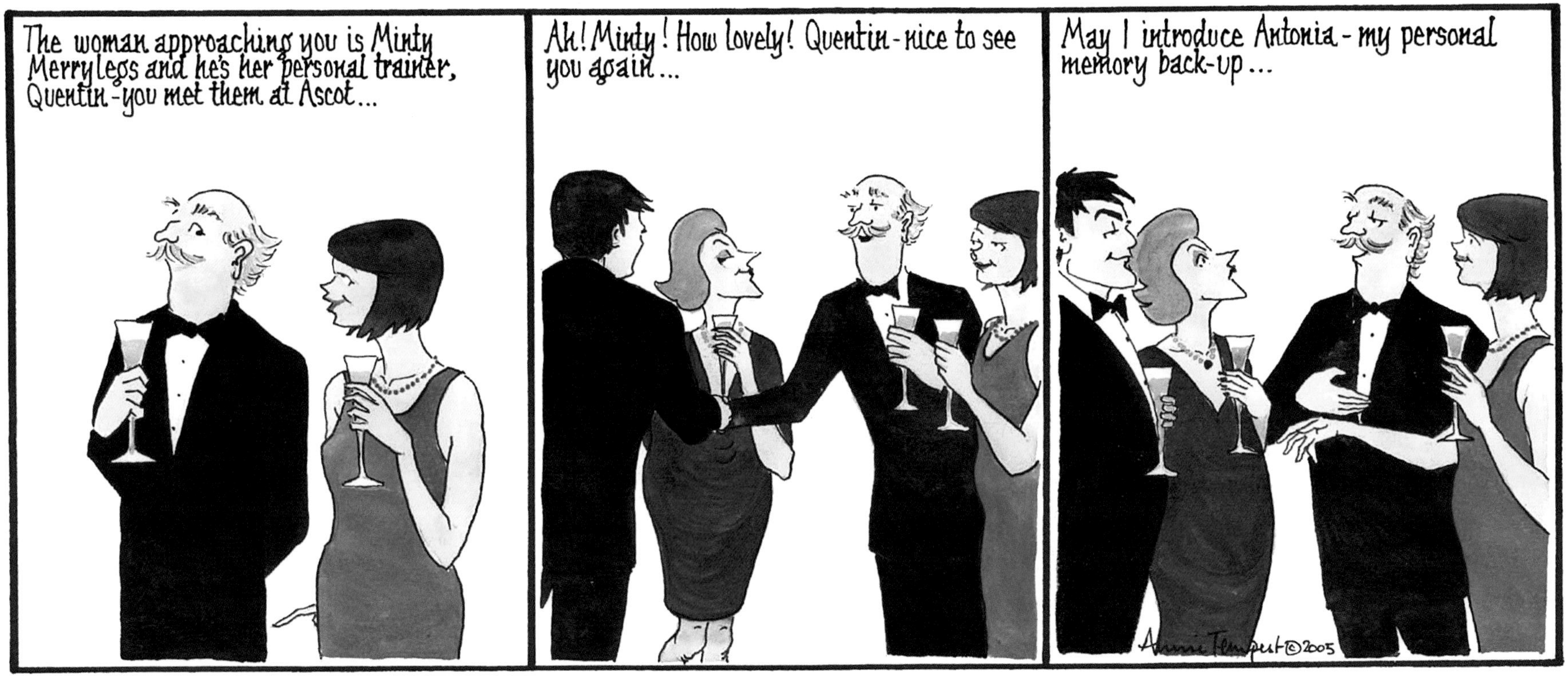

The woman approaching you is Minty Merrylegs and he's her personal trainer, Quentin - you met them at Ascot...
Ah! Minty! How lovely! Quentin - nice to see you again...
May I introduce Antonia - my personal memory back-up...
Annie Tempest ©2005

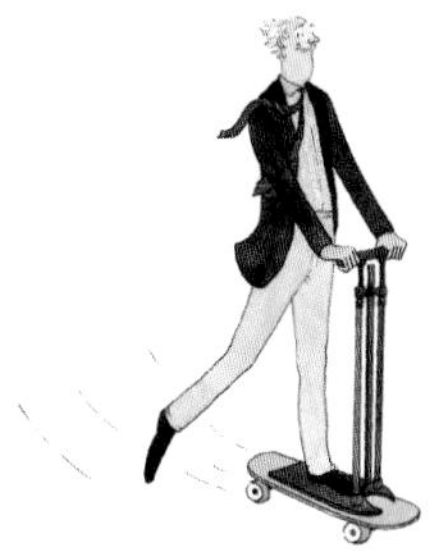

December 8th, 2005

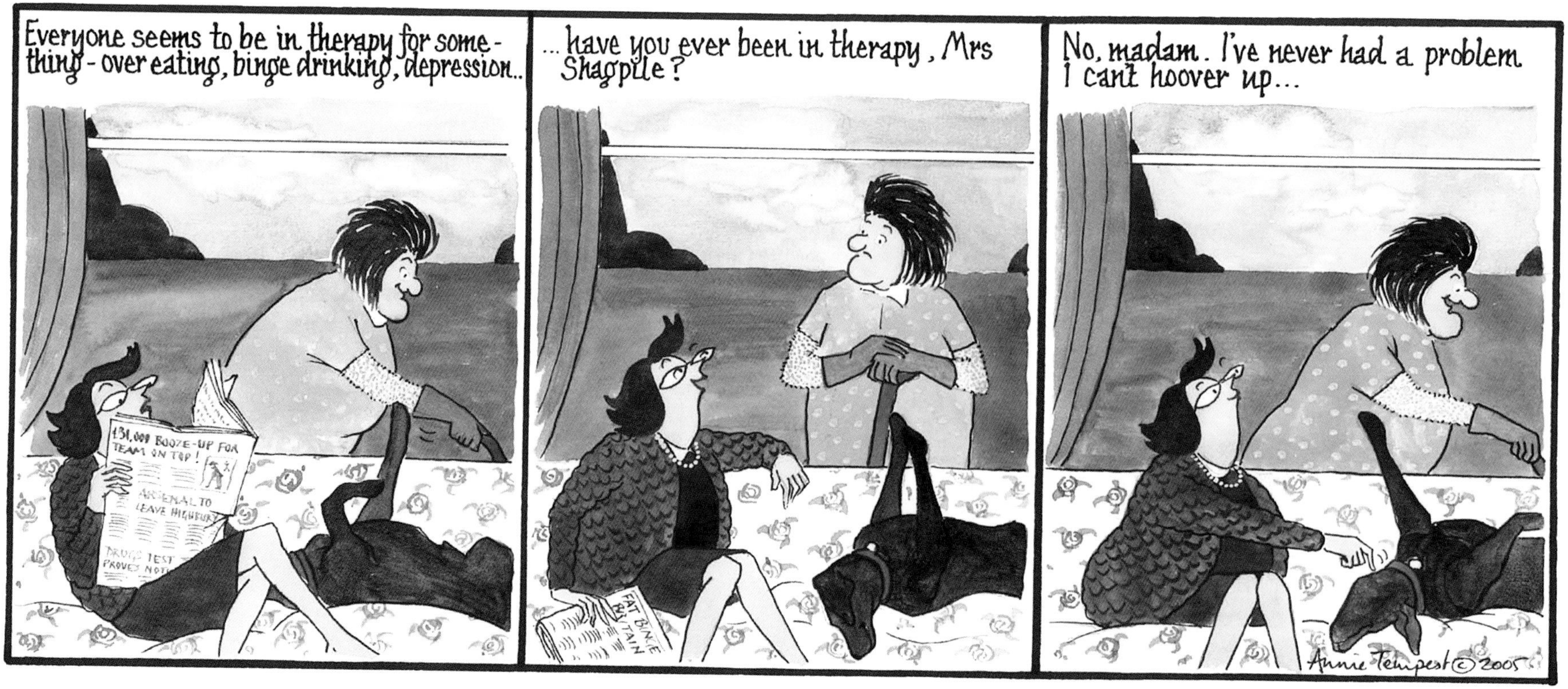

Everyone seems to be in therapy for some-thing - over eating, binge drinking, depression..
£31,000 BOOZE-UP FOR TEAM ON TOP!
ARSENAL TO LEAVE HIGHBURY
... have you ever been in therapy, Mrs Shagpile?
No, madam. I've never had a problem I can't hoover up...
Annie Tempest © 2005

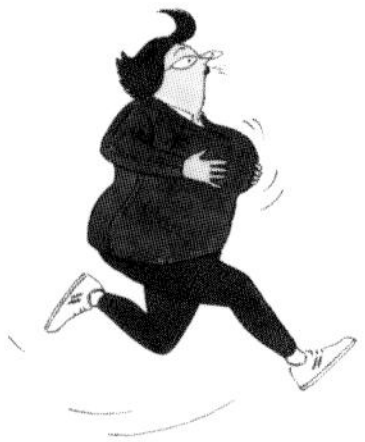

December 15th, 2005

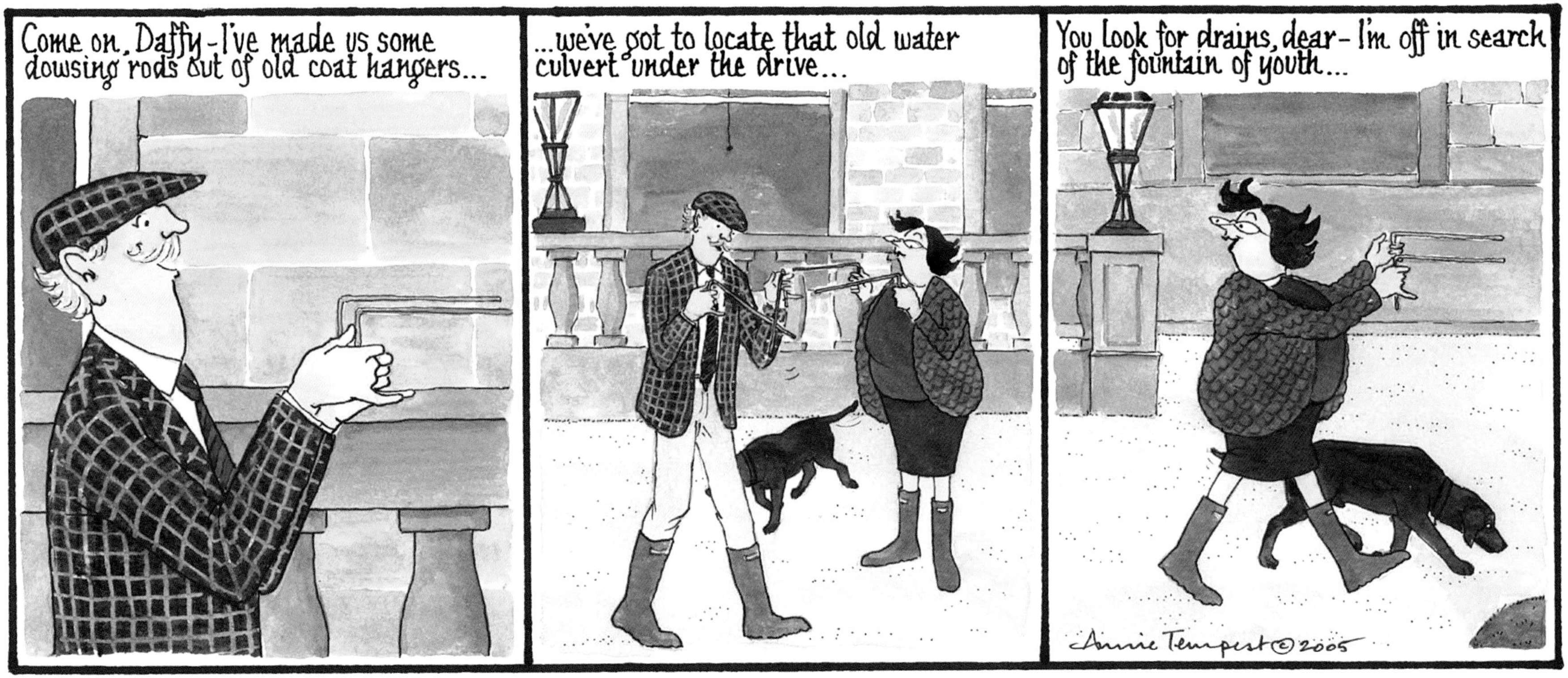
Come on, Daffy - I've made us some dowsing rods out of old coat hangers...
...we've got to locate that old water culvert under the drive...
You look for drains, dear - I'm off in search of the fountain of youth...
Annie Tempest © 2005

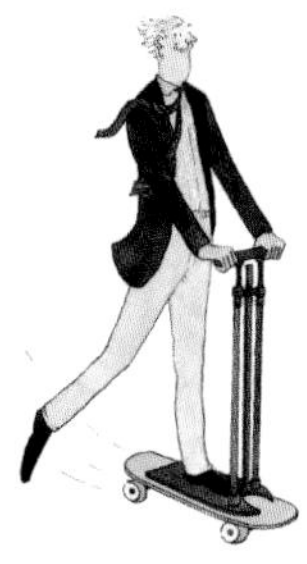

December 22nd / 29th, 2005

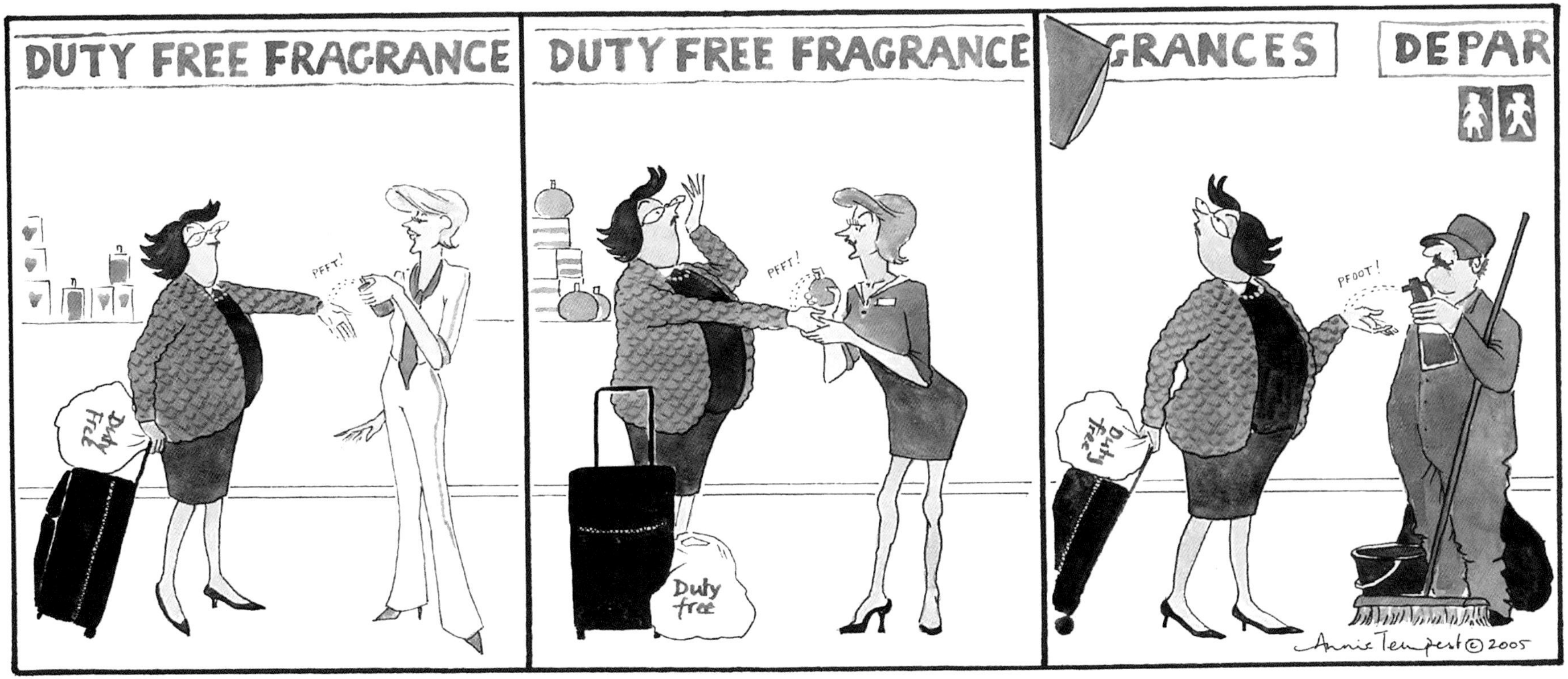
DUTY FREE FRAGRANCE
PFFT!
Duty Free
DUTY FREE FRAGRANCE
PFFT!
Duty free
GRANCES
DEPAR
PFOOT!
Duty free
Annie Tempest © 2005

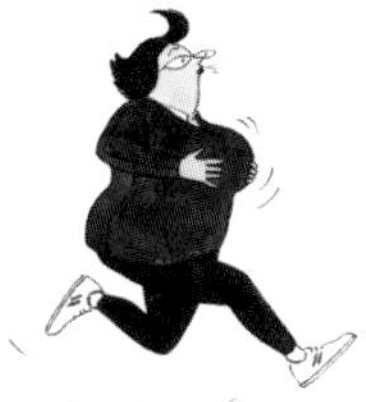

TOTTERING BRAND

It's much quicker if you just pick the ball up and stick it in the hole. There! Can we go for lunch now?..

THE MALE CHARACTER...
A tendency to lay down the law...
...and then accept amendments...

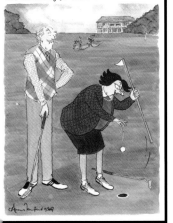

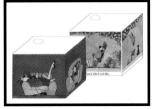

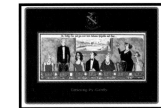

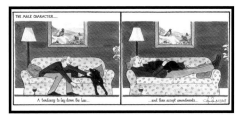

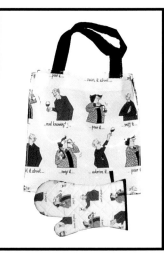

Cartoonist **Annie Tempest's** famous world of **Tottering-by-Gently**, which appears weekly in *Country Life* magazine, has spawned a wonderful range of original and stylish gifts. Her main characters, Daffy and Dicky and their extended family living at the crumbling stately pile, Tottering Hall, provide the vehicle for her wickedly observant humour covering all aspects of the human condition.

The Tottering range of gifts is suitable for everyone with a sense of fun. Gifts include: a large range of Signed Numbered Edition Prints, as well as Digital Prints on Demand (any Annie Tempest image produced as a digital print), books, diaries, greeting cards, postcards, tablemats, coasters, trays, noteblocks, wooden jigsaws, playing cards, mugs, paper bins, silk ties and braces, weekly planners and much more – we even have our own brand of Tottering-by-Gently Champagne . . .

You can telephone us on 01732 866041 for a catalogue, order from our secure website at www.tottering.com or when you are next in London, pop into The Tottering Drawing Room at The O'Shea Gallery, at No.4, St. James's Street, SW1A 1EF, where all the products are available.

www.tottering.com

THE PERFECT MARRIAGE
TRUE LOVE

TOTTERING-BY-GENTLY
VOL.III
ANNIE TEMPEST

Start every day with a smile...
...and get it over with...

"No more Pimms for you, Dicky! - Your face is getting all blurry."

Is it that time already?
12
1
2
3
4
5
6
7
8
9
10
11

TOTTERING-BY-GENTLY®
AT HOME WITH
THE TOTTERINGS
ANNIE TEMPEST

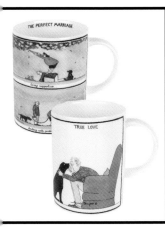

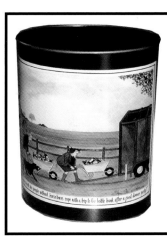

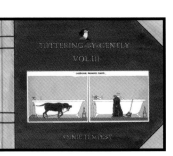

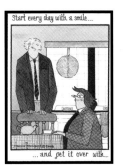

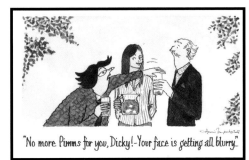

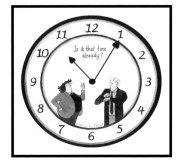

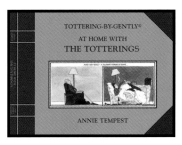

GALLERY OF TOTTERING DESIGNS – Calendar and a selection of greetings cards

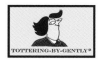

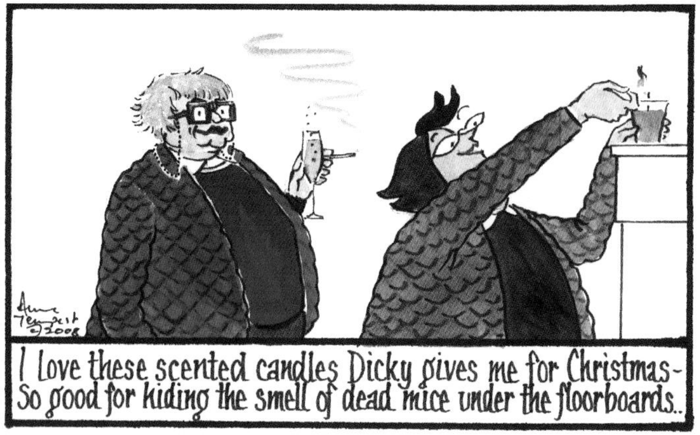
I love these scented candles Dicky gives me for Christmas-
So good for hiding the smell of dead mice under the floorboards..

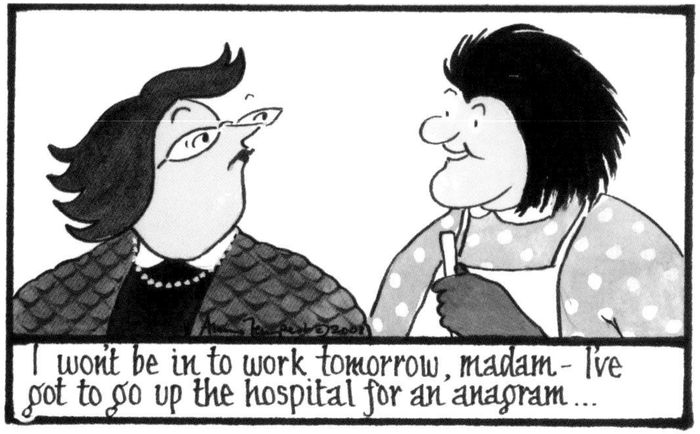
I won't be in to work tomorrow, madam- I've got to go up the hospital for an anagram...

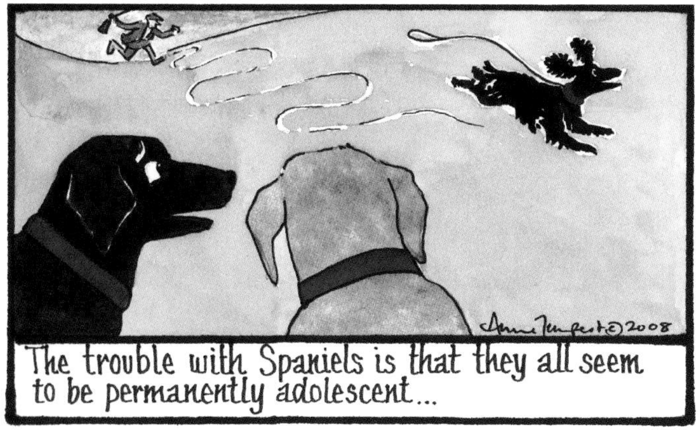
The trouble with Spaniels is that they all seem to be permanently adolescent...

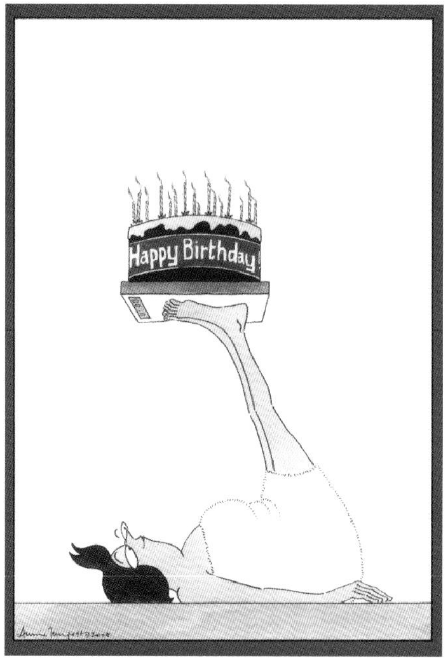
Happy Birthday!

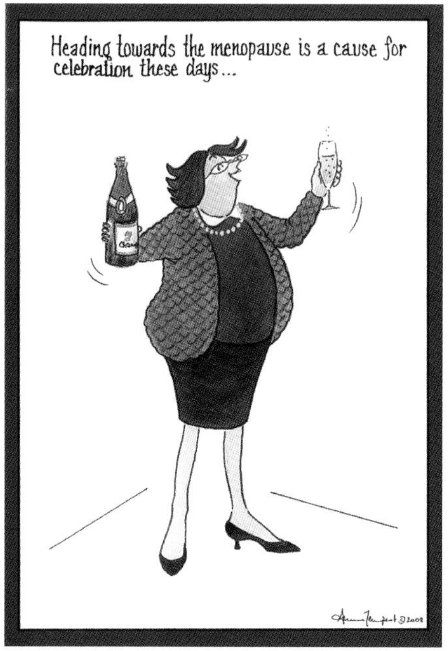
Heading towards the menopause is a cause for celebration these days...

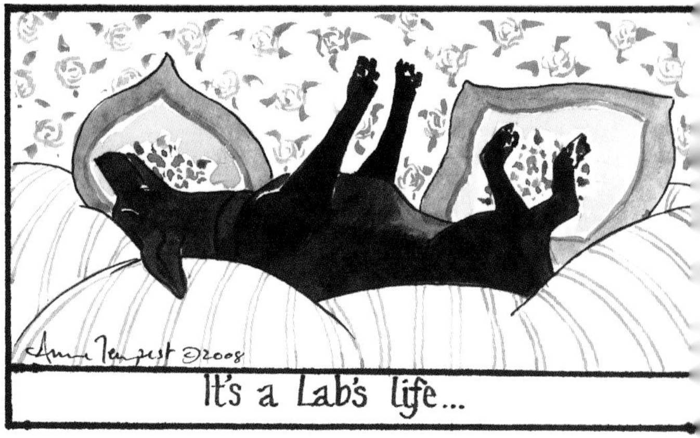
It's a Lab's life...

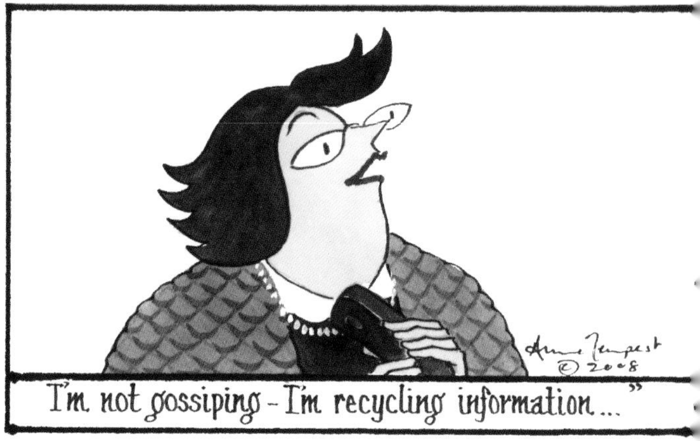
I'm not gossiping - I'm recycling information..."

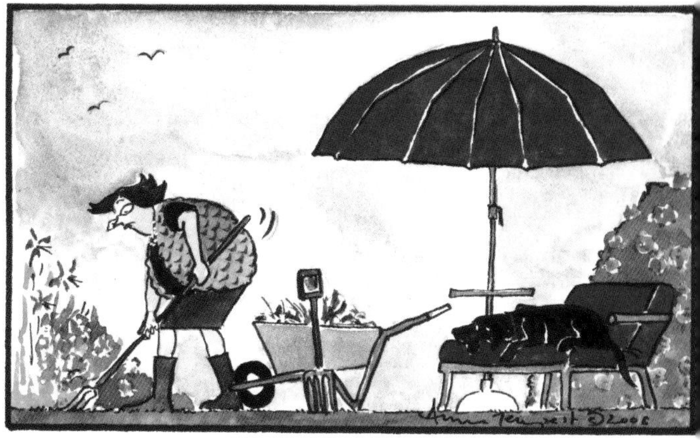

GALLERY OF TOTTERING DESIGNS – A selection of Country Life prints and Specials prints

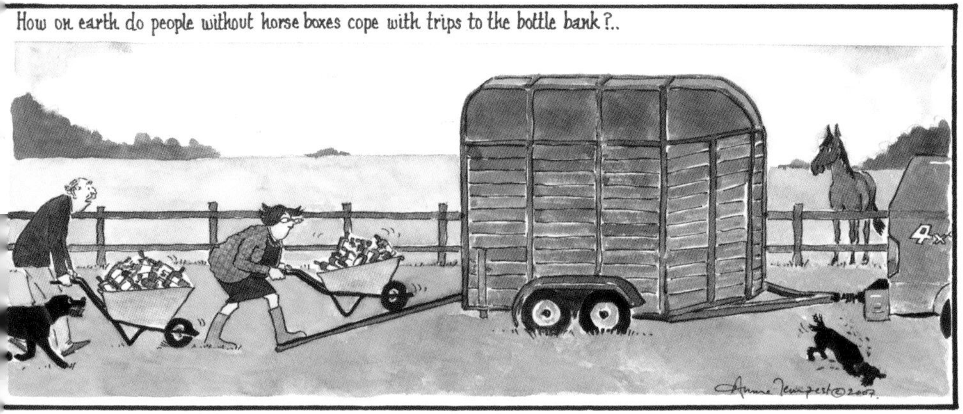
How on earth do people without horse boxes cope with trips to the bottle bank?..
4x

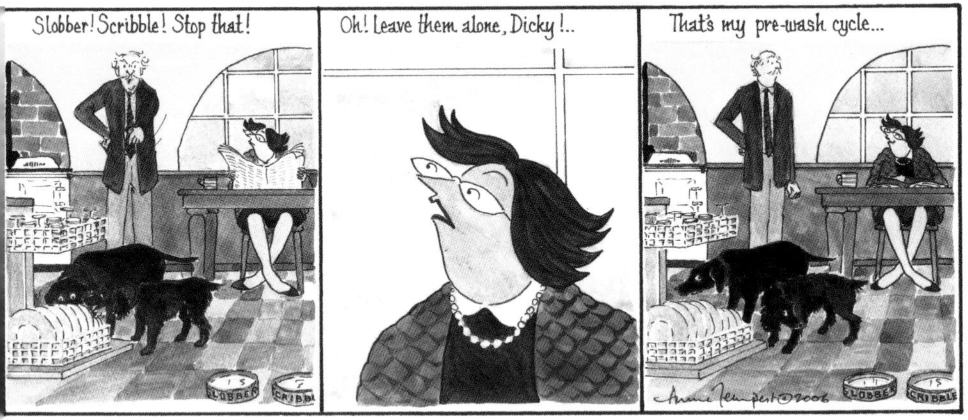
Slobber! Scribble! Stop that!
Oh! Leave them alone, Dicky!..
That's my pre-wash cycle...
SLOBBER
SCRIBBLE

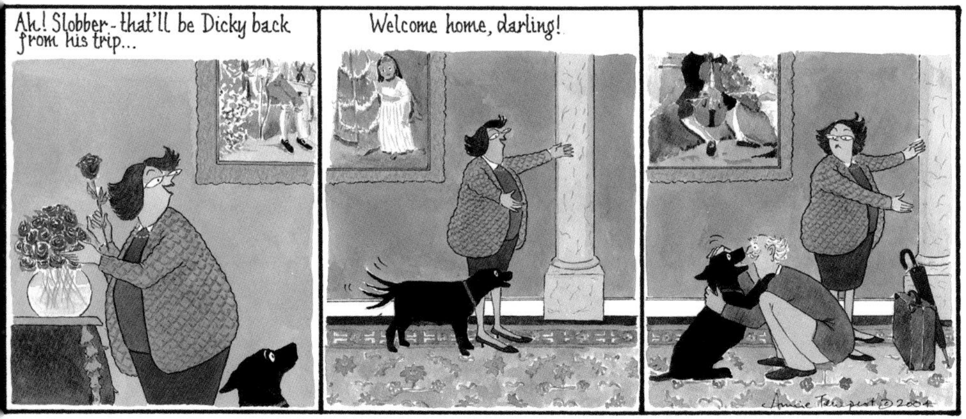
Ah! Slobber - that'll be Dicky back from his trip...
Welcome home, darling!

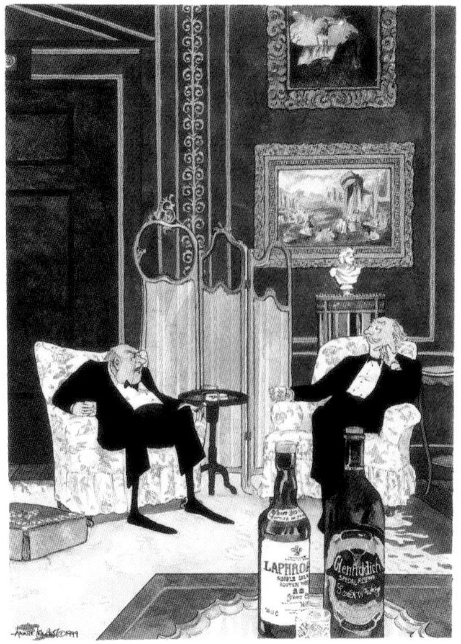
LAPHROAIG
Glenfiddich

"... The future's not what it used to be, Dicky..."

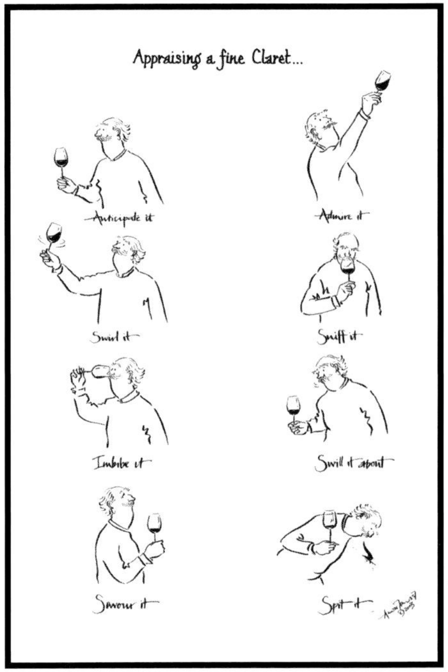
Appraising a fine Claret...
Anticipate it
Admire it
Swirl it
Sniff it
Imbibe it
Swill it about
Savour it
Spit it

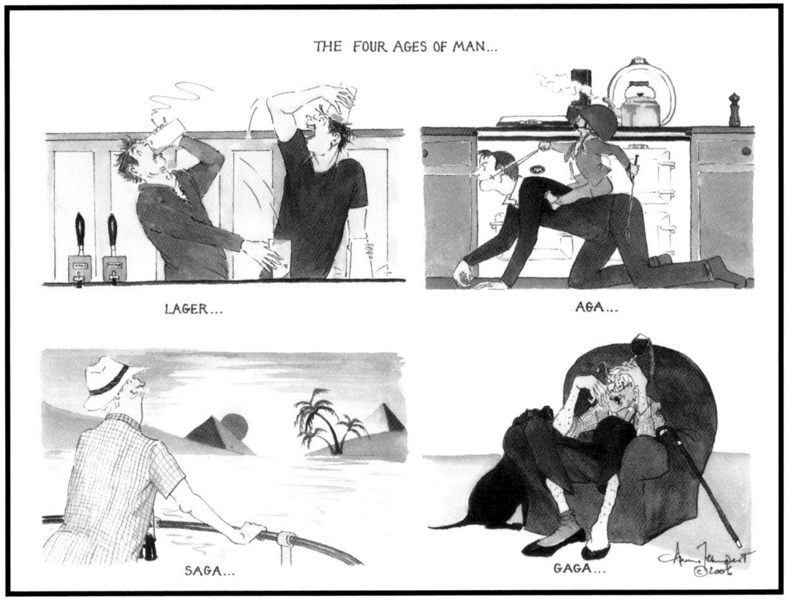
THE FOUR AGES OF MAN...
LAGER...
AGA...
SAGA...
GAGA...

TOTTERING-BY-GENTLY®

GALLERY OF TOTTERING DESIGNS – A selection of Country Life prints and Specials prints

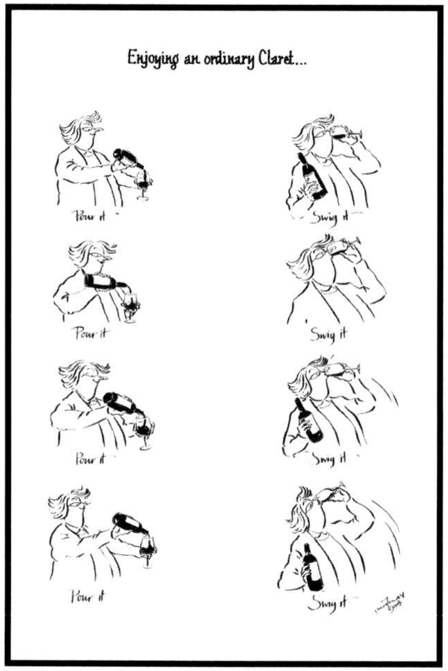

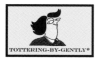

Enjoying an ordinary Claret...
Pour it
Swig it
Pour it
Swig it
Pour it
Swig it
Pour it
Swig it

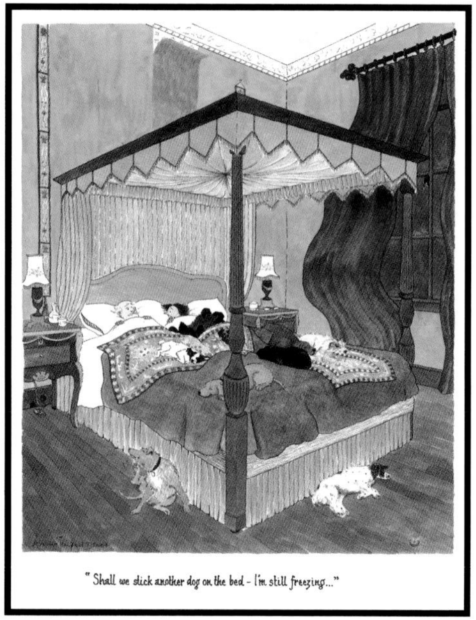

"Shall we stick another dog on the bed – I'm still freezing..."

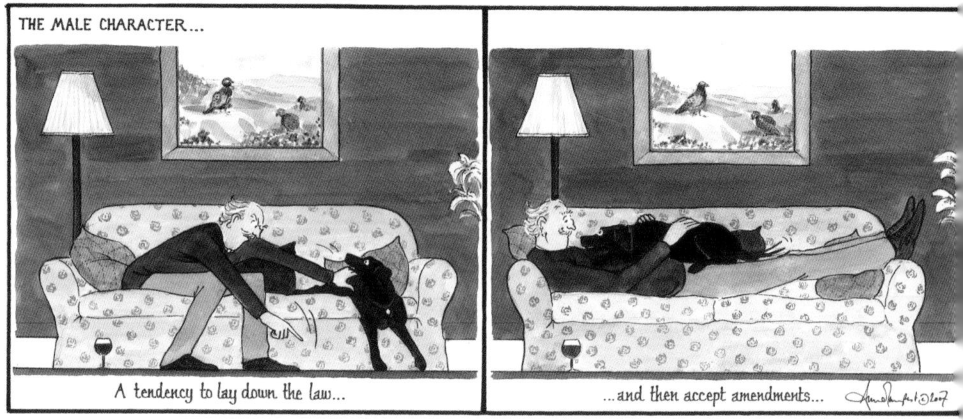

THE MALE CHARACTER...
A tendency to lay down the law...
...and then accept amendments...

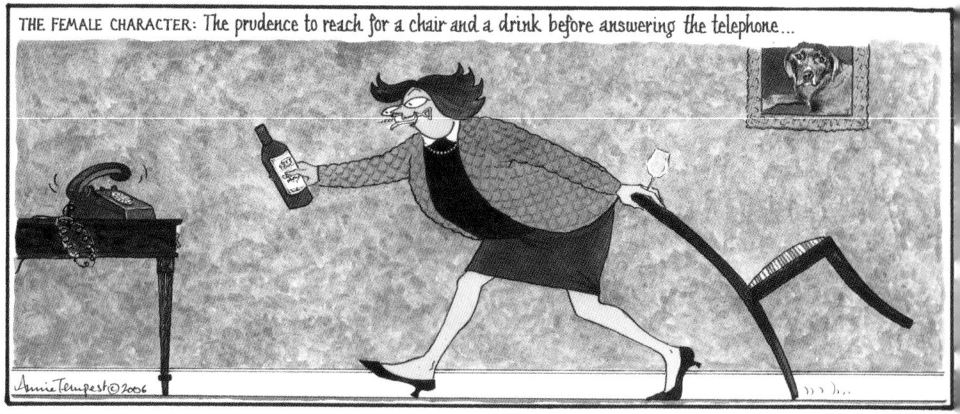

THE FEMALE CHARACTER: The prudence to reach for a chair and a drink before answering the telephone...

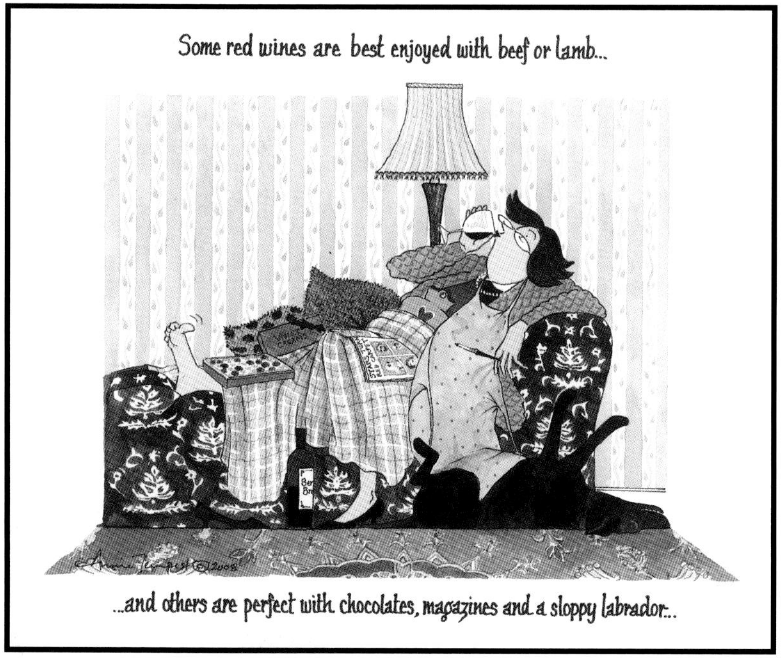

Some red wines are best enjoyed with beef or lamb...
...and others are perfect with chocolates, magazines and a sloppy labrador...

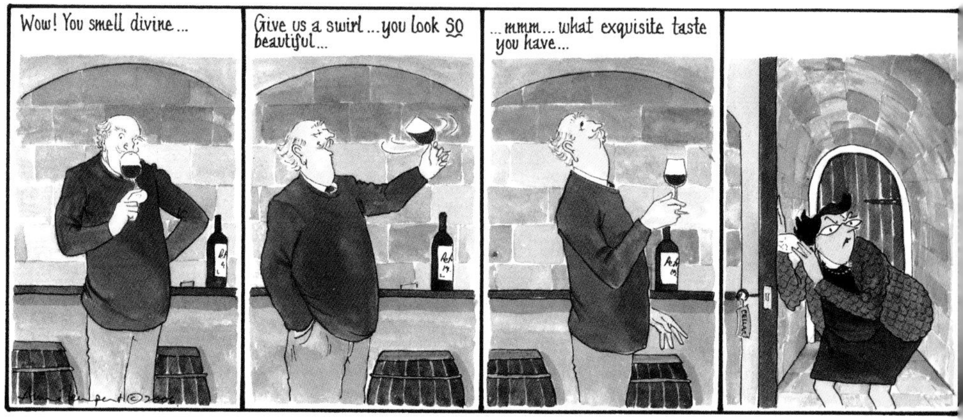

Wow! You smell divine...
Give us a swirl ...you look SO beautiful...
...mmm... what exquisite taste you have...

GALLERY OF TOTTERING DESIGNS – Postcards and greetings cards

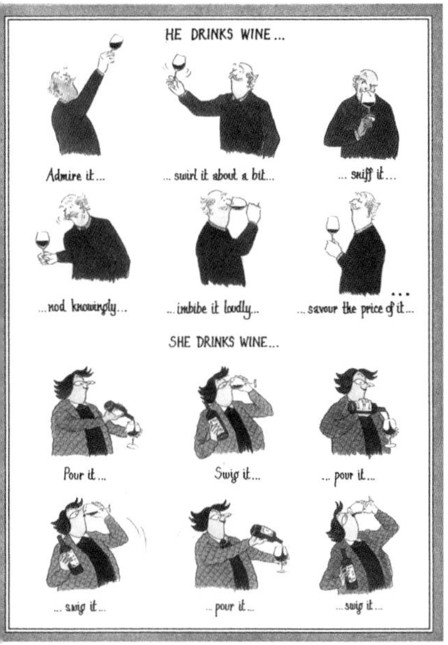
HE DRINKS WINE...
Admire it...
... swirl it about a bit...
... sniff it...
...nod knowingly...
...imbibe it loudly...
...savour the price of it...
SHE DRINKS WINE...
Pour it...
Swig it...
... pour it...
... swig it...
... pour it...
... swig it...

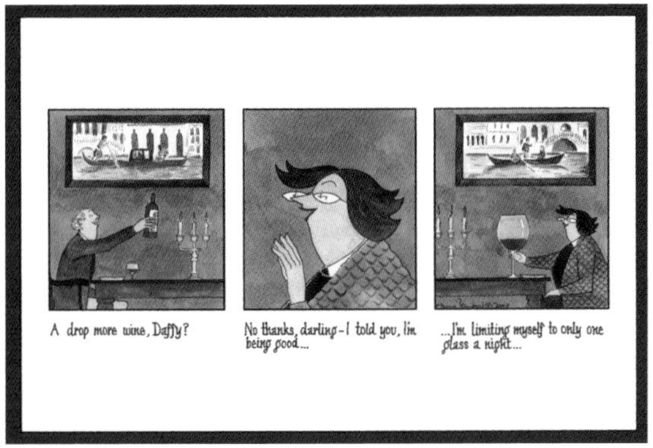
A drop more wine, Daffy?
No thanks, darling - I told you, I'm being good...
...I'm limiting myself to only one glass a night...

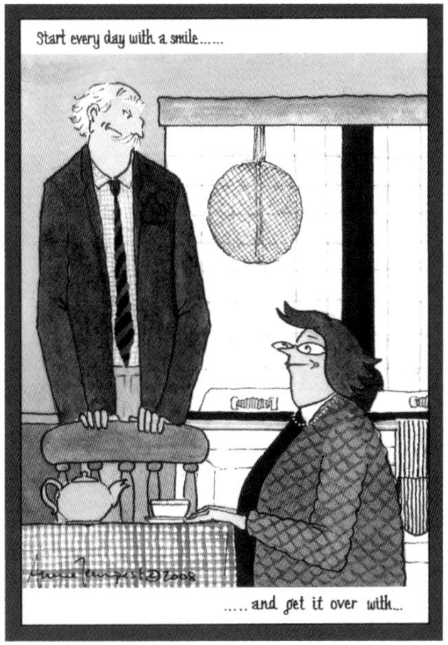
Start every day with a smile......
..... and get it over with...

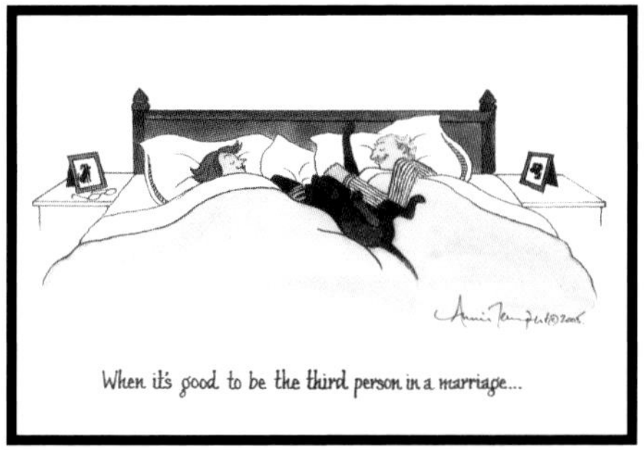
When it's good to be the third person in a marriage...

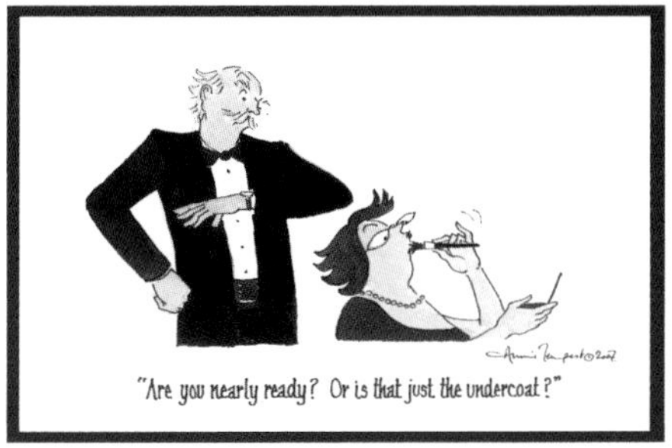
"Are you nearly ready? Or is that just the undercoat?"

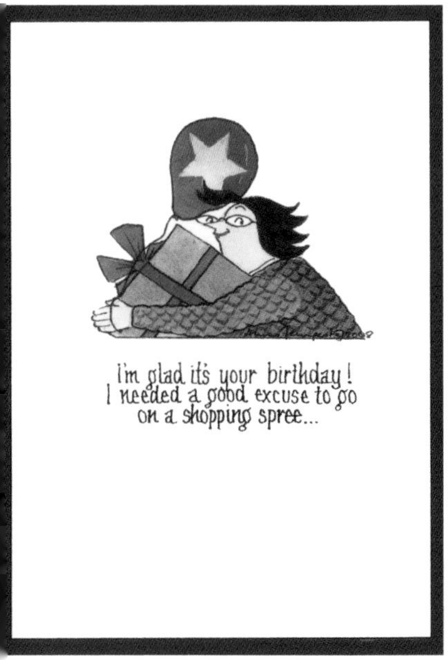
I'm glad it's your birthday!
I needed a good excuse to go on a shopping spree...

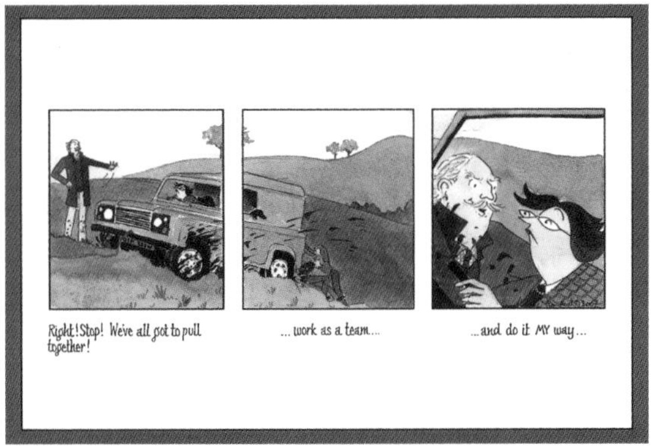
Right! Stop! We've all got to pull together!
... work as a team...
...and do it MY way...

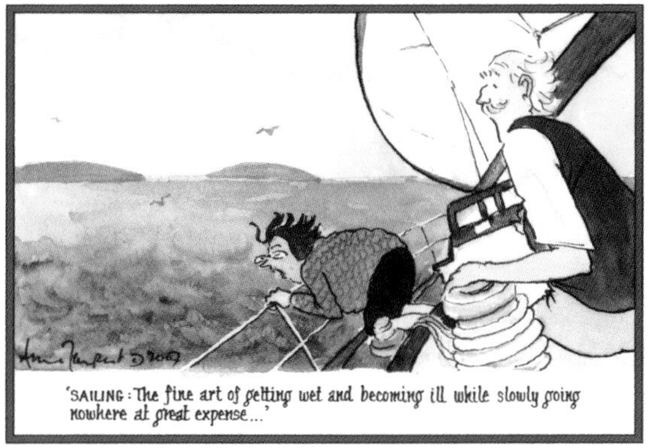
'SAILING: The fine art of getting wet and becoming ill while slowly going nowhere at great expense...'

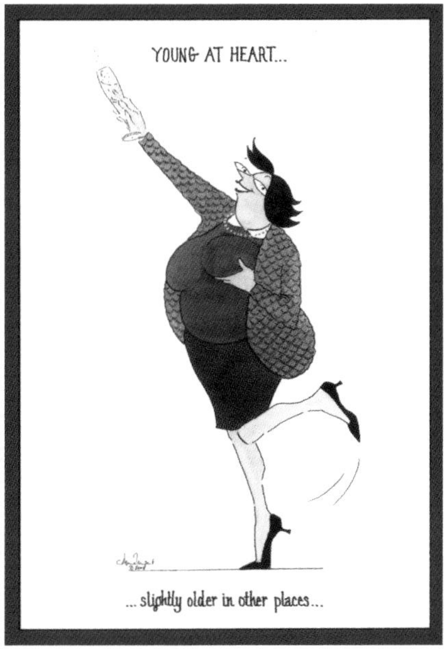
YOUNG AT HEART...
... slightly older in other places...

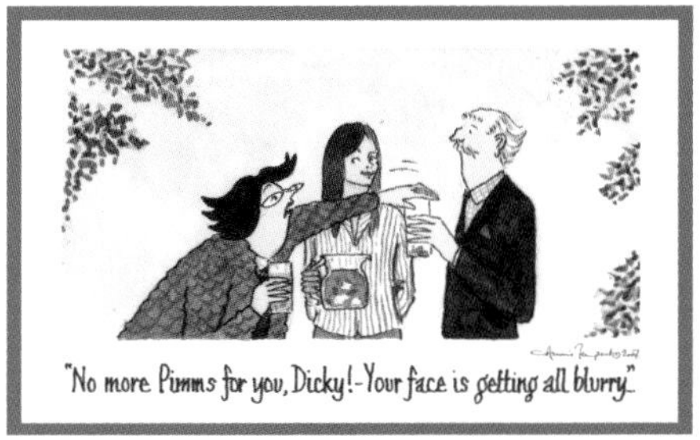
"No more Pimms for you, Dicky! - Your face is getting all blurry."

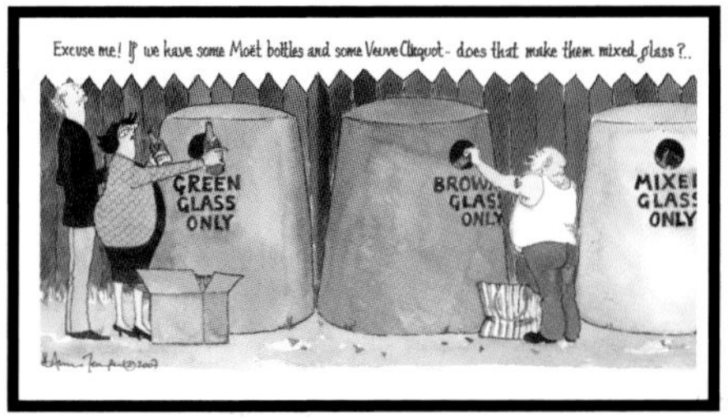
Excuse me! If we have some Moët bottles and some Veuve Clicquot - does that make them mixed glass?..
GREEN GLASS ONLY

GALLERY OF TOTTERING DESIGNS – Selected product images

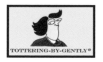

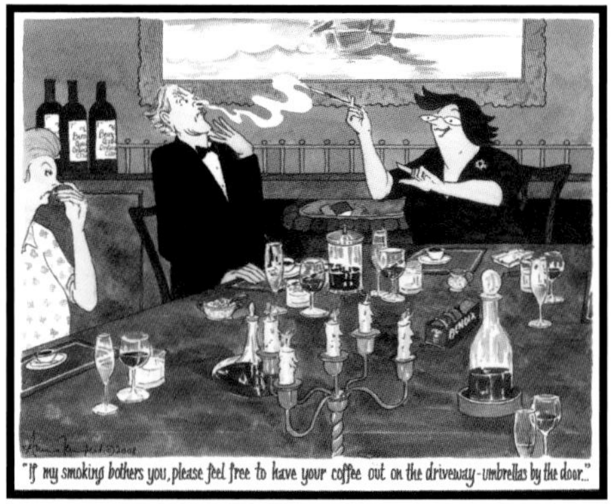
"If my smoking bothers you, please feel free to have your coffee out on the driveway - umbrellas by the door."

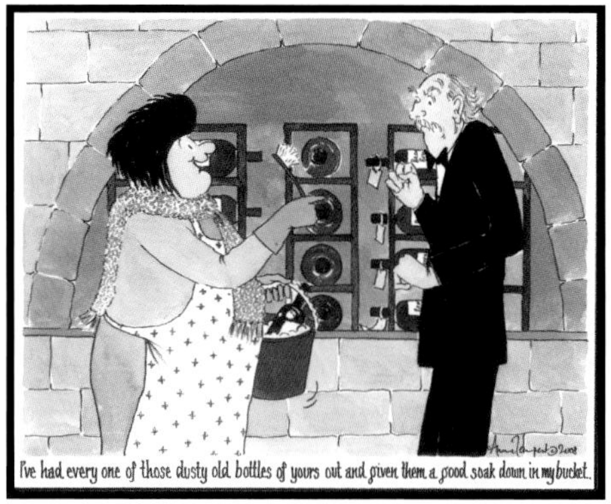
I've had every one of those dusty old bottles of yours out and given them a good soak down in my bucket.

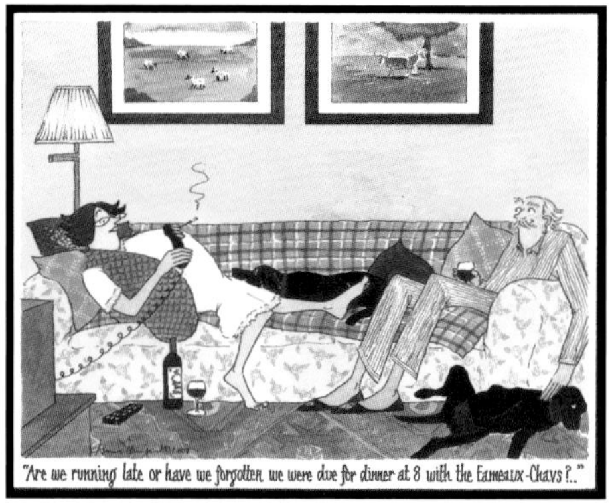
"Are we running late or have we forgotten we were due for dinner at 8 with the Fameaux-Chavs?.."

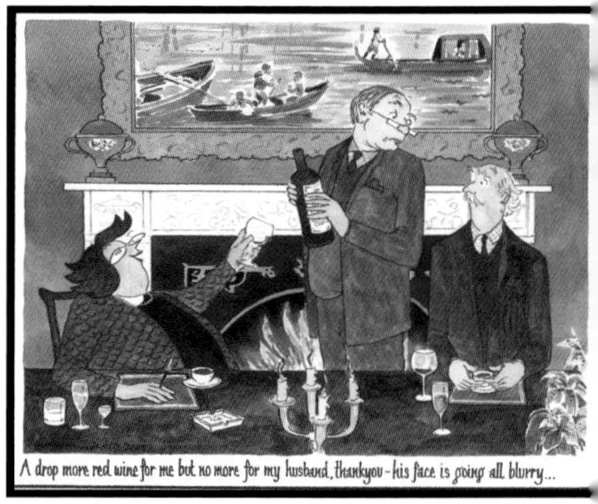
A drop more red wine for me but no more for my husband, thankyou - his face is going all blurry...

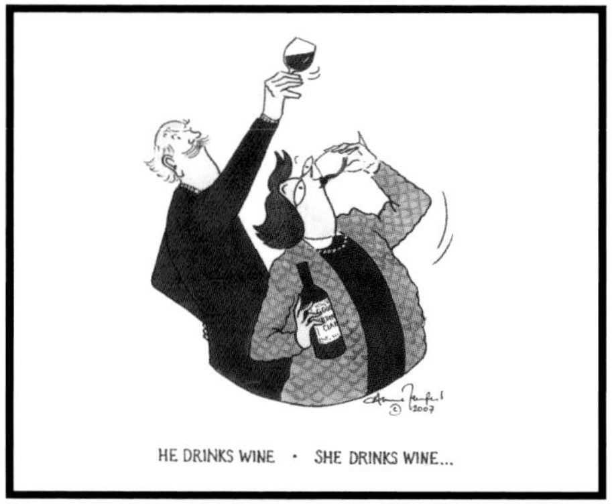
HE DRINKS WINE · SHE DRINKS WINE...

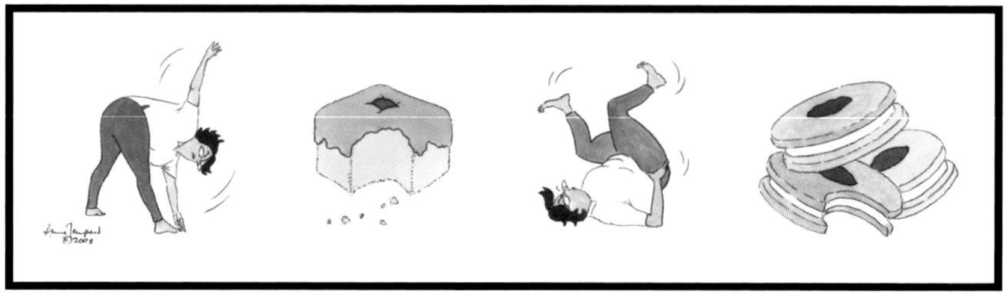

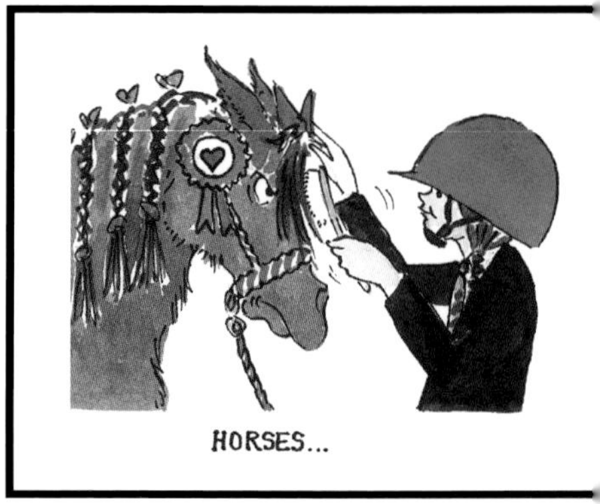
HORSES...

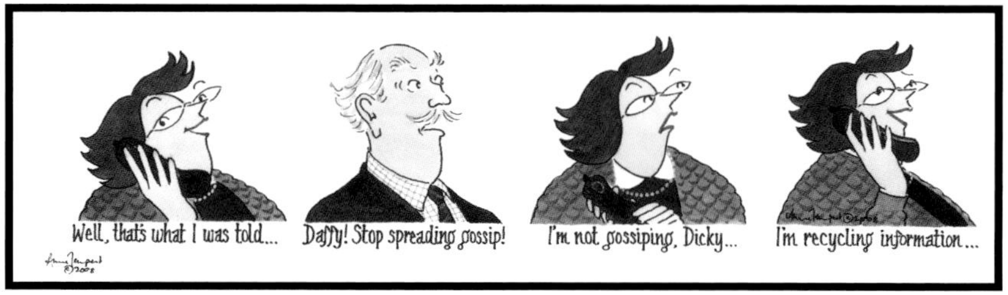
Well, that's what I was told...
Daffy! Stop spreading gossip!
I'm not gossiping, Dicky...
I'm recycling information...

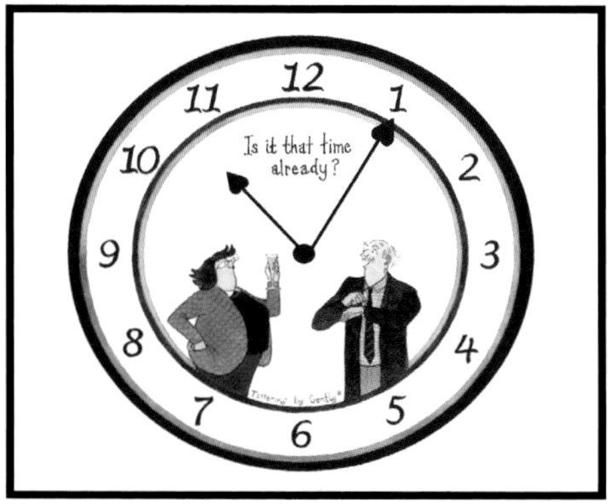
12
1
2
3
4
5
6
7
8
9
10
11
Is it that time already?

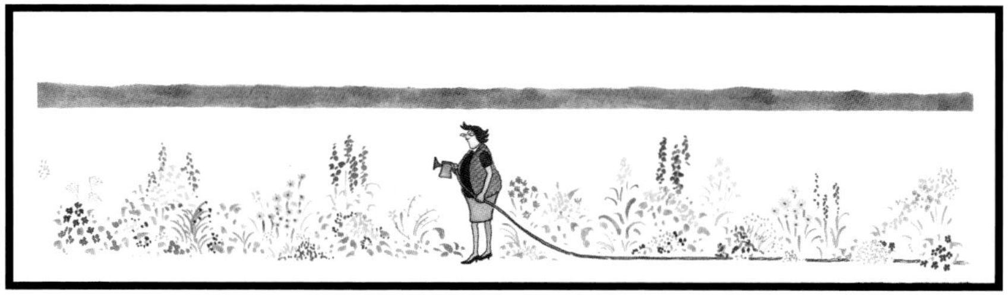

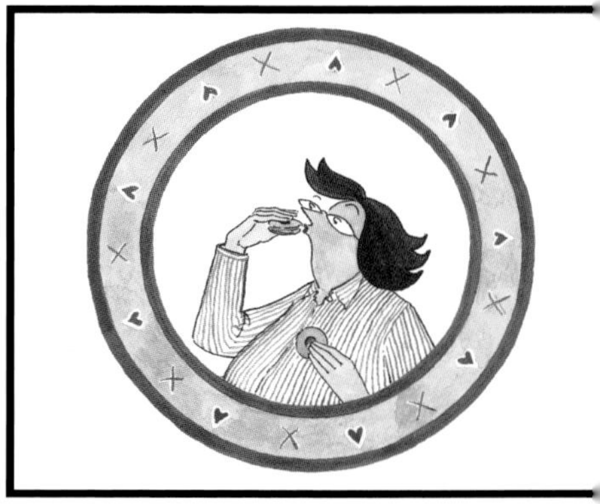